The Muslim Private Sector in Southeast Asia

The **Institute of Southeast Asian Studies (ISEAS)** was established as an autonomous organization in 1968. It is a regional research centre for scholars and other specialists concerned with modern Southeast Asia, particularly the many-faceted problems of stability and security, economic development, and political and social change.

The Institute is governed by a twenty-two-member Board of Trustees comprising nominees from the Singapore Government, the National University of Singapore, the various Chambers of Commerce, and professional and civic organizations. A ten-man Executive Committee oversees day-to-day operations; it is chaired by the Director, the Institute's chief academic and administrative officer.

The **Social Issues in Southeast Asia (SISEA)** programme was established at the Institute in 1986. It addresses itself to the study of the nature and dynamics of ethnicity, urbanism, and population change in Southeast Asia. These issues are examined with particular attention to the implications for, and relevance to, an understanding of problems of development and of societal conflict and co-operation. SISEA is guided by a Regional Advisory Board comprising senior scholars from the various Southeast Asian countries. At the Institute, SISEA comes under the overall charge of the Director while its day-to-day running is the responsibility of the Co-ordinator.

Islam and the Economic Development of Southeast Asia

The Muslim Private Sector in Southeast Asia

Edited by
Mohamed Ariff
University of Malaya

Social Issues in Southeast Asia
INSTITUTE OF SOUTHEAST ASIAN STUDIES

Published by
Institute of Southeast Asian Studies
Heng Mui Keng Terrace
Pasir Panjang
Singapore 0511

Cataloguing in Publication Data

Islam and economic development of Southeast Asia: the Muslim private sector in Southeast Asia / edited by Mohamed Ariff.
1. Economic development — Religious aspects — Islam — Asia, Southeastern.
2. Muslims — Asia, Southeastern — Economic conditions.
3. Islam — Asia, Southeastern.
I. Mohamed Ariff, 1940 –
BP173.75 I82 1991 sls91–204567

ISBN 981–3016–09–4 (soft cover)
ISBN 981–3016–10–8 (hard cover)

Typeset by Alpha-Text Publishing Services.
Printed in Singapore by Kin Keong Printing Co. Pte. Ltd.

CONTENTS

LIST OF TABLES

LIST OF FIGURES

FOREWORD

Ethnic and religious issues have, in the last few decades, confounded many social analysts by refusing to disappear. The "liberal expectancy" among social analysts used to be that modernization would blur ethnic distinctions, achievement would replace ascription and particularistic criteria, and wide-ranging communication and education systems would homogenize populations. The "radical expectancy" was that differences in religions, languages, and culture would be swallowed up, perhaps even across national boundaries by emergent class consciousness. Instead, religion and ethnicity continue to cut across and envelop almost every facet of Southeast Asian life. Indeed, if anything, such divisions in many societies have become sharper, ethnic and religious interest groups more insistent, and opposition more politicized and strident. Much of this activity seems to be increasingly played on the urban stage—and this at a time when the pace of urbanization in Southeast Asia is increasing rapidly, to the extent that by the turn of the century, cities such as Manila, Bangkok and Jakarta could have populations of more than ten million each. In these settings, Southeast Asian ethnic, religious and linguistic complexities are likely to be even more challenging than in the past.

It was therefore only natural that among other aspects of the Southeast Asian social and cultural scene, the Institute should identify the study of contemporary religion as one of its key areas of interest. Southeast Asia is after all not only home to all the major religions of the world—Islam, Buddhism, Christianity, and Hinduism—but the geographical spread of these is such that the bonds that bind their adherents at one and the same time defy and accentuate political and territorial divides and boundaries. The case of Islam is especially striking in this respect, as its followers are present in significant numbers in almost every Southeast Asian country, and in several of these across constraining political borders. Acting on this, a group of Southeast Asian scholars met in 1980 and proposed a project to increase our understanding of Islam in its regional context.

Towards this end, two clusters were identified. The first of these was centred on the nature of Islam in the region, Islam and societal change, and Islam and education. The second concentration was to be on Islam and problems of economic development.

The completion of the first cluster of research activities saw the publication of three volumes: *Readings on Islam in Southeast Asia*, *Islam and Society in Southeast Asia*, and *Muslim Society, Higher Education and Development in Southeast Asia*.

Building on the foregoing studies, work commenced on the second cluster of research, that is, "Islam and the Economic Development of Southeast Asia". The research here too is in three phases, spread over three years. They are: Islamic banking; Islam and resource mobilization through the voluntary sector; and Islam and the role of the private sector in economic development.

The project on Islam stimulated considerable interest in not only other major religions in the region, but also issues relating to ethnicity and development, another of the Institute's long-standing and primary areas of research. Moreover, the experience gained in managing the project on Islam proved valuable in terms of co-ordinating comparative research involving numerous scholars from diverse backgrounds and disciplines—with the result that the Institute was encouraged not only to plan parallel projects on developing a longer-term *programme* of research that would encompass all its projects on contemporary religions, together with those that might grow out of the Institute's interests in ethnicity, urbanism, and related areas.

To facilitate this, the Institute convened a meeting in 1985 of senior Southeast Asian social scientists to discuss issues of social change in Southeast Asia, in order to identify firm areas of research and a sharper focusing of such research and associated activities. The group were unanimous in their conclusion that it was "essential and desirable" to encourage research on social issues in Southeast Asia, in particular religion, ethnicity, urbanism, and population dynamics.

To allow for proper planning and incremental research, the group felt that work in these areas could be most effectively developed within the structure and support of a *programme*, rather than as *ad hoc* projects. Accordingly, it was proposed there be established a programme of research to be known as the "Social Issues in Southeast Asia (SISEA)" programme. This programme would address itself to the nature, persistence, and impact of religions, ethnicity, urbanism, and population change in terms of their intrinsic dynamism and potential for societal conflict, co-existence or co-operation in the context of development, stability, and nation-building.

SISEA would also allow for the consolidation of the various publications emanating from the Institute's work in ethnicity, religion, urbanism, and population change within a single and integrated series, "Social Issues in Southeast Asia" with *The Muslim Private Sector in Southeast Asia* edited by Dr Mohamed Ariff being the latest addition to the series.

SISEA and the preparation of *The Muslim Private Sector in Southeast Asia* have benefited greatly from the financial support provided by the Konrad Adenauer Foundation of the Federal Republic of Germany. The Institute would like to record its appreciation of all such help and support and to express the wish that the various numbers of "Social Issues in Southeast Asia" will circulate widely amongst all concerned with the social dynamics of the region.

K.S. Sandhu
Director
Institute of Southeast Asian Studies

ACKNOWLEDGEMENTS

The papers in this volume were first presented at a workshop which was held in Singapore on 26–27 September 1988. Preeda Prapertchob, Taufik Abdullah, Jamilah Ariffin, Syed Othman Alhabshi, Mehrun Siraj, Carmen Abubakar, and Ataul Huq participated as discussants for the various papers which were presented and I would like to thank them for their stimulating contributions to the discussions at the workshop.

The generous financial support of the Konrad Adenauer Foundation is gratefully acknowledged. Due acknowledgements should also be given to Sharon Siddique, then Co-ordinator of the Social Issues in Southeast Asia (SISEA) programme and presently Deputy Director at ISEAS, for her help in organizing the workshop and for facilitating work on the papers which make up this volume. Thanks also go to Jane Ong, also of SISEA, and the Institute's Publications Unit, for their professional assistance in the preparation of this volume. Last but not least, I would like to gratefully acknowledge the valuable assistance provided by Dr Ananda Rajah in putting this volume together.

Mohamed Ariff
University of Malaya

CONTRIBUTORS

Amina Tyabji is a Senior Lecturer in the Department of Economics and Statistics, National University of Singapore.

Bahauddin Darus is President, PT Bahana, Jakarta, Indonesia.

Chaiwat Satha-Anand is an Associate Professor in the Faculty of Political Science, Thammasat University, Thailand.

Faridah Shahadan is a Lecturer in the Faculty of Economics at Universiti Kebangsaan Malaysia, Selangor, Malaysia.

Mohamed Ariff is Professor of Analytical Economics in the Faculty of Economics and Administration, University of Malaya, Kuala Lumpur, Malaysia.

Mohd. Musib M. Buat is Commissioner, National Labor Relations Commission, Manila.

Monzer Kahf is with the Islamic Research and Training Institute, Islamic Development Bank, Jeddah.

Nor Aini Haji Idris is Lecturer in the Faculty of Economics at Universiti Kebangsaan Malaysia.

Salleh Ismail is Director, Division of Economic Services, Public Bank, Kuala Lumpur.

Syed Waseem Ahmad is a Visiting Fellow at the Institute of Strategic and International Studies (ISIS) Malaysia, Kuala Lumpur.

1 INTRODUCTION

Mohamed Ariff

Man is dignified in Islam as the finest of God's creations and as the vicegerent of God on earth. Such dignity bestowed upon man stems not only from the faculties he is endowed with that are denied to other creatures but, more importantly, also from the freedom of choice that he is able to exercise. It is this freedom that forms the marrow of human existence. The supremacy of human freedom is such that the Qur'an categorically disapproves of compulsion in religion. However, freedom of individuals is by no means absolute in the Islamic order, as Islam disallows actions that infringe the freedom of others. Besides, man is accountable to his Creator on the Day of Judgement. Thus, it is free will and accountability that distinguish man from all other beings.

Private enterprise forms an integral part of the overall freedom that man enjoys in the Islamic framework. The Qur'an clearly states that the universe and everything therein have been created to meet the multifarious needs of man (e.g. 2 : 29; 6 : 165; 7 : 10; 45 : 13) and urges man to seek out the bounties of God (61 : 10), warning that man can have nothing but what he strives for (53 : 39). The Islamic economic system thus places a high premium on human initiatives. There are numerous sayings of the Prophet in the Traditions (Hadith) which underscore the importance of human efforts, equating righteous earnings of individuals with worship (*ibadat*) itself. It is incumbent upon man to fulfil his own needs, meet his family liabilities, make provision for future contingencies and for posterity, and to render social service, thereby contributing to the cause of Allah.

Islam does not decry wealth and the wealthy. In fact, there are Qur'anic verses (e.g. 2 : 198; 5 : 2; 22 : 28) which refer to wealth as the "Blessings of God". Of course, wealth carries with it additional responsibilities for those who possess it. For, one has to account for every penny earned and spent, on the Day of Judgement. According to the Hadith, wealth rightly acquired is a good thing for the righteous man (Bukhari). For, in Islam, both wealth and the lack of it are seen as a trial. And the Qur'an severely warns those who hoard their wealth (9 : 34) and urges them to circulate their wealth for the common good of all (59 : 7).

Thus, getting rich through righteous means and using the wealth in righteous ways is considered a good thing in itself. However, in Islam, wealth is not an end, but only a means for incurring the pleasure of the Almighty. In fact, Islam requires all human activities to be directed towards the achievement of *falah*, a term which is interpreted to encompass welfare in this world and in the Hereafter. In other words, material well-being is an important ingredient of *falah*.

Although Islam permits the acquisition of wealth through legitimate economic pursuits, private ownership is not absolute. For, in the final analysis, everything in the Heavens and on the Earth belongs to God, and man can use his property, dispose of it or pass it on to his heirs, but he has no right to destroy it. Man only acts as a trustee.

Islam represents the middle path, which is clearly divorced from extremes. Thus, extravagance, on the one hand, and stinginess and meanness, on the other, are condemned. The key element in the Islamic ideology is moderation. Extremism is *not* an Islamic virtue.

The Islamic perception of the private sector provides an interesting case in point that underlines the need to drive a middle course. Unlike communism and socialism which throttle private enterprises, and unlike capitalism that glorifies the private sector in a no holds barred fashion, Islam not only permits but also encourages private sector initiatives that are hedged by salutary checks. To achieve *falah*, one must be just. The notion of justice (*adl*) provides the basis for all human endeavours in the Islamic social order. Such considerations would seriously question the applicability of conventional economic theories in an Islamic system. In particular, the principle of profit maximization seems antithetical to the philosophy of the Qur'an and the Hadith. To be sure, profits have a legitimate place in the Islamic order as a motivating factor, but maximum profits cannot be the hallmark of Islamic entrepreneurship. In other words, profits are legitimate, but profiteering is not.

It is well known in conventional economics that the profit maximization principle ensures efficiency. The absence of profit maximization in Islam, however, does not mean that Islam condones inefficiency. Far from it, economic wastes are forbidden in Islam and "economizing" is an Islamic virtue. Efficiency and thriftiness are among the essential constituents of the Islamic way of life. It is an Islamic imperative that God-given resources are put to the best possible use. But, the Islamic entrepreneur would share the benefit of such efforts with others instead of converting them into maximum profits for himself. To put it in technical terms, the Islamic entrepreneur will push his production to a point where average cost is equated with average revenue so as to earn "normal" profits and will not stop short by equating marginal costs with marginal revenue. Such a behaviour would result in higher output at lower prices than would be the case under a profit-maximizing situation.

Clearly, there is no place in Islam for competition that is based on naked self-interest and total indifference to the well-being of others. While Islam does not decry competition, it stresses the need for competition to be fair and just. Islam aims at a blending of co-operation and competition, consistent with its "middle-path" approach. The Qur'anic verse "then strive together (as in a race) towards all that is good" (2:18) sums it up.

To be sure, the private enterprise system is not incompatible with Islam. In fact, such a system is only consistent with the principle of freedom that is fundamental to the philosophy of Islam. The Prophet (peace be upon him) was reported to have exhorted his followers to take up a variety of economic activities, including trade, farming, horticulture, and animal husbandry, which were then in vogue. Islamic history is replete with evidence indicating that the entrepreneurs in the Islamic states were left to manage their businesses without much state intervention, with the Islamic legal system determining the legitimacy of transactions and providing protection to private investments. According to Islamic jurisprudence (*fiqh*), private enterprise is permissible in all fields except those reserved for the state which include rivers and mineral resources.

The market had played a key role in the early days of Islam and in the heyday of the Islamic Empires. It is significant to note that the Prophet had refused to fix the prices of goods even when they rose very high, leaving them to be determined by anonymous market forces. It is equally significant to observe that the Prophet had disallowed traders to intercept farm producers on their way to the market-place, before the latter could monitor the market trends, in an attempt to buy their produce at low prices. Thus, it is unambiguously clear that well-informed market operations have a legitimate role to play in the Islamic economic system. Government intervention is warranted only in the face of distortions caused by monopoly and monopsony, collusion, coercion, and other unfair practices.

In Islam, exchange is lawful only if it takes place with the full satisfaction of the seller and the buyer. In other words, Islamically legitimate exchange is one that is mutually beneficial to both the seller and the buyer. Islam does not legitimize transactions that are shrouded in ambiguities of sorts (*gharar*), i.e. transactions involving unspecified price, quantity, quality, delivery, etc. Islam rejects all transactions of fraudulent nature. Every transaction (*muammalat*) must be free from deceit and exploitation. It is unlawful for a third party to offer a higher price for a good whose price has already been agreed upon. By the same token, it is unlawful for a merchant to underprice his product in such a way as to cause losses to other merchants. The seller must make known the defects of the goods he sells before he transacts his business. The trader is not allowed to transact the sale of something that is not in his possession or the procurement of which is doubtful. Those who cheat in weights and measures are condemned in the strongest terms. In the same vein, usury (*riba*), adulteration, hoarding, misleading advertisements and other unscrupulous practices are forbidden. Black marketing is regarded as a form of "forced trade" which Islam prohibits.

Needless to say, transactions involving goods or services whose consumption is categorically prohibited in Islam are illegitimate. Thus, the sale of pork, alcohol and idols is forbidden. Similarly, transactions involving gambling and games of chance (*maisir*) are disallowed.

It is clear from all this that the private sector has an important and responsible role to play in an Islamic economy. The problem, however, is that an Islamic economy hardly exists these days. Southeast Asia is no exception, although Islam is the religion of millions in this region. Under the impact of Western influence, Islamic norms, values and criteria seem to have taken a back seat.

For most Muslims in Southeast Asia, Islam has ceased to be a way of life and become a religion of rituals. Some remain "nominal" Muslims exhibiting complete disregard for or total indifference to Islamic injunctions; some are conscious of their faith, paying little more than lip-service; the majority observe what may be termed as the "basics" including prayers and fasting, without fully incorporating Islamic precepts into their day-to-day life; and there are still others who tend to rationalize their actions under adverse circumstances. Islam, being a practical religion, allows its followers some leeway under special or extenuating circumstances. It is not incorrect to say that Muslims of today are operating in what may be termed as a "hostile" environment which makes it extremely difficult if not impossible for them to Islamize themselves perfectly. Many have begun to look at it as a challenge and seem determined to face it, thanks to Islamic resurgence in recent times.

An effort is made in this volume to focus on the Muslim private sector in Southeast Asia through a number of case studies that bring out clearly the conflict between theory and practice. These studies provide valuable insights not only into the ways in which Southeast Asian Muslims attempt to resolve such conflicts but also into the socio-economic structure of the Muslim communities of the region.

The present volume comprises ten chapters and is organized as follows. Chapter 2, by Monzer Kahf, discusses the Islamic perspectives of the private sector. In Chapter 3, Musib Buat takes a close look at the Muslim business community of Mindanao in the Philippines. A profile of businesses owned by minority Muslims in Singapore and their business practices is presented by Amina Tyabji in Chapter 4. Chaiwat Satha-Anand provides an insight into the role of Bangkok Muslims in the tourist trade of Thailand in Chapter 5. Nor Aini Idris and Faridah Shahadan discuss the role of Muslim women entrepreneurs in Kelantan (Malaysia) in Chapter 6. An Indonesian experiment with venture capital financing is analysed in Chapter 7 by Bahauddin Darus. Chapter 8, by Syed Waseem Ahmad, examines Malaysia's experience in Islamic insurance. In Chapter 9, Salleh Ismail addresses the question of the Islamic law of inheritance and its impact on landownership and land use in the Malay community. Finally, an attempt is made by the editor of this volume in Chapter 10 to wrap up the preceding chapters in a coherent fashion so that the major issues can be highlighted and some broad inferences can be drawn.

The substantive chapters which constitute the core of this volume were first presented and discussed at a workshop which was held in Singapore in September 1988. The papers were subsequently revised and edited for publication in the present form.

2 THE ROLE AND IMPORTANCE OF THE PRIVATE SECTOR IN ISLAMIC PERSPECTIVE

Monzer Kahf

Introduction

Two axiomatic characteristics describe the economic system of Islam, its response to the nature of the human being and its adherence to the principle of justice. Therefore, the student of this system will always notice that its pillars and principles go along with the intrinsic intuitions of man with little superimposition and much coherence and harmony. This is seen in the organization of the market and in the behaviour of consumers and producers.

Prophet Muhammad (peace be upon him) repeatedly mentioned that Islam is the religion of human nature. This is perhaps the reason why it takes a middle path between the two extremes of individualism and collectivism. It strikes a reconciliation or a balance between the human drives and desires on one hand, and social needs and responsibilities on the other. It calls for a balanced mix of dogmatism and pragmatism.

This chapter consists of five sections. The next section deals with the objectives of the Islamic economic system on the role of the private sector in the economy. It will cover issues relating to the overall aim of the economic pursuits, the degree of individualism which is tolerated or promoted in the Islamic system, and the place of altruism. Section 3 scrutinizes the means for achieving the economic objectives and the role of the market. In Section 4, the basic economic rights of man in the Islamic economic system is discussed. This section will cover the right to economic freedom, the right of private ownership and its corollaries, and the right to adequate means of living. Finally, Section 5 addresses the restrictions placed on the economic rights of individuals in the Islamic system.

The Objectives of the Islamic Economic System with Respect to the Private Sector

What objectives does the Islamic system assign to the private sector? To answer this question, one has to look into the objectives of this system with regards to human beings. The overall purpose of creating the human beings is stated in the Qur'an as worshipping and glorifying God (51 : 56). To be more specific and to derive the economic implication of this overall objective, we will need to delve into details. Therefore, two broad objectives are focused upon in this section. They are (1) the objective of material pleasure and (2) the objective of construction and prosperity.

The Objective of Material Joy

The Qur'an is full of verses[1] which directly indicate that men and women are permitted, called upon and even asked to enjoy all that is on the earth, i.e. the bounties God has created for them. These verses suggest that the material joys of this worldly life are indeed legitimate, permissible; and they are given a moral value of being bounties of God. This principle may be considered the first axiom of human behaviour in the Islamic economic system. A closer look at this axiom reveals that it closely approximates human nature, as it is common to all human beings despite different interpretations in different cultures, religions and doctrines. It is as applicable to Robinson Crusoe in his isolated island as much as it is applicable to most sophisticated men and women in the middle of a large metropolis.

This axiom also implies that more of these joyful goods is preferred to less and it goes without saying that this, like all other decisions of human beings, is always subject to certain constraints. Consequently, talking about restrictions of the Islamic system on this axiom does not seem very important for two reasons. Firstly, restrictions which result from self contentment and ideological beliefs are always reflected in the preferences people reveal in their choice; and such restrictions in any case are taken into consideration in drawing maps of individual preferences. Secondly, restrictions which come from the system on the material environment are not totally different from those that exist in societies, e.g. the prohibition of drugs in many countries. Thus, on the one hand, there are restrictions which reflect the likes and dislikes of individuals which are derived from their style of life, culture, beliefs, faith, ideas, tastes, emotions, social environment, and so forth. All these and similar factors explain why people choose a certain act or course of action and outline their preferences. On the other hand, there are restrictions which reflect either legal and economic conditions which determine the attainable set of material joys available to individuals or economic variables which interfere in the individual choice among different available choices. The latter includes elements such as prices, income, wealth, and so forth. Non-availability can be caused by a legal prohibition or by the scarcity of available resources and the level of technology.

From the above discussion of the first axiom it follows that rational individuals like to increase their material joys, regardless of their faith and beliefs, but they are subject to many limitations that curb this desire. Therefore, they turn to reconciling themselves with the surrounding inner and outer restraints by resorting to a process of optimization instead of maximization. Optimization is, indeed, nothing more than maximization under constraints whereby individuals maximize their material joys within the limits of attainable goods and subject to the restrictions of the economic variables. This kind of behaviour is common to all people under all systems.

But does the Islamic attitude differ, in this respect, from the attitude of non-Muslims? The answer to this question is affirmative, because Islam inculcates in its followers a strong awareness of life after death and the Reckoning therein. This consideration puts certain restraints on the inner desires of the believers in the sense of forsaking some joys for God's sake on the one hand, and urges them to divert some of their available means from the objective of obtaining material joys in the present worldly life to the objective of increasing the amount of joys in the Hereafter, on the other. The Qur'an and the Sunnah (Traditions of the Prophet) have made references to the material joys in Heaven. Many of these statements make quantitative comparisons between the joys of the Hereafter and their counterparts in the worldly life as well as comparisons between the joys of the Hereafter and their cost or prices in the present life. This approach to the Divine rewards (and punishments) is unique to the religion of Islam, nourishing a sense of calculation and mathematical rationalization in the minds of the believers.

Taking into account the fact that people differ in the level of internationalization of their pronounced faith and that an Islamic society may even have disbelievers and non-Muslims within its fold, the incorporation of any such consideration of the Hereafter into the determinants of human behaviour must influence their optimizing functions. This necessarily means that the pattern of individual economic behaviour in Islamic society entails the forsaking of certain pleasures and some diversion of resources to be used in the way of God.

Spending in the way of God may take the form of personal charity to the poor and needy, expenditure on public utilities which benefit all members of the society (e.g. roads, water, mosques and orphanages), contributions to finance the activities of the state. All of these may increase consumption or raise the stock of capital. Thus, for instance, the poor may be given consumption goods or capital assets which would make them self-productive and reliant in the future.

Islamic philosophy weaves a cohesion between selfishness and altruism by asserting that the way to personal salvation goes through being good to others. The ultimate goal of man in Islam is to please God, enter Heaven and salvage one's self from the Fire of Hell. This can be achieved by obeying God, observing His commandments and following His teachings. The success of men and women in achieving this goal depends on two requisites, namely faith in the heart and good deeds. The Qur'an and the Sunnah repeatedly emphasize the idea that good deeds include doing good to other creatures.

Moreover, the concept of asceticism (*zuhd*) in Islam is such that it is personal and does not cover others. One is urged to be ascetic with regard to his own consumption and material pleasures, but when a person acts for others, he/she is required to opt for the maximization of the pleasures of others. The Islamic *fiqh* (jurisprudence) does not permit a person to contribute to charity out of the property of those on whose behalf he/she acts, without a prior authorization, because such donations contradict the material interests he/she is supposed to look after. Consequently, maximization of material prosperity and joys of people is the duty of the state, although the ruler may opt for an ascetic standard of living for his/her own self.

Additionally, there are certain actions of benefit to the whole society or community, for which self-interest does not provide sufficient motivation. These are usually taken care of by the state. In the Islamic system, these actions are given a moral and religious support through what is known as Fard al Kifayah. This is a personal religious obligation on everyone in the community until the job is done by someone. Once this is done, persons become individually relieved of that obligation. In other words, Fard al Kifayah provides personal incentive for the achievement of public benefit by expressing collective actions in the form of individual duties.

All the above make altruistic feelings, sentiments and actions indispensable ingredients of the individualistic selfish pursuit of personal interests. In this kind of matrix, altruism takes the dimension of selfishness and receives the same backing selfishness has in the nature of human beings.

Finally, it is worth noting that this treatment of altruism inculcates in the Muslim mind a sense of responsibility towards other people and the community at large, and provides an outward looking direction in the fulfilment of good and righteous deeds. This attitude is very much supported by the second objective discussed below.

The Objective of Construction and Prosperity

The Qur'an refers to this objective as 'Imarah of the earth (11 : 61, 30 : 9, 9 : 19 and 52 : 4). It seems that from this use of the word Ibn Khaldun derived the title of his sociological science al 'Imran. 'Imarah or 'Imran means populating the earth, constructing it, making progress and prosperity, filling it frequently with activity, maintaining it in proper shape, and so forth. Verse 11 : 61 specifically mentions that God charged the human race with the responsibility of making 'Imarah of the earth. In many other verses, the Qur'an refers to the same objective in terms of doing good and continuously improving all aspects of life and surroundings. The concepts of good deed, perfection and improvement are very much repeated in the Qur'an and they usually cover material as well as spiritual matters, as one would find very little distinction between spiritual and material uplifting and betterment in the Islamic teachings. Moreover, the Sunnah also contains many references to the same objective. Some of the sayings go as far as making this objective imperative even when one thinks that there will be no opportunity of collecting the fruits of such a construction.

The objective of constructing the earth and improving the living conditions therein rests on a major pillar of the Islamic doctrine that God created mankind as the best of His creatures and entrusted them with the earth and what is on it so that they make the best use of all which is under their control. God also empowered the human race and submitted the earth to them. Therefore, resources needed for achieving this as well as the first objective are put under the disposal of men and women, and they only need to apply their minds in the allocation of these resources and to organize their distribution in accordance with the principle of justice. Divine revelation is given through God's Messengers in order to provide guidance in this regard. The construction of the earth and the prosperity of its inhabitants are considered as an individual as well as a collective responsibility of all human beings and this task includes beautification and enrichment of human life and the earthly environment.

Means of Achieving the Objectives of the Private Sector

As was seen, an intrinsic characteristic of the Islamic religion is not to deny but to assist and guide human nature and rationality. It can therefore be inferred that the Islamic economic system must count on human initiatives. Thus, the market mechanism becomes highly relevant to the Islamic system as it can help fulfil its goals. Obviously, the market is also supplemented by certain inherent tools of readjustment as well as by casual state interventions.

It is a known fact that the market, as an institution, is as old as exchange itself. The Qur'an refers to exchanges during the time of some ancient prophets such as Yusuf and Shu'aib. In the Islamic system, individuals are left to manage their economic affairs wilfully through contractual exchanges. Obviously, the legal system determines the forms of legitimate transactions.

Islamic doctrine relates the results persons get to the quantity and quality of effort they put in. The Qur'an reads "That man can have nothing but what he strives for" (53 : 39). Efforts are made in producing and exchanging, both of which are encouraged and urged in Islam. Working to provide for one's self and one's family is considered as worship. The whole Islamic economic system is geared towards promoting and protecting productive human efforts.

Role of the State in Promoting the Private Sector

Since the Islamic system is based on co-ordinated coexistence of public and private ownership, it is only natural that the Islamic state be assigned the responsibility of looking after the welfare of the whole society. This obviously implies that the state administers public property to discharge this responsibility. Nevertheless, the Islamic state is assigned a significant role in elevating and stimulating the private sector. In addition to its traditional role in maintaining law and order, the following points are emphasized in the Islamic literature on economics and *fiqh*.

1. In the Islamic system, an important use of public property is its distribution to individuals in order to encourage and help them make productive projects. The Islamic jurisprudence calls for this practice. The Islamic principles which regulate *iqta* (public property) are given in *fiqh* books. These rules suggest that distribution may be on a permanent or temporary basis, it may be free or for a nominal fee, but insists that in all cases such distribution must serve the interests of the society and must not be restricted to selected individuals or groups.
2. Land which is not owned by anybody is let free for all potential users. Revivification of land and making it productive through land reclamation and improvement is called *ihya* in the *fiqh* literature. This system entitles the person who revivifies it to claim full ownership of the land under certain conditions.
3. Except in very limited cases, which can be described as cases of daily needs, state-owned lots were entrusted to individuals against some rental fee by the Prophet and the four Khalifahs (Caliphs) after him. This principle was applied by the Prophet to the lands of Khaibar and Fadak in the northern part of the Arabian peninsula and later, on a mass scale, by the Second Khalifah, 'Umar, to the lands of Syria, Iraq and Egypt. These lands are known as the lands of Kharaj. The implication of this principle is that public property should best be invested by means which link it to the private incentive of profit making as far as feasible. Furthermore, the Islamic state is not encouraged to engage in economic activities to compete with the private sector. The rare cases when the state decided to run its land directly by employing workers were those lands used for grazing livestock collected as *zakah* or horses designated for soldiers. This is called al Hima and it was applied on a very small scale to a few plots of land only. Here again, the *fiqh* writings provide many details stipulating the conditions of al Hima, its objectives and its permissible utilization.
4. The Islamic state is also assigned the responsibility of helping, encouraging and supporting the private sector. An often narrated parable is the story of a man from al Ansar who came to the Prophet asking him [for financial help]. [The Prophet] said: isn't there anything in your house? [The man] said, yes, a piece of cloth part of which we wear and part of which we lay [on the floor] and a jug with which we drink water. [The Prophet] said: bring them to me. Then, he brought them in and the Messenger of God said: who buys these two [things]? A man said: I buy them for one *dirham*. [The Prophet] said: who offers more than a *dirham*? [He said that] two or three times. [Another] man said: I take them for

two *dirham*. [The Prophet] gave them, took the two *dirham*, gave to the man from al Ansar and said: buy food with one of them and send it to your family, and buy an axe with the other and bring it to me. Then, with his own hands, the Messenger of God tied to it a piece of wood [as a handle] and said to the man: go cut [fire] wood and sell it, and let me not see you for fifteen days. The man went cutting wood and selling, then, he came with ten *dirham* which he gained. With some [of the money], he bought a piece of cloth and some food ... The Messenger of God said: This is better than begging which will come, on the Day of Resurrection, as a dark spot on your face. [Reported by Al Tirmidhi, al Nasa'i, Abu Dawud and Ibn Majah]

The behaviour of the Prophet, in this incident, indicates that the state is responsible for helping private individuals find decent employment which suit their capabilities. It is worth noticing, however, that resources of both the individual and the state, in addition to publicly free goods, were utilized in the process of finding remunerating work for the unemployed. Moreover, the state's responsibility toward the well-being of all Muslims in general, and its citizens in particular, thus include the obligation to help them support themselves, thereby raising their standard of living.

5. Taxation is a last resort in the Islamic economic system. In principle and in general, private property is protected even against taxes. The Islamic state can only impose taxes as an ultimate solution and after exhausting all other means. Even when they are levied, they can be levied only to the needed extent and they should not be a means of penalizing the wealthy. To this, one should also add the protection of private property against confiscation, usurpation or any kind of seizure by the state or any other authority or individual.
6. Shari'ah (the Islamic law) also provides another protection to private investment under what is called the principle of al Hima. Al Hima literally means protection. If a person digs a well at a place, other persons are not permitted to dig well(s) within certain radius of that well in order to protect its sources of water. This principle has several other applications in agriculture, industry and retail trade.

   Similarly, Shari'ah recognizes a right of pre-emption in both private and public land and other forms of investments.
7. The institution of Al Hisbah is another means for supporting the activities of the private sector. The responsibility of this institution is to see to it that moral and ethical norms, and safety and health conditions are observed by all actors in the market, and to maintain an environment in which fairness and prosperity can prevail.
8. The social insurance system in Islam is structured to support and promote

the private sector's activities. Among other things, it provides for the poor and the needy, regardless of any contributions they might have made in the past; it includes a guarantee of dependants and the handicapped; and, provided resources permit, it has a debt insurance scheme which covers all legitimate debts in society if the debtor fails to repay them. The principal source of financing social insurance is *zakah* which is a well-defined tax on wealth and income. Most of the regulations of *zakah*, including its rate structure, subjected items of wealth and income and its exemptions, are given in the texts of the Qur'an and the Sunnah, and cannot be altered by man.

9. The institution of *zakah* also provides a sort of debt payment guarantee under the item of al Gharimin. Al Gharimin are those who are under the burden of debts. The origin of these debts must be lawful such as legitimate business, trade, provision for self and family, carrying a responsibility of blood money or any other financial responsibility in the process of reconciling disputes among people or tribes, and so forth. What is relevant here is that it includes business debts. Disbursement to al Gharimin is mentioned in the Qur'an as one of the eight categories for which *zakah* proceeds must be spent. Such a guarantee would encourage individuals to be innovative and productive in business.

At the end of this section, it must be reiterated that the role of the state in the Islamic economic system is to enhance, assist, and correct the market but not to eliminate and substitute it.

Basic Economic Rights of Man in the Islamic System

The religion of Islam in general and its economic system in particular ensures the basic economic rights of individuals which include the right to private ownership, the right to economic freedom and the right to decent means of living. These basic human rights are guaranteed on the spiritual and moral levels, as Islam teaches its followers to honour and respect these rights. They are also cherished on the legal level, as they are protected in the Qur'an and the Sunnah. Moreover, the whole Islamic system and its institutions are structured to promote them as part of the intrinsic rights of mankind. These basic rights are bestowed by God on to mankind; therefore, they are in a sense Divine and sacred. Thus their protection is considered a religious obligation on all Muslims, individually and collectively to the extent that Muslims are permitted, and even called upon, to fight for the protection of these rights for themselves and for others (4 : 75). Their essential scope and regulations are given in the Divine revelation, a fact which makes any change or alteration outside the reach of man. The Islamic *fiqh* gives in detail a whole listing of the implications of these rights and whatever conditions, restrictions or circumstances the Shari'ah has in regard to their application.

The Right to Private Ownership

Like the rights to freedom, safety and security, the right to private ownership is granted by God to man. The Islamic doctrine treats all these basic human rights as God-given. They do not stem from nature, society or any convention or tradition of men.[2] Ownership is a relationship between an owner and a thing, implying exclusiveness in utilization and disposition.[3] The Arabic term for ownership is *milk*. It is mentioned twenty times in the Qur'an with explicit reference to private property. In many verses things are related or attributed to men and women in terms of private ownership. For example, "Your riches and your children may be but a trial" (64:15), and "Out of their wealth take *zakah*" (9:103). In addition, there are hundreds of explicit references in the Sunnah.

Private ownership in Islam applies to material things such as a horse or an apple and covers the rights of utilization and disposition. It may apply to utilities which can be derived from things owned by others such as the utility of a rented car. It may also apply to intangible matters such as authorship and trademarks.[4] Islamic law describes the right of private ownership as inclusive, exclusive and perpetual. It is inclusive to all authorities of utilization, exploitation and disposition. It is exclusive in the sense that it provides these rights to the owner alone, and it is permanent to the owner as long as he/she owns the property.[5]

Before looking into the principles which govern the different aspects of private ownership, it is important to understand the concept of dual ownership in Islamic economics and jurisprudence. Islamic jurisprudence provides for two coexisting kinds of ownership: public and private. Certain properties are assigned to public ownership. These include rivers, public roads and bridges, all kinds of minerals whether in gaseous, liquid or solid form, besides state property such as government buildings and projects. Things which are publicly owned may be opened to all people to get whatever benefit they desire from them (e.g. using the rivers for drinking and irrigation) or they may be for the exclusive use of the state (e.g. government offices); but in both cases the public property is to be devoted solely to the benefit of the people. It is of interest to note in this context that mines are not permitted to be privately-owned according to many Muslim scholars.[6] It is also of relevance to note that the early rulers of Islam had devoted huge natural resources (land at that time) to public ownership both as a source of public revenue for the running of the government and as means of economic policy to achieve the objectives of the state, especially to ensure economic justice.[7]

The institution of private ownership is predicted in Shari'ah upon principles which clarify its position and role in the Islamic economy. These principles are briefly stated in the following:

1. The desires to acquire and accumulate is inborn in human nature. See, for example, verses 3:14, 17:100, 89:20, 100:8, and so forth and several sayings of the Prophet such as "If the son of Adam has two valleys of wealth, he would seek a third valley". [Reported by al Bukhari and Muslim]
2. Benefits of accumulation are preserved to one's posterity after one's death. Thus the Islamic law of inheritance provides an additional enhancement to promoting saving and capital accumulation by keeping the wealth of the deceased in the hands of his/her beloved ones. In this regard, the Prophet encouraged his companions to leave their heirs rich rather than poor.
3. The right of private ownership is founded on the general Islamic doctrine that man is created by God as His vicegerent on earth. God bestowed on man certain mental and physical abilities and authorized him to act in fulfilment of the responsibilities he is charged with. In this meaning, the ultimate and final owner of every and all things and creatures is God. The implication of this philosophy is that the Grantor/the Ultimate Owner has the right of determining the conditions of the trust and the trustee is supposed to behave accordingly. Therefore, the right of private ownership must be purposive. It should be instrumental in the effective discharge of man's responsibilities of vicegerency and in achieving well-being in this life and in the Hereafter.
4. This nature of the right of ownership, coupled with the doctrine of the oneness of mankind and equality of all human beings, necessitates that the bounties of God be accessible to all men alike and that they do not become the monopoly of a few. In other words, Divine trusteeship is granted to all men equally and not to any group, race or people.
5. The right of private ownership is protected by several moral, spiritual and legal means such as the prohibition of theft, coercion, fraud, cheating, and so forth and the imposition of legal penalties on violators.
6. The right of ownership has a limited extension beyond death in the form of a last will which is limited to a maximum of one third of the estate, and in the form of inheritance which is given in Shari'ah in such minute details that even remote possibilities are not lost sight of.
7. Private property is an individual right which has a social role. Individuals are required to observe the social function of private property. But as the society and the state are not the grantor of this right, they have no right to limit, restrict, confiscate or eliminate private ownership except through the due process of the Islamic Shari'ah which specifies the cases and circumstances of such restrictions, their objectives and conditions.

8. The Shari'ah itself provides regulations and means which assure the fulfilment of the social objectives of private ownership and the prevention of abuse and infringement. However, the Islamic principles do not impose limitations on the size of wealth or the amount of accumulation individuals make, nor do they call for absolute equality in distribution. Furthermore, these principles do not restrict the right of private ownership to consumption goods nor do they exclude means of production from being owned privately. This is in spite of the fact that these principles also draw a balanced position which does not allow non-compensated utilization of others' property or manpower.

The Right to Economic Freedom

Economic freedom in the Islamic economic system is part of the general freedom of choice which is entrenched in the Islamic way of life. People are free even to select the religion, and because of this liberty they are held responsible for their actions both in this worldly life and in the Hereafter. Freedom of decisions, beliefs and actions makes the foundation of religion in Islam the basis on which God sent Heavenly guidance; otherwise He could have created the human race in a form similar to that of the angels who, by their own nature, cannot disobey His orders. Human beings are given the opportunity to choose between the right and the wrong both of which are made accessible to men, to decide their own path in life, and to take the actions they deem appropriate. God sent His Messengers in order to point out the path which is most acceptable to the Lord, and which is the most beneficial and rewarding in this life and in the Hereafter. This is the essence of the doctrine of Islam.

The doctrine of accountability and reckoning in Islam is based on the premise of freedom of choice. As human beings are individually free, they are also accountable on an individual basis. Every person will be reckoned on the Day of Judgement. In no way can one atone for his/her misdeeds except by seeking God's forgiveness and doing good deeds.[8]

Economic freedom is only one aspect of the overall freedom of choice enshrined in Islam. It is significant to note that the Prophet refused to fix prices even when they rose very high. His refusal was based on the principle of fair-dealing in business, according to which the producers cannot be forced to sell their goods at lower than the market price as long as changes in prices are caused by changes in supply and demand without any monopolistic or monopsonic intervention. Furthermore, the Prophet was keen to minimize the information gap in the market when he rejected the idea of intercepting the farm producers before they reached the marketplace and became familiar with what was going on there. He was very forceful in dealing with cheating and monopoly, to the extent that he equated them with the worst sins and disbelief.

Throughout many centuries of Islamic history, Muslim society has preserved this cherished principle of freedom. The concept of supervising the moral behaviour of the market was introduced by the Prophet himself. During the early centuries of the Islamic era, various thinkers wrote books on the role and duties of the market supervisor, al Muhtasib. The theme that prevails in all these writings is the preservation of freedom in the market and the elimination of monopolistic elements. The principle of freedom was carried by many Muslim jurists to such an extent that it even threatened the system by depriving the government of its right to interfere in the case of monopoly. This compelled Ibn Taymiyyah to write his book, *Al Hisbah fi al Islam*, to show that individual economic freedom must be limited in such cases, even if such limitations include government intervention in the pricing of goods and services. Ibn Taymiyyah could confidently make a strongly-worded statement that individuals are fully authorized to keep their property and to dispose of it the way they like, and that no one, including the state, has any right to take all or part of it without their consent, except in some clearly specified cases where they are obliged to give it up with complete and fair compensation.

According to Abu al A'la al Maududi, it is the individual who is more important in Islam than the community, society or nation. The individual, he argues, is not meant to serve society, and that it is society which should ultimately serve the individual. No community or nation is responsible before Allah as a group but each member is responsible before Him individually. The ultimate reason behind the existence of a social system is the individual's welfare and happiness, and not that of the society. Hence, the true measure of a good social system is the extent to which it helps its individual members to develop their personalities and to improve their personal abilities and capabilities. Thus, Islam disapproves of any type of social organization and any social welfare scheme that suppress individuals and tie them very strongly to the social regime so that their independent personalities perish.

In *The Economic Enterprise in Islam*, M.N. Siddiqi points out that Islam relies upon the market mechanism to a very great extent. Some implications of the doctrine of economic freedom in Islam in relation to the market are found in Ibn Taymiyyah's *al Hisbah*. These can be reformulated as follows:

1. People are free to enter and to leave the market.
2. An adequate level of information about the market forces and commodities is necessary. Ibn Taymiyyah investigated contracts in which one of the parties did not comply with this condition, whereupon he gave the other party the option to revise the contract. He also saw it as the responsibility of the government (al Muhtasib) to rectify the situation.
3. Monopolistic elements should be eliminated from the market. Ibn Taymiyyah did not permit coalitions of professional men, whether they were groups of sellers or buyers. He allowed the Muhtasib to interfere and determine the price of the equivalent should monopolistic elements exist in the market.

4. Within this freedom, he recognized the effects of increasing demand or declining supply on prices. He approved the resulting increase in prices, since forcing people to sell at a given price is compulsion without any right; and although the seller should not be forced to give up profit, at the same time he should not be allowed to hurt others.
5. Any deviation from the honest practice of economic freedom (e.g. false oaths, incorrect weights, and ill will) is criticized by the Islamic writers along with production and trade in commodities which are condemned as bad for health or moral reasons (e.g. alcoholic beverages, drugs, prostitution, and gambling).

The Right of Means of Living

Islam essentially regards the satisfaction of basic material needs of men and women as part of the respect and value of human dignity. Human beings are honoured to the extent that their basic needs must be fulfilled under all conditions. Hence, the guarantee of a minimum standard of living is an inherent constituent of the Islamic economic system. This calls for indigenous devices or mechanisms as well as state intervention under special circumstances.

Guaranteed minimum standard of living is biologically, socially and religiously determined. There are certain minimum religious requirements relating to clothing, cleanliness, housing, knowledge, etc. Obviously, these religious requirements need economic means; and the provision of these means is the duty of every Muslim individual, and society. In addition, traditions, customs, social habits and ways create several economic needs, whose non-fulfilment results in social life becoming tough and sometimes untenable.

In addition to resource allocation, employment and production policies which are available to the state in the Islamic economic system, there are a few other tools which guarantee the fulfilment of sufficient means of living. Some of these tools are inborn in the system itself in the sense that they are internal and they work automatically and continuously within the system without being invoked by any special state action. Other tools are resorted to only under special circumstances especially when the indigenous tools show inadequacies for achieving the targets within a reasonable period of time. The inborn means include the following: *zakah*, obligatory interpersonal transfer, *kaffarat*, the principle of granting the surplus and the charitable *awqaf*. In addition to these tools, the state can use public funds and, if necessary, impose special taxes on the rich in order to secure sufficient resources to guarantee the basic needs of all.

The Islamic economic system provides for a dual concept of ownership: private and public. Public ownership covers a considerable area of natural resources and public utilities. Public property may take one of two forms: firstly, property which is owned by the state on an exclusive basis, and secondly, property which is shared by all people together under the supervision of the state. The latter includes public roads, forests, river water, ground surface minerals such as salt, state's treasury, and so forth, while the former includes underground minerals, waterfalls and other natural resources.

The Islamic state is required to ensure that all people have the right of accessibility and utilization of the shared public property, although there are limitations and conditions governing this right. As far as the property owned by the state on an exclusive basis is concerned, all people have equal right to this kind of property and the Islamic state guarantees equal opportunity to this property. This right of the public to the state's property is unequivocal in the Islamic system to the extent that it goes as far as to consider each person in the society as a sort of an owner, on a collective basis, of the state's property.[9] The Islamic government is responsible for distributing the benefits of the state properties to all people in a fair manner.

It is the duty of the state to supervise the application of *zakah* and obligatory transfers in addition to generating sufficient resources for meeting its responsibilities. The Islamic state is obliged to see to it that individuals discharge their responsibility with regard to *zakah*, and the obligatory transfers of income. Thus, the Islamic state is required to take direct charge of the collection and distribution of *zakah* if individuals fail to perform it properly. If the indigenous or voluntary means of financing transfers are insufficient to ensure the basic needs of the people, the Islamic state must impose taxes on the rich.

Restrictions On Economic Freedom and Private Ownership

Like any other system, the Islamic economic system also has certain restrictions on private ownership and economic freedom. Such restrictions aim at enhancing the private and social functions of private ownership and at reducing the likelihood and scope of possible abuses of these rights. These restrictions make the God-given concept of private ownership an intrinsic component of Islam, since man is only a vicegerent of God with regard to property whose real and absolute owner is the one who has the right to define its meaning.

For example, the consumption of certain items (e.g. alcoholic beverages and pork) is prohibited in Islam. Likewise, there are prohibitions on the production of materials the consumption of which is prohibited, and on certain practices such as exorbitant profits emanating from monopolistic power.

Most Muslim scholars are of the opinion that minerals, rivers and similar natural resources must be owned by the state and used for the benefit of the whole society. On this basis, it appears that private ownership is not allowed to enter the domain of the state's property.

The major sources of private property in Shari'ah are increments of already owned property, exchange, inheritance and last wills, gifts and donations, revival and reclamation of non-owned land, and acquisition of free things such as water from a river or wood from a forest. On the other hand, coercion, theft, bribery and gambling are examples of unlawful means of obtaining property which are prohibited in Shari'ah.

Islam also considers *riba* (interest) and sale of prohibited items as illegitimate sources of private property. By implication, income generated by *riba* and sale of prohibited items cannot be owned by the recipient.

Whatever is prohibited for consumption is also considered forbidden for production and/or for spending any man hours in its connection except for its removal and destruction. On the other hand, Islam encourages productive work and considers working to earn a livelihood, to improve one's economic status and to give for charity as a form of worship which is rewarded by God. Moreover, the religious standards of Islam do not permit abstention from productive activities under the pretence of spiritual uplifting or devotion to practices of worship.

Two kinds of restriction on consumption exist in Islam. Firstly, certain items are prohibited. These are alcoholic beverages, pork and all harmful substances. Secondly, there is a quantitative prohibition of extravagance. This second type of restriction is moral to a large extent, although there are occasions of excessive extravagance being regulated when it may be enforced by law. It must be noticed that all societies usually put certain restrictions of the first kind on grounds of proven harmfulness of certain items or on traditional and religious grounds. But, it must also be noticed that prohibitions, which are mentioned in the texts of the Qur'an and the Sunnah, are of a permanent nature not subject to circumstantial changes. As for quantitative restrictions, it may be pointed out that the morality of thrift, which is fundamental to the spirit of capitalism, is not far from that of abstention of extravagance. Besides, there are legally enforceable checks on excessive extravagance in other societies too.

There are only a few restrictions on investment in Islam. In general, Islam calls for productive uses of wealth and discourages hoarding. Of course, items prohibited in consumption are also prohibited in production. Additionally, forms of investment which involve injustice, such as *riba*, are also not permissible. The Islamic business code defines the relations between investors and entrepreneurs in a way that distributes the risk in a balanced manner through equity participation and profit-sharing procedures. Also prohibited are unfair use of one's rights with the intention to cause harm to others, reckless acts which hurt the interests of the society, etc. according to Islamic jurisprudence.

Expropriation of private property is allowed under special circumstances. The right of preemption, forced liquidation in case of bankruptcy and forceful acquisition of loaned property are examples of expropriation for private purposes. The construction of roads, mosques and other infrastructure is an example of the public interest which can be served by means of expropriation. However, expropriation must be done by the proper authorities with full access to the jurisdiction for raising objections.

In addition to normal restrictions, there are exceptional cases in which the state is allowed to interfere and impose certain restrictions on private property and economic freedom. The most important among them is the case of forced pricing when a monopolistic situation is unavoidable such as in some public utilities, transportation, and industries. Additionally, certain temporary and exceptional limitation or ceiling on the size of private property may be imposed, if proven indispensable for securing benefits to society as a whole.[10]

NOTES

1 See, for example: verses 2:168 and 172, 5:91, 6:141 and 142, 7:31, 16:114, 20:54, 34:15, and 67:15.

2 'Abd al Salam al Abbadi, *al Milkiyyah fi al Shari'ah al Islamiyyah*, vol. 1, pp. 133–34.

3 Ibid., p. 169.

4 Ibid., pp. 170–200.

5 Ibid., pp. 391–93.

6 For more elaboration, refer to my paper on "The Public Sector and its Role in Financing Development in Islam", which was presented at the Cairo Seminar on Resource Mobilization in the Islamic State, April 1986.

7 Monzer Kahf, "Financial Resources of the Early Islamic State". Unpublished paper submitted to the Islamic Research and Training Institute, Jeddah 1987.

8 There may be very few examples of collective responsibility in the Shari'ah. For instance, the two cases of al 'Aqilah and al Qasamah may well be about the only two examples, though their occurrence is rare. Al 'Aqilah refers to the responsibility of the family of the person who mistakenly killed or injured someone for blood money due to the family of the deceased or injured. Al Qasamah refers to the procedure of exchange of oath in the case of a person killed without knowing the killer.

9 There are several implications of this rule, the least of them is the inapplicability of severe punishment in case of theft.

10 'Abd al Salam al 'Abbadi, op. cit., vol. 2, pp. 408–10.

3 MUSLIM BUSINESSES IN MINDANAO

Mohd. Musib M. Buat

Introduction

The purpose of this study is to inquire into the entrepreneurship and business practices of the Muslim Filipinos in an urban setting with particular focus on the Moro inhabitants of Zamboanga City, Western Mindanao. It will trace their savings and investment practices and the profile of their business in terms of organization of structure, nature of business, scale of operation and modes of transactions.

The research tools utilized in the collection, validation and updating of data are collation and analysis of data from official sources (for example, agency reports and official records),[1] information from interviews of key informants and a perception survey through the use of prepared survey questionnaires on a random and stratified sample of the population. In the perception survey, a modified cluster sampling method was employed with the aid of research assistants (Tables 3.1 and 3.2).[2] The sample size formula was observed to minimize the margins of error. The statistical tools employed to determine central tendencies are the mean and computed percentages of responses.

It is hypothesized that there is a close link or connection between the habit of saving and capital formation with the increase in economic activity and entrepreneurship among the Muslims. The higher the savings the greater the opportunity for capital formation and investments. Saving habits and capital formation are treated as independent variables. Favourable and/or unfavourable business climate/environment are the intervening variables. It is assumed that the improvement of the peace and order climate and the return to political stability and normalcy are considered the influential intervening variables, together with readily available credit and financing facilities for business expansion and opportunities.

TABLE 3.1
Cluster Distribution of the Sample Population
(N = No. of Respondents)

Sample Area/District	Area Code	N
Downtown Area or Poblacion	A	21
Office of Muslim Affairs, Region IX	B	20
National Labour Relations Commission, Region IX	C	18
Barter Trade Center, Pettit Barracks Area	D	22
Suburban Area (Sta. Catalina & Tetuan Districts)	E	22
Total	5	103

TABLE 3.2
Demographic Characteristics of the Sample Population*

Variables	Frequency of Distribution						
Civil Status	A	B	C	D	E	N	%
Marriage	18	14	13	12	17	74	72
Single	2	4	5	10	2	23	22
Divorced	–	1	–	–	2	3	3
Widow/Widower	1	1	–	–	1	3	3
Total	21	20	18	22	22	103	100
Sex	21	20	18	22	22	103	100
Male	14	11	11	10	15	61	59
Female	7	9	7	12	7	42	41

* Table 2 in the Tabulation of Survey Results.

Zamboanga City

Zamboanga City is situated at the Southernmost tip of the Zamboanga peninsula. The city has a total land mass of about 1,420.99 square kilometres.[3] About 25 other islands fall within the territorial jurisdiction of the city with an aggregate area of 6,248.5 hectares, giving a total land area of about 148,338.49 hectares.[4]

Generally, the terrain of the city is sloping from the shoreline and gradually becoming hilly and mountainous towards the core of the peninsula. The seasons are not very pronounced, relatively dry from November to April, and wet during the rest of the year. This makes the city an ideal haven for commerce, trade and shipping, especially in view of its favourable climate all the year round.

Early History

The native inhabitants of the coastal areas of the Zamboanga peninsula are the Sama-Balangingi and the seafaring Badjaos (Samal-Laut). The highlands are inhabited by Subanon tribes (predominantly non-Muslims) and their close kin, the Kalibugans (Islamized Subanons). The Southeastern part of the peninsula along the Illana Bay or the Moro Gulf is populated by Iranuns (Ilanuns) and Maguindanauns, with a sprinkling of Chinese and Malays.

The Southwestern part of the Zamboanga peninsula and its environs fell sway under the sphere of influence of the Sul Sultanate in the latter part of the sixteenth century. The Spaniards colonized Zamboanga in 1597 and established a fort at La Caldera (presently Recodo, Zamboanga City) which was later abandoned. It was re-occupied in 1635 to check the punitive raids of the Moros of Visayas and Luzon. The Spaniards again abandoned the Zamboanga Fort in 1663. And as soon as the Spanish left, the Moros took over Zamboanga and almost two-thirds of the Christian population returned to Islam. Spain again re-occupied Zamboanga in 1718 and allowed Catholic missionaries to set up new missions.[5]

After the signing of the Treaty of Paris in 1898, the United States occupied Zamboanga on 10 November 1899. In order to consolidate its position in the area, the American administration entered into the infamous Bates Treaty and Carpenter Agreement with the sovereign of Sulu.[6]

Zamboanga was formally organized into a municipal government under Republic Act No. 135 in 1901 through the union of Zamboanga and Tetuan districts. It became the capital of the Moro Province from 1903 to 1913. It became a chartered city on 12 October 1936 under Commonwealth Act No. 39, embracing the island of Basilan. Basilan was separated as a city in 1948 under Republic Act No. 288.

Population and Ethnic Profile

Zamboanga City has a population of about 343,722 according to the 1 May 1980 National Census with an annual growth rate of 5.3 per cent between 1975 to 1980. The average growth rate of the population of Western Mindanao (Region IX) is about 4.3 per cent compared to the average national growth rate of 2.7 per cent for the same period. It has been projected that by 1990 the city will have a population of 443,279.[7] About 93.4 per cent or 113,000 of the labour force are employed. Only about 8,000 or 6.6 per cent are reported to be unemployed (Table 3.3).[8] The age group of 15 and above forms 55.1 per cent of the city population. The sex composition of the city is fairly even (50.5% male and 49.5% female).

TABLE 3.3
Distribution of Labour Force Participation by Sector and Class, Zamboanga City
(In thousand persons)*

Sector	Total
Agriculture, Fishing and Forestry	16,000
Industry	20,000
Services	77,000
Total Employed	113,000
Class of Workers	113,000
Wage and Salary Workers	69,000
Own Account Workers	38,000
Unpaid Family Workers	6,000
Urban (Total Employed)	21,000
Rural (Total Employed)	92,000
No. of Males Employed	79,000
No. of Females Employed	34,000

* NEDA, ibid.; NCSO, Preliminary Report.

TABLE 3.4
Distribution of Population by Ethnic Origin, Zamboanga City, 1980*

Ethnic Origin	Total	% Distribution
Chavacano	224,998	65.37
Cebuano	34,763	10.10
Tausug	28,057	8.15
Sama (Samal)	19,241	5.59
Tagalog	15,675	4.55
Ilocano	11,791	3.43
Chinese	2,019	1.14
All Others	3,934	1.67
Total	334,162	100.0

* Zamboanga City, Socio-Economic Profile, 1984. The 1980 Census reported the population of Zamboanga City to be 343,722 as of May 1980. The Zamboanga City data on population is short of 9,560.

The Tausugs are the dominant ethnic group in the region, followed by the Samal (Sama) and the Subanon. The Muslim population of Western Mindanao is estimated to exceed one million. The Muslim population in Zamboanga City numbered 86,100 as of 1980.

If we extrapolate the population of Zamboanga City at the rate of 2.6 per cent annual growth, the Muslim population of Zamboanga City in 1989 would be about 108,648. This probably is an underestimate, as it does not take into account immigration from the islands.

In terms of ethnic origin, the Chavacano-speaking Zamboanguenos (pidgin Spanish) form about 65 per cent of the population, followed by Cebuanos (10.1%), Tausug-Sulu (8.2%), and Sama (5.6%) according to the data from the City Government of 1980 (Table 3.4). By religious affiliation, three-fourths of the city population profess the Catholic faith and the rest profess Islam and other religious denominations.

Natural Resources

Zamboanga City has its own share of the rich natural resources of the Zamboanga peninsula and the marine environment around it. Its forest and timber lands constitute about 6.9 per cent of the resources region-wide and 8.2 per cent of the aggregate alienable and disposable lands to Western Mindanao (Table 3.5). About

TABLE 3.5

Land Use Classification of Zamboanga City, 1984

(In hectares)

Land Use Classification	Zamboanga City Data[1]	NEDA, RO IX Data[2]	% Region-Wide
Timber/Forest	64,909.88	63,345	6.9
Alienable/Disposable	64,445.97	78,125	8.2
Swamps, Saltbeds, Fishponds & Marshes	8,771.64	–	–
Urban Area	3,963.50	–	–
Islands	6,247.50	–	–
Total	148,338.49	141,470[3]	

1 Zamboanga City, Socio-Economic Profile, 1984.
2 NEDA IX, 1987 Socio-Economic Information on Western Mindanao.
3 Incomplete.

12.4 per cent of the marine fish in Western Mindanao are landed by commercial vessels in Zamboanga City.[9] The Zamboanga peninsula is rich in metallic and non-metallic deposits, representing about 1.8 per cent and 2.5 per cent, respectively, of the national deposits.[10]

Industrial Sector

There were about 749 cottage industry firms registered in 1985 in Western Mindanao, with a total capitalization of 29.7 million pesos, generating 4,653 jobs and posting 9.5 million pesos in sales. There are about 35 major existing industries in the region. Out of these, 17 (49.2%) are located in Zamboanga City. There are 14 mining firms operating in the Zamboanga peninsula, two of which are located in Zamboanga City.[11]

There was an uptrend in the overall performance of the region's economy in the seventies. The Gross Regional Product (GRP) grew at the rate of 8.3 per cent per annum in real terms from 1.5 billion pesos in 1971 to 2.95 billion pesos in 1979. Western Mindanao (Region IX) was the fastest growing region in the country with an annual growth rate higher than that of the Gross National Product (6.6% in the seventies).[12]

Zamboanga City has been recently declared a highly urbanized city under the Local Government Code.[13] The city also has pleasant tourist facilities by local standards and tourist attractions such as the white beaches of Sta. Cruz island, Pasonanca and Abong-Abong Parks, the exotic Taluksangay Moro Village and the famous Yakan Weaving Village, the Public Market that abounds with tropical fruits, the Barter Trade Center, San Ramon and Penal Farm, the Zamboanga Golf and Country Club, and shorelines ideal for fishing and water sports.

Economic Sectoral Performance

The shares of agriculture, industry and services in the Gross Regional Product stood at 52.4 per cent, 18.5 per cent and 29.1 per cent, respectively in 1971. These ratios shifted to 44.7 per cent, 12.0 per cent and 43.3 per cent, respectively, in 1979. The agricultural sector grew at the rate of 10.6 per cent, while the services sector expanded at the rate of 11.5 per cent. The industrial sector registered a slower growth of 8.8 per cent per annum. The contribution of Western Mindanao to the Gross National Product increased from 3 per cent in 1971 to 3.4 per cent in 1979.[14]

The share of the Muslims in Western Mindanao's economic activity is limited to municipal or small-time fishing, seaweed culture, local services and island trading, based mostly on barter trade. The reason for this is the lack of technical know-how and capital. A similar picture also prevails in the rest of Mindanao and Palawan.[15]

Muslim Finance and Trade Practices

Land Tenure and Customary Contracts

Titling of private lands is relatively new to the Filipino Muslims. By tradition, many of them still adhere to customary land tenure based on communal land ownership (*harta pusaka*) in the Malay Adat (customary) Law. Ancestral domains are regarded as tribal preserves or trust lands, a parallel of *kiraj* (state lands) and *waqf* lands (endowments) in *figh* (Islamic jurisprudence).

During the American regime and in the early post-war period, Muslims were only encouraged to register their lands under the so-called Torrens System for convenience since land was then abundant. But after the influx of Christian settlers from the North (Visayas and Luzon), starting in the pre-war commonwealth period and the early fifties, the Muslims felt the growing scarcity of land as ancestral domains were now being encroached upon. By then, land titles were handy instruments for surety and bonding purposes. Private trust lands handed down from a common ancestor have remained undivided among the members of the clan. However, when some unscrupulous member of the clan or family wanted to transfer a portion of the common property to a stranger, say a Christian settler, troubles would arise. In most cases, the shrewd newcomers through connivance of some government land officials succeeded in titling vasts tract of communal lands. To the rest of the members of the clan, the party who sold his rights only conveyed a portion that belongs to him by ancestral right and never the whole tribal property.[16] This was one of the major root causes of the bloody feuds between the Muslims and the new land settlers that led to the present secessionist movement in Southern Philippines.[17]

As a rule, individual members of the clan who personally cultivate a portion of the communal land delineate their rights of usufruct by means of natural boundaries or tree plantings. And, whenever they wish to raise funds, they either mortgage or lease their farms or orchards, granting the lessor or mortgagor the right to till and cultivate the land or harvest the fruits under a customary contract of *sanla* or *arindao*, a familiar practice among the Malays.

The transaction may either be for a shorter or longer period. When it involves a long term or perpetual lease (*padjak*), it takes the form of *bai'-bi-al-wafa'* contract known in *figh* whereby the vendor (or lessor) retains the right of redemption,[18] similar to the *pacto de retro* sale in civil law.[19] When the transactions are for shorter periods, they take the form of partnership contracts known in *figh* as *musagat* (lease of orchards or land for a definite period or cropping season), or *mukhabarah* (cropping lease) where seeds are provided by the cultivator and *mudara'ah* (cropping agreement) where farm inputs are provided by the landlord.[20] This is known as *partida* (leasehold) among Christian Filipinos in Mindanao.

Partnership and Joint Stock Company

The Moros of Southern Philippines, particularly in Western Mindanao, have traditionally practised partnership ventures in trade and commerce since time immemorial under the general term of *sharikat*. They are generally familiar with the two forms of partnership (*sharikat-al-ain*) and the joint stock company (*mudaraba*). The first type is common in trading. A leader in the community or businessman announces his commercial project, say a trading voyage to Sabah, Malaysia. Prospective investors contribute to this venture and they share in the profits and losses proportionate to their investments. The partnership agreement may be for a definite period or on a continuing basis.

Among the natives, the traditional term for association or co-operation is *sama* which literally means togetherness or community association. In the Maguindanao and Maranao tongue, it is known as *upakatan* (*muafakat* in Malay), meaning association or consensus or agreement. *Sama* also refers to the tribal group along the coastal areas of the Zamboanga peninsula (Sama Balangingi) and in the Sulu archipelago (Sama Taw-Tawi).

Corporate property ownership and investment in stock company shares among the Muslims of Southern Philippines is still undergoing a transitional stage from the short-term limited partnership venture (*sharikat-al-ain*) to the corporate association or joint stock company (*qirad* and *mudarabah*).

The *sharikat-mudarabah* type is very common among the Tausugs of Sulu, particularly in commercial fishing ventures. It is not unusual for a group of Muslim businessmen or partners to contribute to a common fund to finance the purchase of a *payao* (a native fishing vessel). They agree to appoint a manager or designate a partner to run the business and share in the profits and losses to the extent of their contributions. The business relationship continues during the lifetime of the partners. Strictly, it has not yet attained the continuing juridical personality of the modern corporation. However, big time businessmen usually incorporate their business venture under the private Corporation Act or register their partnership under Philippine Laws (Civil Code). But even with this, such enterprises have remained family corporations or partnerships. As a rule, the Moro Muslims have not yet reached the stage of running a sophisticated corporate business.

In the City of Zamboanga, the majority of Muslim business organization is still in the category of sole proprietorship. The Partnership ventures are of limited duration and are informally entered into.

Other Forms of Civil Contracts

Business and commercial practices among the Moros have been earlier influenced by Islamic law and jurisprudence with the blending of Adat law.

Other Forms of Partnership. As in civil law, there are also other forms and types of partnership mentioned in *figh*, namely: personal partnership (*sharikat-al-abdan*), a contract whereby the parties enter into a trade or professional association for the purpose of exercising their trade or profession, holding their profits in common and dividing it amongst themselves; universal partnership (*sharikat-al-mofawada*) whereby the profits gained by each partner is held in common and all partners are held jointly liable for the debts of each; and commercial partnership (*sharikat-al-wujuh*) whereby the partners buy the merchandise on their own behalf under particular conditions, but the goods are sold in common, dividing the profits among themselves. Except for the short-term limited partnership (*sharikat-al-ain*) which is generally permitted under the *shafi*' school (*madhab*), all the above three are considered illegitimate or unlawful, because the share of each partner is not clearly specified and the agreement is no more than a mere trade combination.[21] As a general rule monopolies and trade combinations are prohibited under Philippine laws and are declared offences under the penal code. The other three partnership types are uncommon among the Moros.

There is, however, some controversy in the current barter trade practices in Zamboanga City. The local *ulama* (jurist) in the city has rendered a *fatwa* (legal opinion) that the current barter trade practices in the city involve *riba* (usurious transaction).[22] If this refers to the barter trade association of traders, it does not fall under any of the above objectionable partnership contracts. The legally and traditionally recognized practice among the Moro traders is to entrust their capital to a team leader, in groups of ten per team, to undertake the trip to Labuan or Singapore to trade and purchase goods. They share in the expenses of the trip and the purchased merchandise is distributed in accordance with individual orders and the size of the capital contributed by each. In a sense, the transaction resembles that of an agency (*wakala*) with the features of a partnership association. Hence, from the juridical point of view, the transaction does not involve *riba*. The shares of the partners are clearly specified, including the kind of merchandise purchased, and the liability of each partner is limited to his/her contribution.

Agency and Guarantee. Contracts of *wakala* and guarantee (*kifalah*) are also known to the Moros. In the native language, agency is termed as *wakilan* or *pag-wakilan* but is more common in non-commercial transactions such as agency in marriage contracts or deputization of a political agent in the traditional sultanate of Sulu. The term *wakil* has been interchangeably used with *wazir*, meaning district governor or ranking state minister.[23]

Pledge or Security. Pledge or security (*rahn*), as known in *figh*, is common among the Moros of Western Mindanao. The generic term used is *padjak* or *padjakan* (pawnbroker). The contract involves the pledge and security for a simple loan. In Maguindanao, this contract is known as *tihaya* (literally, guarantee or security for an obligation).

This accounts for the proliferation of the pawnshop business in the town of Jolo and Zamboanga City. The Muslims who prefer to invest their savings or surplus capital in gold or silver (usually in jewellery) find the *padjakan* a convenient means of raising cash. It is impersonal because the transaction could be concluded through an agent (*wakil*) and there is no direct contact as in bank transactions. In other words, the Moro pride (*maratabat*) is preserved and protected. To a Muslim of noble and royal birth, contracting a personal loan is most distasteful as it affects one's social standing in the community.

The other reason for investments in gold and silver is because of the traditional trade practice of using the gold and silver as the basic means of exchange in trade and commerce. These commodities are likewise less influenced by the price fluctuation of foreign exchange in the money market. Despite interest (*riba*) involved in the pawnshop trade, the Muslims resort to it for lack of an alternative. The urban-bred among the Moros have more or less accepted the value of opening savings and current accounts in local banks. The prevailing peaceful climate in the city and the region have encouraged traders to keep their money in banks for safekeeping and not necessarily to earn interest.

This is generally true among the traders in Zamboanga City. They, however, prefer to transact their banking needs with private commercial banks than with government banks. The reasons for this are that they find private banks more efficient and that their anonymity is sheltered in private banks.[24] The rise of property-related crimes and lawlessness has made many of them wary about their asset holdings, especially cash.

Simple Loans. Under the generic term of *padjak* customary transactions, simple loans known in *figh* as *gard* and *ariyah*, in the form of loan or lease of chattels and movables, usually implements in trade or business such as a fishing craft (*payap*), goods and merchandise and even firearms, are common among the island folks. It is known in *figh* as *gard* if the loan transaction is gratuitous and *ariyah* if it is for a fee, while a leasing arrangement is referred to as *ijarah*.

Contract of Deposit. Rural folks usually entrust or deposit their funds or valuables to an affluent relative who is engaged in business either for safekeeping or investment. The funds or valuables are returned whenever needed by the depositor. If the deposit is for investment purposes, it becomes *musharaka* (partnership) or *mudaraba* and not merely *wadi'ah* (contract of safekeeping deposits).

Many Muslims in Western Mindanao, including Zamboanga City, find this arrangement to avoid *riba* more practical and convenient for business beginners instead of keeping their money in banks.[25]

Buying and Selling (General Commerce). The most common and prevalent practice among the Muslims in the islands and Zamboanga City is trading in agricultural and marine products. The "comprador" or middlemen (known as *tauki* in Sabah) used to be dominated by local Chinese merchants. Some Moros who have accumulated enough capital through hard work and industry are equally competitive in the trade. This usually takes the form of *murabaha* whereby the purchaser will buy and contract goods for resale to a prospective customer on a "cost-plus negotiated profit margin".

Credit Unions. The national governments had earlier encouraged the formation of credit unions to mobilize funds for rural development under the co-operative programme. This, however, did not make much headway, especially among the Muslims. Among Christian Filipinos, this is simply known as *paluwagan* (credit association). The cultural transplant did not receive popular acceptance among the Moros who are still paternalistic and clannish.

The Islamic counterpart is the *gard hasan* which is a benevolent loan extended by a well-to-do member of the community in favour of a needy brother Muslim, free of interest and repayable whenever the borrower's circumstances improve. In case of default, the benefactor may either ask the borrower to repay it in terms of personal services or condone the loan by way of *sadaqah* (charity).

The Role of Ibadah and Waqf

An interesting and significant aspect of the savings and investment practices among the Moros is the role played by *ibadah* (Islamic devotion). It is an accepted article of faith that the act of giving to *sadaqah jahiriyah (zakat al fitr, zakat al mal* and *waqf*),[26] is a form of purifying one's income and wealth from physical impurities and spiritual pollution.

Muslims in Zamboanga City, both the affluent and the poor, readily contribute their *zakat* and *sadaqah* to their respective district mosques (*daira masjid*) and to the endowment of the local *madrasah* (Arabic and Islamic school) usually attached, or an adjunct, to the mosque.

Successful Muslim businessmen and professionals in Zamboanga City vie with each other in giving endowments (*awqaf*) for the development and upkeep of their respective district mosques which number about a dozen within the city suburb.[27]

Family Enterprises

The great majority of Muslim business organizations in Western Mindanao and Zamboanga City belong to the category of the single proprietorship characterized as "family enterprises". Big-time business in local trading and general merchandise in the barter trade and in agri-marine products are dominated by a score of Muslim families, besides some Chinese and Christian Filipinos. The successful business families among the "oldtimers" (Zamboangueno Muslims of Sama-Tausug descent) are represented by the Sakaluran, Camlian and Nunion families. The latecomers include successful individuals from the Alam, Jammang and Mohaymin families.

Hadji Ahmad Sakaluran, who runs A & S Enterprises, is a big-time dried fish dealer, barter trader, seaweed merchant and cobra dealer. Starting his business operations in the early seventies in joint venture with his brother-in-law Julkipli Camlian, who was then a successful businessman in the dried fish business, the Sakaluran enterprise expanded into a chain of successful business operations. His equally enterprising wife built an inter-island vessel, the *Radin*, in 1975 which became one of the pioneer barter trading vessels to Labuan, Malaysia. The Sakaluran enterprise is reputed to be worth from twenty to twenty-five million pesos in terms of assets and capital. In addition, the family owns coconut plantations in the islands. They also operate a warehouse with refrigeration facilities.

The Camlian family is equally successful in business. Julkipli Camlian, the former business partner of Sakaluran, is reported to have suffered some economic reverses due to his alleged complacency. Once a more successful businessman than Sakaluran, his economic losses were due to uncontrolled spending in non-productive ventures.[28] Hadji Bahari Camlian, a brother of Julkipli, is engaged in barter trading and shark fins business. Other Camlians, Hadji Sali and Qureshi, are also engaged in similar lines of business. The Sakalurans and Camlians market their merchandise as far as Davao and Manila. Shiek Abdulhamid Camlian, a recognized religious and political leader in the city and an ex-rebel warlord (in the seventies), is their family patriarch. Reportedly, they patronize the Bank of the Philippine Island, Solid Bank, and the Philippine Amanah Bank for their banking needs. They transact business both in cash and on consignment. Another successful merchant in the warehousing and refrigeration business is Hadji Abdua.

A close kin of the families mentioned above is the Usman family. Hadji Umar Usman owns a line of business enterprises such as foreign money exchange, film distribution and the Sitti's Film Production with branches in Manila and Zamboanga City.

The Nunio family is also among the oldest Muslim families in the city. The family owns real estate and a pearl farm in Taluksangay, a joint venture with a Japanese group. Aida Nunio operates the pearl farm. The Nunios are reputed to be a family of professionals, religious and political leaders among the Muslims.

Another Nunio, Abdulrahman, is engaged in the profitable bangus fry business, exporting the product to Taiwan and Japan, while another kin, Mohammad Zin Nunio, is in the real estate business.

Amil Abdulrahman, who is related to the Sakalurans, is engaged in trading and owns coconut plantations in the islands. Harun Kiram, the Mayor of Alicia municipality, owns real estate and coconut plantations within the city environs. The Abdulrahim brothers, Aldam and Yasin, are real estate owners in the city.

Another success story is that of the youthful Hasan Alam, who hails from Parang, Sulu. In 1977 he was elected president of the Zamboanga Barter Traders Kilusang Bayan, Inc. (ZBTKBI), a cooperative of barter traders. After initial success in the barter trade, he diversified into real estate, agribusiness and prawn culture at his newly bought farm in Taluksangay. His assets are also reputed to be worth millions of pesos. Hadji Hassan Hassiman, Alam's vice president in the barter trade cooperative, is also a successful businessman and a millionaire in his own right.

A more classic example of a success story is that of Hadji Mahmoud Jammang, formerly a town policeman of Jolo, now business tycoon and a shipping magnate. Like Sakaluran, his success is also attributable to the husband-and-wife business team. He is the president of the Samahang Kabuhayan Traders Association (SAKATA), also a cooperative of barter traders. Jammang owns the Alma Shipping Lines, Inc. with the main office in Zamboanga City. His shipping line operates three vessels, the *Dona Alma* (3,000 tonnage) that plies the Singapore barter trade route, the *Queen Alma* and *Princess Almalyn* (1,000 tonnage each) which are engaged in domestic shipping, loading passengers and cargo (Manila-Cebu and Davao routes).

Other professional/business Muslim sector groups in the city are represented by the Ali and Unga families. The Ali brothers (Basal and Rizal) used to own and operate porterage and *arrastre* services in the city. Due to some personal and business rivalries with some vested groups in the city during the previous regime, their business suffered some reverses. Lawyer Unga owns and operates a local lodging house (Unique Hotel) and a private protective agency, the Unique Security Agency. The other Unga brothers are engaged in barter trade. Another individual successful businessman is Singh Abubakar. He belongs to the influential Abubakar family of Jolo. He owns and operates a gasoline station in the city and a chain of movie houses in Jolo. The Muslims are not left behind in other economic fields. Hadji Yacob Lim (a Muslim convert and self-styled sultan of Zamboanga) owns and operates a domestic airline around the islands known as Swiftair.

Success Factors and Implications

The success of the above businessmen may be attributed to the husband-and-wife business tandem, aggressiveness, ability to take risks, and above all, the native business acumen. In the Islamic tradition, trading is almost a way of life and the rewards are not only earthly but even heavenly if one properly observes the Islamic injunction on business ethics. To some Moro businessmen, any business malpractice, whether intended or unintended is subject to *taubah* (repentance) provided one fulfils his *ibadah* (devotion) by performing the haj (pilgrimage to Mecca) and purifies one's property and wealth through giving *zakat* and *sadagah*. This may sound innovative (*bida'a*) to Muslim orthodox thinking, but the fact is that in the Moro commercial world, a re-interpretation of Islamic business ethics and values is in the moulding stage. Among the Moro legal thinkers, Muslims are justified to resort to any available business and trade practices on considerations of urgent necessity known as *darurah* in *figh* (Islamic jurisprudence) such as resorting to Western type of banking, finance and insurance, for lack of an alternative, to survive under a minority situation.

The Barter Trade

Historical Background

Trading is an age-old preoccupation of the Islamized Malays (Moros) of the Southern Philippines, particularly in the Sulu and Tawi-Tawi archipelago. They have traded as far as the Malaysian and Indonesian Islands.[29]

This traditional border trade has been branded by the national government as a form of "smuggling" because it deprived the national treasury of custom duties and revenues. Ironically, however, "big-time" smuggling is done by capitalist non-Muslim syndicates. If at all some Muslims were involved, they were used as mere proxies for powerful and influential groups. As traditional Moro barter trading continues, the national government has instituted guidelines to control the entry of contraband and to systematize the trade.

Liberalization of the Barter Trade

On 9 January 1973, Presidential Decree No. 93 was issued by former President Marcos liberalizing the barter trade. It was primarily intended to discourage the Muslims from joining the secessionists movement that surfaced earlier before the declaration of martial law on 21 September 1972, and to keep the Muslims pre-occupied with a legitimate source of livelihood.[30]

The three-fold objectives of the liberalization of the barter trade were to (1) provide economic benefit for former Muslim rebels and the Muslim community in general; (2) legitimize the traditional trade in the Sulu Archipelago, Balabac and Zamboanga de Sur; and (3) promote greater participation of the banking system in the trade.

Early Barter Trade Operations

The Philippine National Bank (PNB) initially handled the documentation of the barter traders and provided for their credit services. Each trader was issued a trading certificate of registration (TCR) and allotted five thousand (P5,000.00) pesos worth of goods per trading trip, not exceeding two trips a month. The military commander of the Southwest Command (Southcom) was given the task of co-ordinating barter trading activities and issuing appropriate guidelines.

As part of the liberalization policy, the Monetary Board of the Central Bank has been authorized to waive the usual requirements on foreign exchange transactions, while the PNB has been primarily assigned to handle banking facilities, including designation of correspondent banks. Imported goods and merchandise sold and consumed either in Zamboanga or Jolo are free from import duties and taxes, except those bought outside the trading zones in large commercial quantities which are taxable. An inter-agency task force headed by the Southcom Commander has co-ordinated the barter trade operations.

The traders were also encouraged to form associations or cooperatives. The Zamboanga Barter Traders Kilusang Bayan, Inc. (ZBTKBI) is the pioneer registered traders' cooperative in Zamboanga City.

In the beginning, from 1973 to 1975, there were only a few interested in investing in barter trade. After the burning of the town of Jolo in 1974 in the wake of the MNLF-Military confrontation, many Sulu traders moved to Zamboanga City and they were the ones who later constituted the backbone of the barter traders in the city.

The signing of the Tripoli Agreement on 23 December 1976 and the ceasefire agreement between the MNLF and the government brought back normalcy and relative peace in the Southern Philippines. In due time, the barter trade in Zamboanga City prospered. Private commercial banks opened branches in the city and the local tourist industry likewise boomed.

Some Tausug traders who dominated the barter trade in the city were followed by their business rivals and political enemies, converting the city into a battle arena. This alarmed the once peaceful local residents. Economic progress, however, has its social concomitant side effects.[31] Bad elements from the neighbouring islands and provinces found their way into the city and preyed upon hapless traders. Petty and personal rivalries among some trader groups sometimes ended in violence.

In 1982, a group of traders, tagged as the "Tuvera" group, headed by Enrico Tuvera, son of a former ranking state Minister in the previous administration,[32] approached the ZBTKBI group to ply the Zamboanga-Singapore barter trade route as an alternative to the Labuan-Malaysia) route. The venture was initially a flop because there were only a few investors. When the Tuvera group assumed trips in 1983, plying the Zamboanga-Singapore trade route, the Jammang group (which was earlier authorized by Southcom to undertake trips and identified with former Muslim Affairs Minister Romulo M. Espaldon) complained to the Office of the President about the rival trading vessel.[33]

As a result of the controversy, former President Marcos suspended the barter trade operations from 1983 to 1985 on account of rampant smuggling and business-related crimes, pending issuance of new guidelines. The Jolo-Labuan route was also suspended by former Southcom Chief General Castro on April 1984 for similar reasons.

On 9 May 1984, Presidential Letter of Instructions No. 1409 was issued authorizing the resumption of the barter trade under the Kilusang Kabuhayan at Kaunlaran-Processing Center Authority (KKK-PCA), a subsidiary of the defunct Ministry of Human Settlements. The Samahang Kabuhayan Traders Association (SAKATA), headed by Jammang, was allowed to operate under the new authority. Meanwhile, the Alam group was also allowed to resume operations in August 1985.

From 1985 to 1986, the barter traders' group under Alam operated with the

Tuvera group, competing with the group of Jammang, the SAKATA. The then Human Settlements Ministry sought the transfer of the management of the barter trade from military to civilian authority. The Alam group opposed the transfer, arguing that continuance of military supervision over the barter trade was more orderly.[34]

The Modus Operandi of Barter Trade

During the early operations of barter trade, the Zamboanga traders were required to be members of a unified traders' cooperative, the ZBTKBI, which presently has about 1,300 members.

The ZBTKBI is a service cooperative and a non-stock corporation. Membership fee is 100 pesos. Jolo had about 1,234 traders affiliated with the Jolo Barter Trade Cooperative.

In the early operations, each trader was allotted 5,000 pesos as capital value of merchandise in a group of 5 to 10 members under a team leader. The latter was allowed another 1,500 pesos for his personal effects, in addition to his own capital of 5,000 pesos, while each member contributed 10 per cent (500 pesos) for his expenses in undertaking the trip, with a gross capital of 56,000 pesos for a group of ten members. Reportedly, there were some anomalies in the issuance of TCRs which were allegedly being sold at 3,000 pesos per document.[35]

Under this arrangement, the team leader purchases the goods ordered by his respective team members who represent the consignees. In view of the devaluation of the peso, the amounts allotted to each trader were later doubled.

A common practice among individuals with less capital, even to this day, is to contribute to a prospective trader his capital investment, locally known as the *padala* (consignment or share venture) system. This has enabled some individuals with little capital to participate in the barter trade and earn some income. Generally, the trustee is not liable to the contributor in case of loss due to mishap or robbery at high seas. Depending upon the agreement, either profits and losses are proportionately divided in accordance with individual contributions or the merchandise purchased is distributed in proportion to the individual contributions. These transactions have the features of agency (*wakala*) and/or partnership participation (*mudarabah*).

The big-time capitalists finance their enterprises, the trader-industrial partners share in the profits and losses according to pre-arranged terms, exhibiting the features of equity financing (*musharaka*).[36]

It cannot be denied, however, that in the early operation of the barter trade, some local traders were either used as "dummies" of big-time capitalists or have been the victims of unscrupulous loan sharks. However, when government banks liberalized their lending terms and many traders were able to establish their credit standing as efficient and honest businessmen, many of them could in fact purchase goods in Labuan and Singapore on credit terms. Meanwhile, as the barter trade prospered, many Muslim businessmen themselves provided capital to their fellow Muslims on easy credit terms (*girad* or *gard hasan*).

Present Barter Trade Operation

On 24 July 1986, President Corazon C. Aquino issued Presidential Memorandum Order No. 24 granting the Southern Philippines Development Authority (SPDA) regulatory powers over the barter trade. The authority promulgated on 1 September 1986 new guidelines for barter trade, and also opened another barter trade centre in Cotabato City.

From the original and pioneer ZBTKBI, the present number of barter traders associations has increased to eight which the SPDA has accredited as of 31 July 1987, namely: (1) Zamboanga Barter Traders Kilusang Bayan, Inc. (ZBTKBI), headed by Hasan Alam; (2) Samahang Kabuhayan ng Krislam Traders Association (KRISLAM), headed by Edgardo Gorostiza; (3) Samahang Kabuhayan ng Bansa Moro Traders, Inc. (BANGSA MORO), headed by Junical Angare; (4) Zambasuco Barter Traders Cooperative (ZAMBASUCO), headed by Hadji Anthony Lim; (5) Samahang Kabuhayan ng Traders Association (SAKATA), headed by Hadji Mahmound Jammang; (6) Western Mindanao Barter Traders, Inc. (WESTERN MINDANAO), headed by Hadji Ramon Gonzales; (7) Samahang Kabuhayan ng Viajeros (SK ng Viajeros), headed by Rashdi Sakaluran; and (8) Minsupala Barter Traders, Inc. (MINSUPALA), headed by Ustadz Abdulkarim Ladjamatli.[37]

The SPDA reports that each association has at least 1,200 members, divided into trading teams of 30s, with a team leader and 29 members (consignees) per trading team.[38] This assertion, however, does not tally with the actual consolidated listing of barter traders (Table 3.6). There are a total of 7,893 barter trade members, 5,496 of whom are Muslims (70 per cent).[39]

Each trader is limited to a trading capital of 5,000 pesos worth of goods or 150,000 pesos per team. The monthly quota of trips averages two major vessels for Singapore and four to five *kumpits* (native crafts) for Labuan, with a minimum requirement of 40 trading teams per trip to Singapore and 15 to Labuan. The SPDA Administrator approves the deployment and schedule of vessels, and the slots are awarded by drawing lots.

As of the end of December 1987, the SPDA reported an income (revenue) of P5,489 million from accreditation fees in the two barter trade centres in Zamboanga and Cotabato. In addition to the above nine barter trade associations in Zamboanga City, there are three in Cotabato, one in Basilan, and one in Jolo, with an aggregate total 16,547 barter traders. About 70 per cent are reported to be Muslim traders.[40]

From January to August 1987, ten trips were made to Singapore and 23 to Labuan. As gathered from outward manifests provided by the Bureau of Customs, the value of goods/merchandise from Singapore was 49.9 million pesos and 52.2 million pesos from Labuan (Table 3.7). The value of goods actually exported (from

TABLE 3.6
Distribution of Membership of Barter Traders Per Association/Cooperative by Religious Affiliation, 1987*

Association/Cooperative	Total No. of Members	No. of Muslims	%	No. of Christians	%
Sakata	664	515	78	149	22
Sk Ng Krislam	500	222	44	278	56
Bangsa Moro	900	732	81	168	19
Viajeros	1,164	864	74	300	26
Islamic-Muslim Confederation	450	377	84	73	16
Zambasuco	1,079	367	34	712	66
ZBTKBI	915	838	92	77	8
Wesmin	1,020	697	68	323	32
Minsupala	1,201	884	74	317	30
Total	7,893	5,496	70	2,397	30

* SPDA, 1987 Report.

October 1986 to 31 December 1987) was 107.1 million pesos to Labuan and 108.7 million pesos to Singapore or a total of 215.8 million pesos, while the value of imported goods for the same period was 100.8 million pesos from Labuan and 124.4 million pesos from Singapore or a total of 225.2 million pesos (Table 3.8).[41]

For the first quarter of 1988, the SPDA Barter Trade Center in Zamboanga reported exports of 40.6 million pesos and imports of 19.2 million pesos from ten

TABLE 3.7
Volume of Trade, August 1987*
(In million pesos)

Type of Merchandise	Singapore	Labuan
Agri-Products	26.1	–
Aquamarine	16.6	–
Decor/Furniture	4.0	25.0
Consumer Products	3.2	27.2
Total	49.9	52.2

* SPDA, 1987 Report.

TABLE 3.8
Value of Goods Actually Exported and Imported from October 1986 to 31 December 1987*
(In million pesos)

Barter Trade Centre	Labuan	Singapore	Total
Exports			
Zamboanga	93.2	93.4	186.6
Cotabato	13.9	15.3	29.2
Total	107.1	108.7	215.8
Imports			
Zamboanga	170.8	89.2	160.0
Cotabato	30.8	35.2	65.2
Total	100.8	124.4	225.2
Balance of Trade	6.3	15.7	9.4

* SPDA Report on the Barter Trade, 1987.

trips to Labuan and three trips to Singapore. One vessel, *M/V Crusader*, chartered by the Bangsa Moro Traders, sank, resulting in a total loss of goods.[42]

Balance of Trade
In the last quarter of 1987, there was a trade deficit of 9.4 million pesos and in the first quarter of 1988, a big trade deficit of 20.44 million pesos in the barter trade business.[43] Similar problems were noted in the past. In 1975, there was a trade deficit of 9.48 million pesos or an average trade deficit of 72,000 pesos per trip. This went up to 10.1 million pesos in 1982. As of 1984, there were about eight trading vessels plying the Jolo-Labuan trade route, with four vessels alternating each month, bringing goods worth 800,000 pesos to 1.5 million pesos.[44]

Implications of the Barter Trade
The loss of government revenue due to barter trade is far offset by the economic import of the trade in terms of increase in the income levels of the inhabitants of the area. The trade has also benefitted hundreds of workers, such as support workers, dock handlers, stevedores and the increase in business by trucking companies, support services (local transport and restaurants) and domestic tourism. The trade has afforded a rare and golden opportunity for the Muslims to have a worthwhile livelihood, generate income and capital, promote the export potential of the

Mindanao region, making Singapore and Labuan natural outlets of Mindanao products, and improve the country's external relations through barter trade.

The above barter trade, however, has some negative aspects. One of them is the problem of transhipment of goods outside barter trade zones. But with government regulatory measures, this problem has been reportedly minimized.[45] Another problem is the absence of a border trade agreement between the Philippines and Malaysia, making border patrols by both countries a major hassle. However, a bilateral agreement has existed between the Philippines and Indonesia since 8 August 1984.[46]

There is an on-going controversy over the transfer and phasing out of barter trade in Zamboanga City. Zamboanga barter traders have vigorously objected to this because it would cause serious economic dislocation not only to the traders themselves but also to those who solely depended on such economic activity. The ZBTKBI alone employs no less than 1,000 support workers who earn an average of 50 pesos each daily. If this is multiplied by the number of barter trade associations, there will be about 9,000 support workers affected, with a loss of about 13.5 million pesos in aggregate monthly income.[47]

Savings and Capital Formation

Banking Facilities

There are some 66 banking institutions in Western Mindanao (as of 30 June 1980). Commercial banks rank first (39.4 per cent) or 26, followed by 25 rural banks (37.9 per cent) and 8 specialized banks (12.1 per cent), 7 thrift banks (10.6 per cent) in addition to 22 non-banks or financial intermediaries, yielding a total of 89 financial institutions.

Philippine Amanah Bank

One of the specialized banks is the Philippine Amanah Bank (PAB). It was chartered on 2 August 1973 under Presidential Decree No. 264. It operates as a specialized bank, with the features of a commercial, development and savings bank. It has corporate power to invest in equities of allied undertakings, including trust business.[48] Its headquarters is located in Zamboanga City. Its charter empowers the bank to carry out banking operations on "the basis of Islamic Concept of Banking following the non-interest and partnership principles" (as amended by Presidential Decree No. 541), with an authorized capital of 100 million pesos.[49]

Most of the operations of PAB are still based on conventional banking, while the Islamic modes of finance are in the experimental stage. The Islamic banking component of PAB has been limited to the Pilgrims Special Savings Deposit (PSSD) which was earlier launched on 8 February 1983 upon prior authorization from the Central Bank to maintain interest-free accounts under a separate special passbook.[50]

TABLE 3.9
Comparative Liabilities of PAB and its Deposits*
(In million pesos)

Deposits/Year	1985	1986	1987**
Demand	17.7	26.8	29.7
Savings	22.2	26.1	30.5
PSSD	0.7	0.5	1.4
Time	146.7	132.0	135.1
Total	187.3	185.4	196.7

* 1987 PAB Report.
** Figures have been rounded.

During the initial launching of the PSSD, it generated nearly one million pesos funds from about 1,300 depositors all over PAB branches in Mindanao (including the Makati Branch, Metro Manila). The PSSD scheme also provides facilities for inward remittances by the Filipino Muslim workers in the Middle East.[51] Table 3.9 presents the composition of PAB deposits.

Impact on Corporate Finance
An interesting aspect of the PAB experiment is the opportunity afforded to Muslim investors to acquire and learn the rudiments of corporate investment. During the period September 1974 to June 1986, the PAB had 996 Muslim stockholders, in possession of 1,663 certificates under its Series "C" corporate stocks offered for public acquisition with a total par value of 166 million pesos, as against 154 non-Muslim stockholders, representing 344 shares of stock issued (Series "C") with the total par value of 34,400 pesos.

Trends in Savings Deposits
The records of PAB disclose the following trends in the savings habit among Muslims, namely: the Marawi branch has the highest number of Muslim depositors, followed by Zamboanga, Cotabato and Jolo branches. Jolo, however, discloses greater amounts of deposits by Muslims compared to the Zamboanga branch, with Davao the least, followed by General Santos and Cagayan de Oro (Table 3.10). There is a total of 25,528 accounts by Muslim depositors with an aggregate total deposit of about 19 million pesos, as against the total accounts of 11,193 by non-Muslim depositors with an aggregate deposit of about 160.1 million pesos.

In terms of percentage, 68 per cent of the depositors are Muslims accounting for 9 per cent of the total amount of deposits while there are only 32 per cent

TABLE 3.10
Percentage Distribution of Depositors by Religious Affiliation*
(as of 1986)

	Muslim Borrowers		Non-Muslim Borrowers	
Name of Branch	% of Accts.	% of Amount	% of Accts.	% of Amount
Cotabato	60	47	40	53
Cagayan de Oro	16	30	84	70
Iligan	56	24	44	76
Zamboanga (A)	50	22	50	78
Makati (B)	52	1	48	99
Davao	14	1	86	99
General Santos	11	3	89	97
Marawi	99	92	1	8
Jolo	93	70	7	30
Percentage	70	11	30	89
Mean (Average)	50.1	32.22	49.77	67.77

* 1987 PAB Report. PAB figures have been updated.

TABLE 3.11
PAB Loan Beneficiaries from 1974 to July 1986 by Branches*
(In absolute figures)

Name of Branch	Total No. of Muslim Loan Borrowers	Total Amount Granted in Million Pesos	Total No. of Non-Muslim Loan Borrowers	Total Amount Granted in Million Pesos
Cotabato	752	7.2	181	5.2
Cagayan de Oro	17	0.5	224	10.2
Iligan	96	2.6	192	6.7
Zamboanga (A)	349	18.7	702	34.9
Metro Manila (B)	21	4.1	110	118.4
Davao	33	12.4	259	13.4
General Santos	42	1.2	165	5.0
Marawi	1,921	14.2	78	0.3
Jolo	264	4.9	34	0.3
Total	3,495	65.8	1,945	194.4

* Branch Supervision Department, PAB Report.

non-Muslims accounting for 91 per cent of the amount deposited.[52] It is also of interest to note that Muslims account for 64.2 per cent of the total number of borrowers, but their borrowings represent only 25.3 per cent of the total (Table 3.11).

Muslim Perceptions of Savings, Investment and Finance

The result of the author's structured survey more or less confirmed the earlier information elicited from his unstructured interviews of key informants and from the data procured from official sources on the savings characteristics of the Muslim Moros in the Islands of Mindanao, particularly in the City of Zamboanga.

The majority type of business organization is of the single proprietorship variety, closely followed by partnerships. The corporate type accounts for a negligible proportion of the total. The concentration of business activity is on trading (27 per cent) and retail (23 per cent), followed by agri-business (19 per cent) and aquamarine (16 per cent). About 8 per cent are engaged in the wholesale business, 3 per cent in foreign money exchange and 2 per cent in food processing service (*kadday* or restaurant business) and the rest in transport and shipping business.

In trading activity, the Samas (Samals) and Tausugs (more or less are equal in number) account for about 80 per cent of the total sample population actively engaged in business. About 56 per cent of their business is conducted locally, 26 per cent regionally, 13 per cent on a national scale and only 4 per cent of them engaged in foreign trade. This implies that the majority of those engaged in barter trade business are merely co-partners (*sharikat* or *mudarabah*).

The main mode of transaction is on a cash basis (65 per cent), followed by consignment basis (19 per cent). About 11 per cent engage in both cash, consignment or credit basis and only 4 per cent on pure credit basis.

About 22 per cent are highly aware of the institutionalization of Islamic banking and finance, 37 per cent are fairly aware, 30 per cent are merely aware and only 11 per cent are not yet aware. There is high degree of awareness among the Samas (Samals) and Tausugs combined, 100 per cent among the Maguindanauns and 50 per cent, respectively among the Maranaos and Yakans, in relation to their total number in the sample population. Only about one-third of all the other tribal groups combined (including non-Muslim ethnic groups) exhibit high degree of awareness.

With respect to Muslim businesses problems, the respondents have cited with high frequency distribution political interference, big-time capital domination, lack of both entrepreneurship skills and financing.

About 25 per cent of the population patronize private commercial banks and 33 per cent government banks (PNB, PVB and PAB combined), with the PNB accounting for 18 per cent, and PAB for 14 per cent of the respondents. Details of the survey results are presented in Appendix A.

Summary and Conclusion

There is a growing upward trend in the savings habit formation of the Muslim Moros of Mindanao. By far the most common type of business organization is traditional (*sharikat* and *mudaraba*) and cash transaction is still the major mode of business. Prospects for the institutionalization of Islamic banking and finance as an instrument for the development of Muslim Mindanao are bright.

There exists a close link between increased savings and capital formation and the growth of economic activity and entrepreneurship among the Moro Malays of Southern Philippines.

The findings in this study can be briefly summarized as follows:

1. There is an upward trend in the savings habit formation by the Muslims of Mindanao, particularly in Zamboanga City. This data is likewise strengthened by the official records of the Philippine Amanah Bank discussed in the main text of this paper.
2. The main types of business organization among the Muslims are sole proprietorship and partnership. The Moro Muslims are very familiar with the *sharikat al ain* and the *mudarabah* models, as known in Islamic business and finance. The Islamic values play an important role in the Moro Muslim business ethics and trade practices.
3. Muslims are highly aware of their perceived goals and objectives in development and there is a very strong consensus on the importance of education and business advancement. At the macro level, socio-economic development and regional autonomy occupy top priority.
4. There is a very good prospect for the institutionalization of Islamic banking and finance despite the semi-hostile business environment. On top of this, there is a strong perceived problem of adverse political interference and apparent government neglect with respect to Muslim entrepreneurship development. This accounts for the preponderant sentiments in favour of regional autonomy.
5. The PAB top management has failed to effectively disseminate information concerning basic knowledge on the principles of Islamic banking and finance. This has resulted in the lack of popular support for the Islamic banking component of the PAB operations.
6. Trading is the main source of livelihood among the urban Muslim residents of Zamboanga City. This seems to be the general trend in other urban centres in the Islands of Mindanao. Trading has an Islamic traditional background. The Holy Prophet of Islam himself was a trader during his youth until his call to Prophethood. Moreover, the early merchants known in history were Arabs and Muslims. In fact, Islam was spread throughout Asia and the Southern Pacific basin, up to China and

Japan in the Far East through trade and commerce and not by the sword as erroneously reported by some orientalists.

7. Finally, there is empirical evidence to show that savings and capital formation in the Moro community are closely related to the growth of economic activity and entrepreneurship. Socio-economic development represents an important objective variable of development for the Moro Muslims. The need for the institutionalization of Islamic banking and finance is strongly felt.

This study, admittedly, has its own limitations as it is confined to a particular area in Mindanao, which affects the degree of conclusiveness of the generalizations made by the author.

APPENDIX A

Results of the Survey on Muslim Perceptions on Savings and Finance

I. Description of Research Methodology

Survey questionnaires were administered to a randomly stratified sample of the population on the basis of sectoral and district representation. From a randomly prepared list, the sector/districts were alternately picked out, two from the government agency sector and three from the private business sector.

About 150 survey questionnaires were prepared, 20 of which were earlier pre-tested in the month of June 1988 at the Maharlika Village, Taguig, Metro Manila, among the Muslim residents therein. After some minor revisions on the questionnaires, about 130 sets were sent out to the field with the aid of some research assistants who volunteered for the purpose. A follow-up and field trip was made in the first and second week of July 1988. Retrieval of survey results was a problem, but luckily, about 103 sets of survey questionnaires were recovered. The statistical tools used in the analysis and interpretation of data are the simple mean, computed percentage of responses and the rank order method to determine central tendencies. An allowance of 10 per cent margin of error was employed.

II. Characteristic of the Sample Population

The Muslim population of Zamboanga City is estimated at 86,000 by extrapolation of the 1980 national census of population and housing, although official records placed the Muslim population at about 47,289. The Muslim urban residents are estimated at 20,640. For a population of about 7,000–50,000, the allowable margin of error is 10 per cent for a sample population size of 100. About 5,496 of the Muslim urban population are registered barter traders and another 1,500–2,000 consist of professionals, government workers, privately employed or self-employed individuals and businessmen.

On the basis of the above, we posited that the manageable size of the sample population should be from 99–100. An allowance of 30 sets of questionnaires was provided for possible non-recovery of survey materials, an average of 26 questionnaires per cluster sample size.

III. Analysis and Interpretation of Data

Characteristics of the Population

The sample population is relatively young, clustering between 25–30 years. In the rank order, the median age is between 46–50 years old. About 72 per cent are married and only 22 per cent are single.

A great number of the urban sample population are government employed (40 per cent). About 34 per cent of the aggregate sample population are engaged in business and 26 per cent of them are privately employed. The greater majority are rank and file employees (68 per cent). About 3 per cent of them occupy executive or managerial positions; 15 per cent are in the supervisory group; and 14 per cent are self-employed.

With respect to the ethnic composition of the sample population, the Tausugs consist of 40 per cent, Samas 23 per cent, and Chavacanos 10 per cent. The others are Maranaos, Cebuano/Bisayan and the mixed Moro ethnic groups (5 per cent each), Iranuns and Yakans (3 per cent each), Maguindanao (4 per cent), the Tagalog and Davaweno (1 per cent each).

Income Level and Capital Investments

The results of the survey show that the greater majority of the sample population are middle level entrepreneurs, with capital investments ranging from P20,000–30,000 (20 per cent) to P500,000 (4 per cent) or more. The monthly (average) income level of the sample population is high by local standards, ranging from P4,000–5,000 (36 per cent). But a great majority are within the range of P2,000–3,000 average monthly income.

The general impression among knowledgeable informants is that the Muslims of Zamboanga City are economically far better off compared with other Muslims in urban centres in other parts of Mindanao. This assertion appears to be confirmed by the results of the study.

About 69 per cent of the sample population stated that they have either a member of the family or relative engaged in trade or business (including the respondents in the government sector). Only 21 per cent replied in the negative, and 10 per cent did not bother to respond to the query. Only those with incomes not exceeding P3,000 monthly were more candid in their responses.

About 44 per cent of those who revealed having a member of the family or relative engaged in business, 47 per cent are in barter trade, and a few have relatives in the restaurant business (4 per cent), transport and shipping (3 per cent) and 1 per cent in foreign money exchange, out of a total of 73 respondents. The rest (1 per cent) did not specify the particular line of business of their relative or kin. About one-third (29 per cent) failed to give any specific answer.

Perceptions on Savings and Investments, Banking and Finance

An interesting finding revealed that respondents have rated very high their children's education as the main and primary purpose in saving (about 39 per cent). Other important motives include capital formation (21 per cent), and medicare and/or old age (9 per cent), out of a total of 173 responses. The young age of the sample population accounts for these variables, revealing a higher desire for self-improvement.

Respondents have ranked education (objective variable) as top priority for personal development, followed by business, acquiring higher position and political career in the descending order. These findings belie the impression that the rise to affluence by some members of the Moro population in Zamboanga City pose political threats to local non-Muslim politicians. It is likely that the new migrants will have to go home to their respective island provinces to pursue their political careers and it appears that they are in the city either for education or business purposes.

The rank order of these perceived objective variables may, however, change over time. The Bangsa Moro national aspirations for political identity and self-determination are influential variables that will lure youthful professionals and successful businessmen to pursue political careers in their desire for political pre-eminence. The Zamboanga City political environment will not therefore be spared if continual challenge is put forward by certain non-Muslim politicians. The Muslim population of Zamboanga could easily triple in the next decade. The Chavacano speaking Zamboanguenos will soon be outnumbered by the more aggressive new migrants such as the Tausugs and the Cebuanos.

About one-fourth (38 per cent) of the respondents rated socio-economic development as a top variable for development, followed closely by regional autonomy (35 per cent) and political development (19 per cent). Other objective variables such as peace and order, enforcement of Shari'ah, education, social justice, integration and statehood have an aggregate of only 15 per cent score. The implication therefore is that at the micro level of development, education and business are ranked high, while at the macro level, socio-economic development, regional autonomy and political development are given greater emphasis.

There is a relatively high degree of awareness about the institutionalization of Islamic banking and finance as a government programme (61 per cent); about 23 per cent of the respondents are "very much aware", 38 per cent are "fairly aware", 31 per cent are "merely aware" and only 11 per cent are aware at all.

However, on the operational knowledge and understanding of Islamic banking and finance, only 8 per cent very well understand the principle, 27 per cent fairly well understand. About 13 per cent of the respondents replied that they have no knowledge of this new banking principle. There appears to be more respondents (52 per cent) knowledgeable of the "non-interest" and "profit-sharing" principles of Islamic finance. About 34 per cent have low or little knowledge and 14 per cent have no knowledge at all about Islamic principles relating to banking and finance.

It is of interest to observe that 68 per cent f the respondents regard Islamic banking and finance as an important variable in the development of the Moros, while 32 per cent are unsure, and 4 per cent consider the programme a failure.

With respect to the perceptions of respondents on the privatization of PAB, 44 per cent are in favour of the status quo (i.e. remain under government control) while 35 per cent are strongly in favour of privatization. About 7 per cent are opposed to the idea. About 12 per cent of the respondents have no categorical answers and only 2 per cent have made alternative proposals.

Savings Account and Bank Patronage

Only 22 per cent of the respondents were candid about disclosure of their bank savings, which range from a high of P3,000–4,000 to a low of P500, with one respondent confessing that he did not have any bank account at all. About 21 per cent stated that their bank accounts are confidential and 56 per cent did not bother to give any categorical answer. About 33 per cent of the respondents patronize government banking institutions, and 25 per cent prefer to avail the services of private commercial banks, with the PNB having at least 18 per cent patronage and PAB, 14 per cent.

Types of Business Organizations and Nature of Business

About 23 per cent of the business organizations in Zamboanga City are single proprietorship, 19 per cent are partnerships and 3 per cent are corporate types. This was disclosed by about 45 per cent of the respondents who gave answers to this particular question.

The principal types of businesses the respondents are engaged in are the barter trade (27 per cent), retail business (23 per cent), agri-business (19 per cent) and aquamarine (16 per cent). About 8 per cent are in the wholesale business, 3 per cent in foreign exchange and 2 per cent in food processing service (*kadday* or restaurant business) and the rest in transport / shipping business.

In terms of ethnic distribution, 38 per cent of the single proprietorships types are by Tausugs, and 17 per cent each by Samas and other mixed tribal groups, while Maguindanauns account for 12 per cent and Maranaos and Yakans 8 per cent each. The majority of the partnership types are by Tausugs (53 per cent), and Samas (27 per cent).

Scale of Business Operations and Mode of Transactions

Majority of the Moro business operations in Zamboanga are localized, 26 per cent are region-wide, 14 per cent are on national scale and only 5 per cent have foreign ventures. The focus of "Local" trade is on trading (34 per cent), retail business (32 per cent) and in agri-business (20 per cent). The main areas of the regional trade are agri-business and trading (44 per cent), aquamarine, wholesale and retail (51 per cent) and transport and shipping (5 per cent).

National trade concentrates on aquamarine (50 per cent), trading (17 per cent) and foreign exchange (17 per cent) wholesale business (8 per cent). Aquamarine accounts for 50 per cent of foreign trade, with foreign exchange and agri-business contributing 25 per cent each.

The principal mode of transactions are as follows: cash basis (65 per cent), consignment basis (19 per cent), combination of cash, consignment and credit (4 per cent) and commission basis (1 per cent).

NOTES

1 The author was involved in various programmes for the Muslim Filipinos, having been a co-project director of studies and research on the customary adat laws of the Muslim Filipinos, co-chairman of an inter-agency task force in the preparation of a comprehensive "Muslim Plan for the Autonomous Regions", programmes for Muslim human resource development, seminars, studies and workshops on Islamic banking and finance, *awqaf* (endowments) and in the continuing study, training and research and law reform on Muslim Personal Laws. His experience and field notes were useful for the present study. In many of these activities, he had the opportunity of collaborating with the Filipino Muslim scholar Datu Michael O. Mastura, now a member of the Congress of the Philippines, representing the First district of Maguindanao province and Cotabato City.

2 The research assistants who assisted the author in the collection of data are Abubakar Sansaluna of the Office of Muslim Affairs, Central Office and Amir Mustapha and Banseng Lim of the OMA Region IX Office, Farouk Alawi of the National Labour Relations Commission, Region IX Office, and a dozen informants who voluntarily offered valuable data and information: notable among them are Hadji Abdulla Camlian, Ali Al-Raschid, Shiek Abdulhamid Camlian, Hasan Alam and Farouk Carpizo, incumbent President of the Philippine Amanah Bank.

3 Zamboanga City, "Socio-Economic Profile 1984", mimeographed (Zamboanga: Office of the City Planning and Development Coordinator, 1984), p. 3.

4 Ibid., p. 3.

5 Caesar Adib Majul, *Muslims in the Philippines* (Quezon City: Asian Center, University of the Philippines Press, 1973), pp. 114–65.

6 Ibid., pp. 314–16.

7 NEDA IX, *Socio-Economic Information on Western Mindanao* (Zamboanga: March 1987), pp. 30–39.

8 Ibid., pp. 53–55.

9 Ibid., p. 20.

10 Institute of Small-Scale Industries, University of the Philippines (UP-ISSI), "Baseline Study of Twelve Regions of the Philippines, Region IX" (Quezon City: May 1981), p. 25.

11 Ibid., p. 25.

12 Ibid., p. 29.

13 Batas Pambansa (Legislative Act) Blg. 337. Under this Act, a highly urbanized city must at least have a population of 150,000 as certified by the National Census and Statistic Office (NCSO) with the latest annual income (revenue) of at least P30 million as certified by the Finance Ministry. Cities which have not met the above criteria remain as component cities and may only become highly urbanized after compliance with the minimum legal requirements. (Zamboanga City, op. cit., pp. 132–33).

14 UP-ISSI, op. cit., pp. 29–30.

15 This data has been culled from the background documents of the then Ministry of Muslim Affairs used in the preparation of the "Muslim Plan for the Autonomous Region" wherein the author was a co-chairman of the inter-agency task force that drew the plan in August 1984.

16 Communal Property ownership is recognized under the Code of Muslim Personal Laws (P.D. 1083), promulgated on 4 February 1977, specifically on Title II, Book Five of the Code, Articles 173–74, particularly on trust (*waqf*) lands. Under P.D. 410, which was never implemented, it afforded opportunity for the Muslims and other tribal communities to title and register their ancestral landholdings within the period of ten years from the promulgation of the degree in 1976.

17 On 1 May 1968, the late former Cotabato Governor Datu Udtog Matalam issued a "Manifesto" announcing the grievances of the Muslims over long years of government neglect and their desire to set up their own polity, the Islamic Republic of Mindanao and Sulu, including Palawan. This manifesto caused a furor in the national leadership and generated support and sympathy from Muslim youth, notably former University

of the Philippine Professor Nur Misuari who later on formed the Moro National Liberation Front shortly before the declaration of Martial Law on 21 September 1972.

18 Azizan Abdul Razak, *Introduction to Islamic Law and Jurisprudence* (Quezon City: Philippine Shari'a Institute, Office of Muslim Affairs, 1986), pp. 82–83, (citing S. Mahmassani, *The Philosophy of Jurisprudence in Islam*, English translation by Ferhat J. Ziadeh).

19 The *pacto de retro sale* in the Philippine Civil Code was basically drawn from the Spanish Civil Code which had its origins in Islamic jurisprudence under Moorish Spain and the Code of Napoleon.

20 Among the Sunni school (*madhab*), the Hanafis generally recognize a sale with the right of redemption. They, however, do not approve long-term lease contracts for orchards. Thus, recourse was made through legal fiction whereby the orchard or plantation was sold and the vendor retained the right of redemption. This form of sale (*bai bi-al-wafa'*) was obviously devised by means of legal fiction to circumvent the prohibition on long-term lease contracts which amounts to virtual absolute sale or cession of property rights in perpetuity and is therefore considered a form of *riba*. (Azizan, op. cit., pp. 82–83).

The latter dealings on land are cited from Fathul-Qarib and the Minhaj in Anwar Ahmad Qadri, *Islamic Jurisprudence in the Modern World* (Labore: Sh. Muhammad Asraf Kashmiri Bazar, 1973), p. 326.

21 E.C. Howard (Eng. trans.), *Minhaj Et-Talibin, A Manual of Muhammadan Law According to the School of Shafi'i by Imam Nawawi* (from the French ed. by L.W.C. Van Den-Berg; Lahore: Law Publishing Co., undated), pp. 210–11.

22 This information was gathered from the Zamboanga Barter Trade Center. It was also confirmed by Hasan Alam, president of the barter traders group.

23 After the decline of the sovereignty of the Sulu Sultanate, local pretenders to the Sulu throne designated or appointed their own *wakils* (deputies) and *panglimas* (district governors) to administer and dispense with their respective *diwans* (royal decrees) on customary laws on local marriages and family relations and customary penal laws on the notion that the Sulu Sultanate retained its ecclesiastical powers under the US-Sulu Carpenter Agreement and the Bates Treaty.

24 This has been provided by informant Ali M. Al-Raschid, a Muslim economist and resident of Zamboanga City and who is presently a consultant to the Mindanao Peace Commission.

25 The Arabic word *riba* which properly signifies "excess" does not directly correspond to the English term "interest" and "usury" as understood in Islamic law. But nonetheless, the Holy Prophet of Islam was reported to have expressly prohibited interest on loans because it derives advantage in receiving back from the borrower an amount larger

than what was actually lent as practised in Western banking and finance. Muslim jurists have devised techniques and methodology for avoiding usury. One of them is the simulation of the financial transaction as a trading transaction.

26 See Carmen A. Abubakar, "A Preliminary Study on Zakat and Sadaqqa Practice Among the Moros of Southern Philippines" (Singapore: Institute of Southeast Asian Studies, August 1987) 39 pp., for a detailed discussion on these institutions in Western Mindanao.

27 This information was gathered from the Regional Office of Muslim Affairs (Region IX), Zamboanga City.

28 Hadji Abdulla U. Camlian provided this information.

29 For an account of Arab trade in Southeast Asia, see G.R. Tibetts, "Early Muslim Traders in South-East Asia", *JMBRAS*, Vol. XXX, Part I, No. 177, 1957, p. 2, cited in Majul, op. cit., p. 37 and in "Traditions, Customs and Commerce of the Sulu Moros, in Majul, op. cit., p. 52.

30 Southern Philippines Development Authority (SPDA), "Documents on Barter Trade" (Manila, 1987).

31 This information was provided by informants in Zamboanga City during the field work in July 1988.

32 Hasan Alam supplied this information. The participation of the Tuvera Group is public knowledge in Zamboanga. Enrico "Ike" Tuvera is the son of former Minister Juan C. Tuvera, Presidential Executive Assistant of former President Marcos.

33 Hasan Alam confirmed this information.

34 Reportedly, former Southcom Chief General Jose Magno had acceded to this plan. Alam observes that under the present administration of the barter trade, some traders are emboldened to bring in banned items such as motorcycles. He also observes that transhipment of barter goods have become rampant and with the increase of barter trader associations, civilian authority has failed to enforce discipline among traders, compared to the orderly military supervision of the trade. The SPDA, however, claims that they have made some headway in instituting reforms in the trade operations (SPDA, op.cit.).

35 This information is almost public knowledge in Zamboanga City as confirmed by our informants, including Alam. On top of this, the TCR was reportedly difficult to secure before and only those with the proper "connections" could secure it for a fee.

36 A variation of this is the so-called "dummy" practice among some aliens and big-time capitalists who use nationals as their proxies. Under the Philippine laws,

circumvention of the nationalization policy of the government is an offence under the Anti-Dummy Act or under the Penal Code when it is resorted to as a form of trade monopoly or combinations in trade.

37 SPDA, op. cit.

38 Ibid.

39 Some informants opined that some of these associations do not have 1,200 members.

40 SPDA, op. cit.

41 Ibid.

42 Ibid.

43 Report of the SPDA-Barter Trade Center, Zamboanga City (1 January to 30 March 1988).

44 Data from the Zamboanga Trade Assistance Center, in Michael O. Mastura, "Impact of the Tripoli Agreement on Philippine Relations with the Middle East", *Muslim Filipino Experience*, Philippine Islam Series No. 3 (Manila, Ministry of Muslim Affairs, 1984), pp. 275–76.

45 SPDA, op. cit.

46 Mastura, op. cit., p. 276.

47 This information was provided by Hasan Alam. Hadji Mahmoud Jammang, SAKATA president, advanced the view that the transfer of the barter trade is motivated by the desire of some sectors to pluck the rising affluence of some Muslims in the city. Reportedly, some non-Muslim politicians view the increasing economic power of the Muslims as threat to their local leadership. Politics and the "secessionist" hysteria have also compounded the transfer controversy. On one hand, Sulu politicians are petitioning for the transfer to Jolo to resurrect the town's economy which declined after it was razed by fire in the early seventies. Adding to the tension is the tendency of the local media in sensationalizing the dispute. Reportedly, the transfer is definite. The trade also has its security implications. It is being blamed for the rise of crimes in the city, a convenient excuse for the failure of the local police to enforce law and order thereby prompting local residents to call upon the military to perform police work. Knowledgeable city residents are, however, agreed that the barter trade is not the real culprit but politics.

48 Michael O. Mastura, "Islamic Banking in the Philippines: Issues and Prospects", *Muslim Filipino Experience* — A Collection of Essays (Manila, Philippine Islam Series No. 3, Ministry of Muslim Affairs, 1984), p. 255.

49 Ibid.

50 The PAB project however was not competitive because it failed to open a branch office in Jeddah unlike the PNB which maintains an office there.

51 PAB Annual Report, 1987.

52 Ibid.

4 MINORITY MUSLIM BUSINESSES IN SINGAPORE

Amina Tyabji

Introduction

The Muslims in Singapore may be dichotomized into two groups: Malay Muslims and non-Malay Muslims. According to the 1980 Census of Population, of the population aged 10 and above, 16.3 per cent or 323,867 persons were Muslims. Of these 90.21 per cent were Malays, 0.35 per cent Chinese, 8.6 per cent Indians and 0.85 per cent "Others" (mainly Arabs). These comprised 99.4, 0.1, 21.8 and 6.5 per cent of their own ethnic group, respectively (Table 4.1). Thus, minority Muslims comprise only 10 per cent of the total and are largely of Indian and, to a much lesser extent, of Arab origin. The Arabs originated mainly from Hadhramaut and are more homogeneous compared to the Indians. As is well known, Indians comprise a number of ethno-linguistic groups. Singapore Indians, according to the 1980 Census, include the following in order of importance — Tamils, Malayalees, Punjabis, Sikhs, Bengalis and others (who include a small number of Gujeratis, Sindhis, etc.). There is no reason to believe that this ranking does not hold for Indian Muslims. In fact, Indians Muslims may be divided into two groups: the majority, the Tamils, and the minority comprising all others. These groups are distinct to the extent that they are separated not by religion but by language and, to some extent, culture attributed to the place of origin.

This article is concerned with minority Muslim businesses (MMBs) which by definition are non-Malay businesses. Why focus on MMBs when these Muslims comprise only 10 per cent of total Muslims in Singapore? Two reasons may be put forward to explain the choice. First, the majority Muslims are not prominent in business activity. Second, while the minority Muslims from the days of their earliest settlement in Singapore have been engaging in commerce, they have not

TABLE 4.1
Singapore: Persons Aged 10 Years and Above by Religion and Ethnic Group, 1980
(In number and percentage)

Religion	Total	Chinese	Malays[1]	Indians[2]	Others[3]
Christianity	203,517 (10.3)	161,068 (10.6)	805 (0.3)	15,879 (12.4)	25,765 (60.8)
Buddhism	529,140 (26.7)	520,174 (34.3)	317 (0.1)	1,268 (1.0)	7,381 (17.4)
Taoism	580,535 (29.3)	580,334 (38.2)	55 –	86 (0.1)	60 (0.1)
Islam	323,867 (16.3)	1,122 (0.1)	292,174 (99.4)	27,823 (21.8)	2,747 (6.5)
Hinduism	72,401 (3.6)	65 –	60 –	72,179 (56.5)	96 (0.2)
Other Religions	11,069 (0.6)	1,374 (0.1)	30 –	8,976 (7.0)	689 (1.6)
No Religion	26,433 (13.2)	253,524 (16.7)	679 (0.2)	1,570 (1.2)	5,660 (13.4)
Total	1,981,962 (100.0)	1,517,660 (100.0)	294,121 (100.0)	127,781 (100.0)	42,399 (100.0)

[1] All persons of Malay and Indonesian origin.
[2] All persons of Indian, Pakistani, Bangladeshi and Sri Lankan origin.
[3] Includes Eurasians, Europeans, Arabs and Others.

SOURCE: *Census of Population 1980 Singapore*, Release No. 9, Religion and Fertility, Department of Statistics, Singapore, 1981.

been separately and systematically studied. Besides, the role of the private sector in economic activity is enshrined in Islam which does not condemn the accumulation of material wealth, provided this does not violate Qur'anic norms. In Islam, trading (production, distribution, exchange) is legitimate and this study affords an interesting opportunity to examine how MMBs cope with a secular environment.

The chapter is divided into three parts. This first part sketches the historical origins of MMBs, using available published material. The second part attempts to generate new data and information through a survey and to provide a profile of their present activity in terms of type of organization, nature and scale of operations, investment and saving behaviour, with a view to identifying problems. The third section discusses selectively the problems faced by various strata of MMBs as a result of Singapore's rapid economic transformation, and assesses their role in the economy.

Historical Origins

Like the rest of Singapore's population, minority Muslims are migrants attracted to the island by better income prospects. This section delineates and highlights their historical origins so as not only to provide background information but also to allow for some comparison with the present-day situation discussed in the next section. However, the discussion here is not very extensive due to the paucity of systematic studies in this area.

Indian Muslims in Business

South Indian Muslims. Indian migration into Singapore (including Indian Muslim migration) became a major force only during the second half of the nineteenth century following the consolidation of British rule. While these migrants represent a wide spectrum of occupations, traders, both large and small, are known to have been fairly prominent. For our purposes, the Muslim traders can be classified into two broad groups: south and other Indians. The former, always the more numerous, hail from the Tamil Nadu region where they are recognized to be skilful and shrewd shopkeepers and traders, whose mercantile interests explain much of their migration to Southeast Asia. Their prominence in trade is ascribed to their relatively high degree of education and urbanism. Two other characteristics are of interest here: (1) the stress on economic independence, hard work and frugality as a means of success; and (2) their strong links with their homeland, embodied in close ties with kinsmen and the maintenance of households and families in India to which they return periodically.[1]

Their involvement in the Singapore economy, both in the past and at present, appears to cover a wider spectrum of activities (than the other Indian Muslims). These include running restaurants, eating shops, cigarette-cum-general goods stalls,[2] provision and textile shops and pharmaceuticals, and functioning as hawkers, frame makers,[3] mirror sellers, jewellers, and stationers (at the wholesale and retail levels), money-changers, exporters and importers. Their firm size ranges from one-man operations to small- and medium-scale units, as dictated often by ethnic market size. Some of the above activities could be described as falling into the curb or informal market category, such as money-changing. Indeed, money-changing, cigarette-cum-general goods stalls and butchering[4] (beef and mutton market stalls) appear to be practically a Tamil Muslim monopoly. Concentration in such activities may be seen to stem in part from religious sanctions or their lack, as in the case of money-changing as opposed to money-lending. Other activities are directed at meeting the demand from Indians and Muslims such as tailoring and Muslim cooked food stalls.

The Tamil Muslim activities in commerce and services, as delineated above, exhibit a number of traits which, albeit not unique, should still be noted. First, there is the long trading tradition. In fact, sons were trained on the job from an early age. Second, up till the second world war, employees were recruited from India and their migration was employer-assisted to some extent. Third, management styles were paternal, as was the norm then[5] and was said to elicit loyalty and dedication. Fourth, and as one study puts it, "one of the aims of the Tamil Muslim employee was to open a business for himself".[6] The employees therefore tended to be very thrifty. The same study also refers to the practice of mudharabah, with the employees repaying their employers whatever assistance (usually seed capital) was provided together with a percentage of the profit.[7]

One other characteristic which may be noted is that Tamil Muslims appear to be less settled demographically. Many still maintain immediate families in India, although one or two family members, usually sons, may be stationed in Singapore. Indirect evidence of this is provided by the Indian sex ratio which was 1,323 males per 1,000 females in 1980.[8] This compares with the overall sex ratio of 1,042 males per thousand females. As may be expected, this imbalance is more pronounced for older persons. Another pertinent feature is that 83 per cent of the Indians are citizens (compared to the ratio of 91 per cent for the total population) while 9.3 per cent are permanent residents (compared to the proportion of 3.6 per cent for the total population).[9] The above data may be regarded as being fairly representative of Tamil Muslims, as Tamils and Tamil Muslims constitute respectively the majority of Indians and Indian Muslims. The purpose of drawing attention to it is that it has certain implications for the future. This is discussed in a subsequent section.

Other Indian Muslims. The phenomenal growth of Singapore as a mercantile centre during the nineteenth century also attracted other Indian Muslims. Prominent among them were the Gujerati Muslim merchants who, like their South Indian compatriots, have a strong trading tradition. Important among the Gujeratis are the Khojas, Sunni Vohras, Sulaimani and Dawoodi Bohras and Memons.[10] Although numerically small, all of them are represented in Singapore. They are generally more prosperous and better educated than other Muslim communities. Compared to the South Indian Muslims, the business activity of this group is less diverse; they appear to be heavily concentrated in the import, export and wholesale trade, dealing mainly in tropical produce and textiles. They also generally appear to be more settled demographically.

It appears that only a small proportion of the Gujeratis and those from other groups started as traders. Many owners of present-day businesses started as employees. This phenomenon, apart from population growth, explains the (horizontal) expansion of their involvement in the trading sector which has simultaneously intensified competition in a particular line of business, for example, the spice trade. To put it differently, learning by doing has played an important part.

As noted previously, early MMBs showed a strong preference for the employment of family members, and other kith and kin, within a given sub-ethnic community. This practice persisted up till the early 1950s. Under the (new) immigration law of 1953, (for both Singapore and Malaya) immigration was allowed for only wives, children under the age of 18 and for persons who were able to earn at least S$500 per month. This reduced the pool of would-be employees and (to some extent) would-be entrepreneurs.

Arab Muslims

Migrants like the rest of the population, Singapore's Arabs originated mainly from Hadhramaut, where they have had a strong trading and entrepreneurial tradition. From the days of their earliest settlement in Singapore, they have been traders and shopkeepers (dealing in textiles, batik, pulicat, books and magazines, perfumes and other paraphernalia associated with Muslim life) and landowners (and concomitantly in real estate valuation and management). Their businesses were organized as family enterprises[11] with trading links with Arabia and overseas Arab businesses in Southeast Asia.

Historical accounts refer to their prominence not only in Singapore's entrepôt trade but also in civic life: for example, an Aljunied was a member of the European-dominated Chamber of Commerce in 1837.[12] Their share in business was large, because at that time there were not many large traders. Their wealth and influence as landowners and traders are attested by several streets and mosques named after them.[13] Apparently, their trading profits were accumulated in the form of land. One study notes that "their dependence on landed property was so great, over 80 per cent of the Arabs lived on incomes from rent before the 1920s".[14] These landholdings were both in the city area and outside it.[15] However, their hegemony as landlords appears to have been eroded after the second world war due to the following reasons: some of the properties lapsed to the government on the expiry of their 99-year leases; some lands were compulsorily acquired;[16] the Rent Control Act, 1948 had an adverse impact on owners of rent controlled properties; where properties were jointly owned by families (which in many cases are/were large) their distribution produced some disintegration. It appears that, at present, only one or two families have retained their earlier prominence as landlords.[17] Nevertheless they are generally looked upon as being a prosperous community.

Persian Muslims
One of the tiniest of the Muslim minorities in Singapore is the Persian community, estimated to number between forty and fifty,[18] most of whom have been resident in Singapore for some length of time. Of this, many of the younger generation are Singapore born, while of the early and older generation, many were born in India. The early Persian settlers, who in any case were few in number, were engaged in entrepôt trade. Today, there are only a handful of Persian businesses, other members of the community being involved in the professions. Generally, their importance is disproportionately larger than their small number due to a number of factors, amongst the most important of which is their higher level of education ("almost all the younger members have had or are having some form of tertiary education") and involvement in civic and religious (Muslim) organizations.[19]

In concluding this section, it is useful to pull together several similarities of the different Muslim minority groups identified. Regardless of whether they came as traders or as employees, minority Muslims were attracted to Singapore by the prospects of higher incomes. While some started as employees, their goal was to become self-employed or establish their own businesses. That many ended up in the commerce sector is not very surprising, since most of them originated from communities with strong entrepreneurial and trading traditions. Early MMBs also showed a preference for the employment of family members, kin and other Muslims, if not the members of the same ethnic group. In this regard, they were little different from, say, the early Chinese businesses in Singapore.

Profile of MMBs

As minority Muslim businesses have not been systematically or separately studied in Singapore, it was thought that a survey could yield useful new information and that its findings could help support or reject a priori expectations. Accordingly, a survey was conducted and the results are reported in this section.

Identification of MMBs for Survey
MMBs are largely undifferentiated in the official publications on the manufacturing and the service sectors. These classify enterprises according to the usual descriptive characteristics and according to whether they are locally or foreign owned but seldom according to ethnicity and least of all according to religion. Thus, an attempt was made to trace MMBs through the ethnic Chambers of Commerce, fully recognizing that membership of these organizations would provide only a *partial* picture. The four chambers of commerce relevant for this purpose are the Arab, Pakistani, Malay and Indian. The information available from each is noted below, to explain the basis of the survey and to indicate the difficulties of identification.

The Arab Chamber of Commerce could not be traced at the address stated, although it still exists on the rolls of the Registrar of Societies. While one is unable to explain this contradiction, as noted below, some Arab firms were traced through the Malay Chamber of Commerce.

Fifty-eight members were listed for the Pakistan Chamber of Commerce (as at 20 June 1987). Identification was not easy due to the paucity of information given: name of company, address and name of contact persons. Nevertheless 20 firms were identified as MMBs through other means and questionnaires were mailed. There was, however, no response from this group.

The problem with the Malay Chamber of Commerce list (as at July 1987) was that of separating minority from majority (Malay) Muslim enterprises.

Only some Arab firms were readily identifiable from this list, since in the case of many others Malay nomenclature was employed for the names of the owners/directors. This is understandable, as Arab assimilation with the Malays was particularly stronger than was the case with other minority Muslims. The more readily identifiable numbered 24. The little information provided here suggest that most were engaged in trade, including import, export, and wholesale and retail trade.

For the Indian Chamber of Commerce, the oldest of the four, the latest membership list available was for 1986. Out of a total membership of 427, 81 were identified as MMBs (19.0 per cent), on the basis of both company name (here there is a tendency to use family names) and by examining the names of the owners/partners/directors. These 81 firms certainly do not represent the whole of Indian MMBs, as random inspection revealed that many companies and subsidiaries are not listed.

In terms of business organization, 53 per cent of the Indian MMBs are private limited companies, 26 per cent partnerships and the remainder (21 per cent) sole proprietorships. These firms are largely family enterprises, as evident from the strong kinship relations between partners and directors, and most of them belong to the small-medium enterprise (SME) category. It is interesting to compare this distribution of MMBs by legal organization with the national distribution as revealed by the Survey of Wholesale and Retail Trade, Restaurants and Hotels 1985.[20] Here, in contrast, the predominant form of legal organization is the sole proprietorship (44.3 per cent), followed by private limited companies (28.1 per cent) and partnerships (27.1 per cent). This difference may be ascribed to the more comprehensive coverage of the 1985 Survey. To put it differently, it is the larger firms (however defined) which are more likely to be members of chambers of commerce and to belong to the (private) limited liability type of business organization.

These firms are mostly engaged in the import and export trade almost entirely at the wholesale level, with the majority trading in tropical produce especially timber and products, spices and other foodstuffs. Some are styled as manufacturer's representatives, but it is not known what agencies they hold. Negligible numbers are involved in the manufacturing sector, but many do trade in manufactured goods such as textiles, garments, chemicals, and (more recently) electronic goods and computer peripherals.

To supplement the above sources and to close what seemed to be obvious gaps, recourse was made to the telephone directory to identify MMBs in the oriental carpet trade and money-changing activities. Firms were also selected from the Dawoodi Bohra Directory (1985). Though few in number, questionnaires were also sent to a handful of Persian and Chinese Muslim firms. All in all, some 150 firms were identified for the survey. The survey, conducted during March–June 1988, was supplemented with interviews.

At this juncture, it is important to note the limitations of the methodology employed for identifying MMBs. First, since MMBs could not be identified directly from official sources (which could have provided both a more representative and comprehensive sampling frame) the firms selected cannot be regarded as being representative. Second, while the identification of firms by name of company and owners/directors was useful for the commerce sector, the same method could not be employed for the manufacturing sector. Thus, no firm could be selected from, for example, the *Singapore Manufacturers' Association Directory*. But, this omission may be less glaring than it might appear at first sight, since the role of local firms (which would include MMBs) in Singapore's manufacturing sector is by and large small relative to foreign firms.[21]

Needless to say, the limitations of the methodology in general and the poor response in particular (only 32 firms or 21.3 per cent responded) demand that the survey findings be interpreted with caution, and the conclusions regarded as no more than tentative and preliminary.

Survey Findings

While much of the following discussion is based on the survey and interviews, other observations, where relevant, are also interspersed. A socio-economic[22] rather than a purely economic approach was deliberately taken for the survey as this may yield more useful insights. In order to ensure confidentiality, the findings are presented in an aggregated fashion. Besides, classification of responses according to ethnicity and sub-ethnicity was not possible, given the narrow base of respondents. A wider base would have allowed for meaningful comparisons between groups and sub-groups.

Vintage. The majority of the surveyed firms had begun their operations before the second world war (Table 4.2). All these, except one, are third and fourth generation family firms, and some have been in existence for a century. As most of the owners left Singapore for India during the war, they started afresh, often from scratch and with little capital, after the war. Fifty per cent of the owners/

TABLE 4.2
Age of Firms

Year of Establishment	Percentage
Pre-war	42.9
1950s	21.4
1960s	21.4
1970s	14.3

directors had inherited the business, while the remainder started as employees in similar activities. There are a few long-established MMBs which to this day are managed not by their owners who are headquartered in India but by their appointed managers. How much of the decision making is done locally is not known. These "caretaker" firms are in some respects reminiscent of the modern MNCs.

Nature of Activity. More than half of the MMBs here are concentrated in the export and import business or entrepôt trading. Timber traders have at times been involved in some degree of processing but have not moved into manufacturing. A very small percentage of textile traders indicated that they had branched into the production of garments and batik. The general direction of movement of the surveyed MMBs appears to be horizontal, that is within the commerce sector, rather than vertical, involving a shift from commerce to manufacturing, although the latter has been a leading growth sector. A few other details may be noted regarding the horizontal movement. In the entrepôt trade sector, while specialization in terms of commodities continues, new products have been added to cope with changing market forces.

Their large presence in entrepôt trade is evident from Table 4.3. However, this does not indicate dominance or control. Indeed, it would not be incorrect to state that not only a large number of MMBs, but also other firms are to be found in this sector, given the early foundations and the present structure of the economy.

A further observation is that the markets of the sample firms are mainly in the Middle East, Africa and Southeast Asia and, to a lesser extent, in Western Europe and North America. Although the majority of firms here are Indian, commercial links with country of origin are weaker than in the past. At the aggregate level, India is not a major trading partner of Singapore.[23] It may also be pointed out that India's present exports to Singapore consist mainly of capital goods (engineering products) the marketing of which requires technical knowledge not possessed by the firms in question.[24] But, as discussed in the next section, such links may strengthen in the future.

TABLE 4.3
Nature of Activity

Nature of Activity	Percentage
Export-import-wholesale[1]	56.2
Estate management	6.3
Jewellery	6.3
Stationery	6.3
Transportation	3.1
Financial services	9.4
Other services[2]	12.5

[1] Of spices, tropical produce, timber and textiles.
[2] Includes retailing.

In terms of the nature of activity, most of the surveyed firms may be considered to be specialized rather than diversified. Nevertheless, a few observed departures may be recounted. One firm in particular started in the import and export business, but shortly after the second world war, upon obtaining the agency for an Indian shipping line (and several others subsequently), diversified into transportation and has achieved prominence here. More recently, this particular MMB appears to have diversified both backward and forward; it is also involved in marine technology and containers, a logical development given its anchor activity in shipping. Its other activities now also include properties and restaurants.

Some MMBs are engaged in the provision of financial services, both in the formal and informal sectors. Growth of MMBs in the formal sector seems directly related to the growth of Singapore as a financial sector which has seen the emergence of the international money broking firms, including joint ventures with foreign partners. One MMB has, in the last decade or so, evolved from being a very small money broking firm into a large organization with multinational connections in both developed and developing countries.

As noted in the previous section, money-changing in the informal financial sector is predominantly an MMB activity. Here, too, some diversification is evident. While the precise scale of this cannot be determined, it is observable that money-changing is often combined with the sale of sundry goods. It is also not possible to determine whether this is a result of two (or more) persons joining hands simply to share rents/profits or whether the money-changers on their own decided to enter the market for sundry goods to improve income and to reduce risk.

Another observation relates to the successful involvement of Arab firms in the pilgrimage related business.[25] In a sense, these firms have comparative advantage in this field, given their know-how relating to the demands of the pilgrimage, conditions in Arabia and the like. And its scope is a function of rising per capita income in Singapore. The demand for travel is widely regarded as being income-elastic and this is manifested in the increasing number of persons going not only for haj but also for *umrah* (pilgrimage).

Structure. Generally, the type of legal organization chosen by firms reflects their size and scope. Thus, small firms tend to favour sole proprietorships, while larger firms often prefer limited liability status, with partnerships falling in between. The limited liability form was chosen by 70 per cent of the surveyed firms (Table 4.4). Of the 70 per cent, around one-half had "incorporated" only during the last 10 years. The progression was generally from sole proprietorship to limited liability status. Almost all are wholly-owned family firms. Respondents offered a variety of reasons for the shift in the legal status, ranging from the need to limit liability to reduced tax liability. The latter motivation was particularly strong, given the 15 percentage points difference between the company tax rate (40 per cent) and the top personal income tax marginal rate (55 per cent).

While the above reasons may be valid, other formal reasons may also be adduced by comparing the benefits and costs of different forms of business organization.[26] On the benefits side, the limited liability form provides relatively easier access to finance compared to the sole proprietorship/partnership. It also provides greater flexibility in the areas of transfer of ownership, dismissal of directors, ceasing of business and continuity of business even on the death of owner(s). It also appears that banks and customers prefer to deal with limited liability firms rather than with partnerships and sole-proprietorships. These benefits are offset to some extent by statutory requirements such as submission of audited accounts and filing of returns to the Registrar of Companies. Moreover, both the set up and running costs are higher on account of registration and professional fees for registration and costs of audit.

However, the limited liability option has not resulted in significant changes in the management style and financing modes. With few exceptions, firms with

TABLE 4.4
Type of Legal Organization

Type of Legal Organization	Percentage
Sole proprietorship	21.4
Partnership	8.6
Private limited	70.0

limited liability continue to be managed by owners and partners in a personalized way. Owners are independent in the sense that they do not form part of a larger enterprise and are thus free from outside control in making decisions. Firms continue to be family businesses, run by their owners (frequently with wives and eligible children listed as directors) without a formal management structure. In the majority of the firms, the boss is either the founder of the company or a member of the founder's family. Again, a large proportion of the firms are almost entirely owned by the first, second or third generations of the same family. In this regard, they are not very different from other family firms in Singapore and elsewhere.

Age of Entry. For those who inherited MMBs, age of entry was the early twenties. Individual age varied with the level of education completed, which in most cases was secondary. For those who inherited MMBs say in the 1980s, age of entry was a little higher than that of fathers mainly due to longer years of education received (often tertiary). Sons are expected (perhaps some coerced) to carry on businesses. It has generally been the practice for at least one son to enter the business. Given the preference for small and nuclear families and the possibility of sons training for other professions, a (male) succession problem can arise. This is sometimes mitigated by training female family members who are now being listed as directors. It might be noted that there are some (albeit few) successful MMBs run by women.

For those who started as employees, age of entry ranged between the late twenties and early thirties. This is not surprising, since time is required to accumulate sufficient start-up capital and experience.

Reasons for Entry. The MMB entrepreneurs had knowledge or received training (on the job) either as a family member (sometimes from an early age) or as an employee. For employees, the two most important reasons for venturing into business were prospects for larger income and knowledge of the business. Several respondents also mentioned the desire for greater independence. This appears to be a universal characteristic of especially the small firm owner. Studies on entrepreneurship have shown that many become businessmen because of the lack of alternative employment opportunities, although in our sample the proportion was very small. These studies also report that many began their business on a part-time basis to test the ultimate viability of the enterprise, but this factor seemed irrelevant in the case of MMBs. It appears that low start-up costs, especially in commerce and in some service activities had made new entry relatively easy (Table 4.5). Finally, family pressures also counted. It is interesting to note two responses which reveal the desire for family involvement and control: (1) a business owner had encouraged his sons and even grandsons to enter the business in order to have sufficient manpower for diversification, despite the fact that some of them had received higher education in disciplines hardly related to business; (2) a business

TABLE 4.5
Reasons for Entering Business

	Initial[1] (Percentage to Total)[3]	Subsequent[2] (Percentage to Total)
Inherited business	57.1	–
Had knowledge or received training	42.9	35.7
Prospects for larger income	7.1	42.9
Market potential	21.4	21.4
Required little capital or training	14.3	14.3
Encouraged by family and friends	35.7	21.4
Other reasons	7.1	21.4

[1] Initial occupation.
[2] Started as employee.
[3] Multiple responses.

owner had even repaid government bonds for his scholarship-holder sons in order that they could join the family business upon completion of their studies.

Firm Size and Education Level. There is no agreed definition of size. For our purpose, the 1983 Census definition based on employment will be used, especially since the MMB responses regarding capital and turnover cannot be regarded as reliable.

The 1983 Census of Wholesale Trade, Retail Trade, Restaurants and Hotels defined firm size in terms of employment as follows:[28] (1) small—employing less than 10 workers; (2) medium—employing 10–49; (3) large—employing more than 50.

According to this definition, 71 per cent of the sample MMB firms in our survey are small while only 7 per cent are large (Table 4.6). For those engaged in commerce labour usage is understated, since they make use of the *kepala* (contractor) system which provides the labour for the transport, distribution and warehousing of the goods. A further point to note here is that there is no longer a systematic tendency to favour the employment of Muslims as in the past. Some respondents indicated that merit had replaced religion as a criterion for employment.

While the majority of owners have secondary education, they do not have formal management education qualifications. Many analysts note that tertiary qualifications may be a necessary but not a sufficient condition for entrepreneurial success. They argue that the successful running of a business requires personal

TABLE 4.6
Employment

Number of Employees	Percentage
Below 10	71.4
10–49	21.4
50 and above	7.2

skills which are not necessarily associated with intellect.[29] While the older generation businessmen generally concurred with this, some recognized that the business world today is not only more competitive, but also more complex and demanding, and hence the need for higher education. This explains why sons are now allowed the opportunities of tertiary education before joining the business. In fact, some even view it as a form of insurance. In this regard, MMB owners are not very different from other business owners in Singapore, where the stress on meritocracy of necessity singles out education as an important input. A final point to note here is that the sample firms are all prosperous businesses. The fact that the majority of the MMB owners had a secondary education would seem to support the a priori expectation regarding the correlation between education and income.

Sources of Finance. As Table 4.7 reveals, own and family savings represent the main source of initial investments. This is observed to be the case for those who inherited the business as well as for those who started off as employees. For the latter, the practice of *mudarabah* may have been employed but its extent could not be determined. This reliance on internal sources could be due to the maintenance of traditional norms, low start-up costs or difficulty of obtaining funds from formal

TABLE 4.7
Sources of Finance
(In percentage)

Source of Finance	Initial Investment	Subsequent Investment
100 per cent own/family funds	64.3	21.4
70–80 per cent own/family funds	35.7	64.3
20–30 per cent own/family funds	–	14.3

sources. But, the influence of Islamic teachings must be given its due weight. Excessive consumption or wastefulness (*ishraf*) are frowned upon in Islam while the channelling of savings into productive real investment is highly favoured.

For subsequent investment, though there is increased reliance on financial institutions, reliance on retained earnings for the running of the business remains heavy. A few informants have indicated that the presence of a large number of banks in Singapore made it relatively easy to obtain credit and discounting facilities. This reliance on conventional or non-Islamic financial institutions may be regarded as being inconsistent with the requirements of Islam. It may be noted that their use of non-Islamic financial institutions is presumably due to the absence of formal Islamically institutionalized options available in the country.

Possibly recourse is made to other informal (that is, unregulated by the state) options, such as *mudarabah* and *qard-al-hasan* (benevolent loans). But again the extent of their use could not be determined.

A proposal was made in 1985 by the minister in charge of Muslim affairs to set up an investment institution to be run on Islamic principles. Its aim is to mobilize available Muslim funds for investment in order to increase the Muslim share of the economy. While this proposal[30] has yet to see fruition, it could provide a workable Islamic arrangement in a non-Islamic environment.

Responses to the question on the extent to which profits were ploughed back into the business reveal no systematic tendency. In other words, responses fall into a very wide range. A few of the respondents have indicated that profits were used mainly for the acquisition of assets. Although the nature of the assets was not specified, it appears that some of it took the form of property (real estate) and gold and jewellery. The latter in particular is useful as collateral for small loans since it may be pledged at pawnshops. Again the extent of such use by Muslims could not be determined.

Constraints on Investments. The strength of the Singapore dollar was perceived by respondents as a principal constraint on their investment (Table 4.8). Those who viewed future prospects pessimistically stressed direct trading by neighbouring countries as the main cause. Port and warehouse charges, and levies on the use of labour such as the Central Provident Fund contribution and Skills Development Fund levy were identified as adding to costs. Some look upon government charges as eating into the already low profit margins. The factors mentioned appear to be a problem applicable to all Singapore businesses and not specific to MMBs. Singapore's tight labour market was not regarded as a serious constraint except by those in retailing and for those activities requiring special skills which are in short supply. This is not surprising, since the surveyed firms are not in general large labour users. While a longitudinal question on employment was not asked, it is not unreasonable to state that their direct labour requirements may have remained the same or decreased slightly due, for example, to office automation.

TABLE 4.8
Constraints on Investment*

Reason	Percentage
Taxation	28.6
Tight labour market	28.6
Lack of finance	35.7
Strong Singapore dollar	57.1
Future prospects of activity	50.0
Government regulations	42.9

* Multiple responses.

To gauge whether government fiscal and financial schemes were beneficial to the surveyed firms, respondents were asked to state their usefulness to their business. However, most did not find them useful. One reason indicated by a respondent was that they were "... beyond the reach of small firms ...".

Performance. During the last 25 years, structural change in the economy has reduced in relative terms the share of the commerce sector. Despite this and despite complaints regarding direct trading, 70 per cent of the firms in the commerce sector reported favourable performance as measured in terms of turnover. Several respondents mentioned that, to overcome the problem of direct trading, they were now exporting directly from producing countries. Those who stated that their business was unfavourably affected cited the 1985 recession, competition from government linked companies and exchange rate fluctuations as explanatory factors. For the smaller firms, the need for more capital was often cited as a problem.

Firms in the financial services sector in particular reported favourable performance, as this sector has emerged as a leading growth sector in recent years. Those in the formal financial sector attributed their performance to the growth and diversification of offshore financial activities. Those in the informal or curb market ascribed their performance to the growth of tourism and residents' travel abroad as important factors.

Firms were asked to compare their present activities with those that took place some 10 to 20 years earlier. The observed changes may be summarized as follows:

1. Use of modern communications and office equipment in the form of telex, IDD, and facsimile.

2. Diversification in terms of products and markets.
3. Larger bank loans and facilities.
4. Higher level of capitalization.
5. More overseas travel for business.

However, only a few have diversified into manufacturing, although some are considering this type of diversification. Another salient observation is that management styles have remained unchanged, despite the changing circumstances.

Respondents were also asked to state their views on MMBs. These are summarized below:

1. MMBs are not aggressive enough. This could suggest that they are not profit maximizers. The consequence of this is slower capital accumulation. However, in the case of restaurants, profits are lower because they are unwilling to serve liquor.
2. Especially the smaller MMBs, for religious or other reasons, are wary of dealing with financial institutions. This explains the reliance on internal finance.
3. The lack of knowledge of modern business management practices, especially financial management, was regarded as a factor adversely affecting profitability.
4. There has been very little co-operation among MMBs.

Respondents were asked to rate the success of an Islamic bank in Singapore. Their answers revealed only a negligible degree of awareness and understanding of such institutions and their practices. This is by no means surprising, since Islamic banking practices have been brought into sharper focus only fairly recently in the wake of the world-wide Islamic resurgence.

A question on how closely business ethics (practices and relationships) conform to Islamic ethics was not asked as it might have been construed offensive. However, probably many adhere to the Islamic injunction that private gain is for both private use *and* public use. This is manifest in Singapore in the establishment of Wakaf bodies (largely by minority Muslims), support of Jamat activities where such organizations exist, voluntary payment of zakat to the Majlis Ugama Islam which has not made it a mandatory payment yet, other donations to Muslim activities including Sadaqah.[31] Some of these activities defy quantification. They are nevertheless part and parcel of Muslim life even where Muslims are a minority group.

Problems and Prospects

While the MMB activities are fairly diverse, they generally achieved prominence in the commerce sector. This prominence is reflected in the fact that four out of nine members who signed the Memorandum of Association of the Indian Chamber of Commerce in Singapore in 1937 were MMBs.[32] The survey findings (which admittedly are unrepresentative) also suggest that the majority of the MMBs are concentrated in the commerce sector. This section examines the problems and prospects of MMBs in the light of the rapid economic and social transformation of Singapore during the last twenty-five years. Given the diversity of MMB activity and the paucity of information, generalization would be difficult. Further, the issues and problems vary with the level and type of business. Thus, our discussion is highly selective. It should be emphasized here that the problems identified do not necessarily pertain to MMBs only, but impinge on all businesses affected by the changing circumstances.

In the process of economic development, which involves structural change and urban development, traditional occupations and activities can be expected to decline. This may be attributed to both economic and social causes such as demographic changes, labour shortages, rising wages, rising levels of education, technological developments, urban renewal, and changing lifestyles.

We single out for discussion first a number of activities which potentially face a serious problem of continuity. The activities selected are all one-man operations which were not captured by the survey.

We consider first the case of the cigarette cum sundry goods stalls, often located in the recesses of outerwalls of old rent controlled shop houses.[33] Many of these old shop houses have been affected by urban renewal forcing the stalls to close down, though some have relocated to the Housing and Development Board estates. Relocation to new areas entails higher rents (overheads) which may affect the viability of the activity. Another factor adversely affecting their activities is the change in the pattern of retailing where small scattered establishments are being replaced by shopping centres. Other than the higher rents, relocation to shopping centres would require a higher degree of capitalization beyond the means of many of the stallholders. Recent proposals for the conservation of certain areas such as "Little India", where some of these stallholders may still be found, may prolong their life to some extent.

Our second illustration involves tailoring establishments operated for the most part by one individual. Urban renewal has again required relocation to premises with no rent control. Besides, the redistribution of population to the new housing estates has meant for some a loss of clients. Even for Indian style garments, customized tailoring now has to compete with the manufactured garments industry. An additional factor is the changing lifestyles which reduce the demand for traditional (ethnic) clothing especially by the younger generation.

Our third illustration involves the provision shops and similar small scale traditional retail establishments run by MMBs. This activity is labour intensive and in the past had relied on (cheap) labour from family and kin. Presently they face labour problems due to controlled immigration, and reluctance of younger family members to participate in the activity due to better education and higher income prospects from alternative employment opportunities. Their requests for permission to employ foreign (guest) labour have not been viewed favourably by government due to the low value added nature of the activity. Their labour problem appears to be more acute than those faced by Chinese provision shops. This has its roots in the unfavourable Indian sex ratio referred to earlier. Many Chinese retailers rely heavily on family labour including that of women and children. MMB (Indian) provision shop owners often only have a part of their families with them in Singapore and this increases their dependence on non-family labour which is in short supply. The other problem which they face is a shared problem—that of competition from larger establishments such as supermarkets. For the MMBs and for others, viability requires adjustment to changing factor endowments.[34]

Finally, we shall consider the case of the Indian Muslim cooked food stalls (hawkers), highly visible as a group but again difficult to quantify. Their future role is as much a function of specifics such as the hawker policy as other more general socio-economic changes. During the early days of independence, the high unemployment rate made the official policy towards hawking rather liberal. Unemployment, however, has not been a problem since the mid-1970s and the hawker policy has seen attendant changes. First, street hawkers have been licensed and relocated to markets and food centres to mitigate negative externalities. Second, the licensing policy has become more restrictive. Licences are now granted to resettlement and extreme hardship cases where those seeking a licence must be Singapore citizens between 40–60 years of age, unemployed and with family incomes below S$500 per month.[35] In other words, new entry is now more difficult. A more recent policy decision involves the replacement of wet markets and food centres with mini and supermarkets and eating houses in the new towns.

Our four illustrations above suggest some of the difficulties facing the self-employed or own account workers. Our earlier discussion on the historical origins of MMBs in Singapore pointed to their strong preference for independence—"running their own businesses". This, combined with the low entry costs (which include low educational levels), facilitated their involvement in a variety of activities. Modernization often involves a reduction of the so-called informal sector or bazaar activities, and this poses a potential threat to many MMBs and to similar non-Muslim businesses.

We shall now turn to firms in the formal sector. Some of their problems were identified by the survey findings. They belong largely to the small-medium enterprise category (SME) and their problems lie mainly in the area of finance and marketing. As is prevalent elsewhere, SME studies[36] and policies generally exhibit a manufacturing bias and hence do not directly address the problems of SMEs in non-manufacturing sectors. However, with the recent resurgence of interest in SMEs in official and private circles, help may be on the way.[37] But it would be up to MMBs (and others) to take advantage of these initiatives.

Specifically for those involved in entrepôt trade there is a need to identify both new products and markets and possibly seek other ways of diversification. Singapore's trade policy is now actively seeking new markets, and focusing, *inter alia*, on India, where the easing of trade regulations can provide new opportunities. The familiarity of MMBs and their contacts with the Southeast Asian region would mean that they are in a good position to extend their traditional intermediary role in this (new) market.

Survey findings and observations suggest that MMBs have not diversified into "new" activities despite the structural changes in the economy. Their energies continue to be directed to the commerce sector which has not been the leading growth sector during the last 25 years. In particular, the MMB presence in the manufacturing sector appears insignificant. Is this due to the common contention that Singapore is seriously deficient in industrial entrepreneurial skills? A full discussion of this issue is beyond the scope of this article.[38] Suffice it to note that the following factors are often cited to explain this phenomenon: free entry and presence of foreign firms, the dominant role of government, the lack of access to long term finance, and culture and tradition. These factors appear to affect risk taking adversely. As we have seen, although many MMBs have changed their legal set-up to one of joint stock (private limited) companies, this has not resulted in any real economic change within the organizations, that is, ownership and control are not separated as would be expected of this form of business organization. As family control still remains the norm, new talent from outside is generally not induced to join such organizations. It also implies an unwillingness to expand the equity base which in turn keeps their scale fairly small.

It was seen that MMB activities both in the past and the present have been concentrated in the commerce sector without dominating or controlling the sector. Unlike the early Chinese traders who made a name for themselves in plantation agriculture and mining in West Malaysia and in the banking sector in Singapore, MMBs did not venture into primary activities. Writing on the role of the Indians in Singapore, one analyst observed that "there are plenty of successful Indian businessmen but few stand out as tycoons".[39] This description would appear to fit the MMBs too. Is their low profile a function of their minority status? That would be too facile an explanation since Indian Muslims were/are very prominent elsewhere notably in African countries. A more comprehensive explanation must await further research.

Conclusion

This article does not claim to have provided a fully representative picture of MMBs in Singapore. It is, however, the first such attempt to single out MMBs for special focus. Since data problems have been enormous, the survey findings must be regarded as preliminary.

MMBs are largely family businesses whose behavioural pattern appears to be economically rational. Falling largely into the SME category, they share many of the problems faced by this group. Family businesses have always been their mainstay. As elsewhere they are belatedly getting the recognition they deserve, as manifest in official and private efforts to improve their efficiency and profitability. And it is up to MMBs to take advantage of such initiatives, of course within the constraints imposed by Islam.

Although the diversity of MMBs makes generalization difficult, the impact of Singapore's rapid economic development on MMBs has in general not been very different from that on others. While most have had a share in the country's growing affluence, some have been adversely affected but not on account of being Muslim.

APPENDIX A

Questionnaire for the Survey of Muslim Businesses in Singapore

I. *Organization and Ownership*

1. Name and year of establishment:

2. Address:

3. Address of head office and year of establishment (if applicable):

4. Address of branches and subsidiaries and year of establishment (if any):

5. State the nature of your business activity and specify the main products and levels of production and distribution:

Items

Main Products	Wholesaler	Retailer	Manufacturer	Agent	Importer	Exporter
1						
2						
3						
Main Services						
1						
2						
3						

6. Type of legal organization:

   Sole partnership
   Partnership*
   Private limited company*
   Public limited company*
   Other (please specify)
   * Specify percentage owned by you and your family

7. Names of directors/partners:

   Name *Citizenship* *Place of Residence* *Relationship*

8. Why did you choose this form of legal organization and when?

9. How old were you when you first went into business?

10. Where was your early life spent?

    Place
    Period
    Reasons for leaving:

11. Before you entered this business did you hold any other job(s)? (If yes, state places of work and duration)

12. What are your reasons for going into business or choosing this particular business: (Please rank the four most important)

    1. Inherited business
    2. Had knowledge of or received training in business
    3. Prospects for larger income compared to previous occupation
    4. Has market potential
    5. Requires little capital or training
    6. Encouraged by family/friends
    7. Others (specify)

II. *Employment and Education*

13a.

Category of Persons Engaged	Singapore Citizens			Non-Citizens		
	Male	Female	Muslim	Male	Female	Muslim
Paid employees[1]						
— Full time						
— Part time[2]						
Working proprietors/ partners						
Unpaid family workers						
Total						

[1] Including working directors and workers paid on commission basis.
[2] Working less than 20 hours in a normal week.

13b.

Category of Persons Engaged	Singapore Citizens			Non-Citizens		
	Male	Female	Muslim	Male	Female	Muslim
	Primary	Secondary	Tertiary	Primary	Secondary	Tertiary
Paid employees[1]						
— Full time						
— Part time[2]						
Working proprietors/ partners						
Unpaid family workers						

III. *Financing*

14. State sources of capital and financial assistance received to *start* your business:

Source of Capital	*Percentage Share (%)*
Own capital	
From family	
From shareholders	
Loans from banks	
Other (specify)	

15. State sources of capital and financial assistance received to *run* your business:

Source of Capital	*Percentage Share (%)*
Own capital	
From family	
From shareholders	
Loans from banks	
Other (specify)	

16. Indicate the proportion of net profit after tax that is ploughed back into the business:

17. If not ploughed back, how are the funds used?

(a) (b) (c)

18. Which of the following factors do you consider to be the most important constraints to investment in your business (please rank):

Taxation
Tight labour situation and high labour costs
Lack of finance and general advice
Strong Singapore dollar
Future prospects of the activity concerned
Government regulations

19. Use of Government Fiscal and Financial Schemes: which of the following have you utilised and how useful have they been:

	Useful/Not Useful
Trade Development Board	
Skills Development Board	
Economic Development Board	
MAS export rediscounting scheme	

IV. *Performance*

20. Has the rapid economic transformation of Singapore in the last 20 years affected your business favourably or unfavourably (please elaborate):

21. Please indicate the growth performance of your business over the last 5 years in terms of turnover/sales, employment, and net assets or profit.

22. Please indicate the extent to which your firm is responsible for the introduction of new products, processes, markets in the last 10 years (please elaborate).

23. To what extent do your present operations/activities differ from those 5–10 years ago? Compared to 20 years ago? (Example in terms of capitalisation, use of modern equipment, techniques, management style etc.)

24. Please indicate the prospects for your line of business over the next five years.

25. Please indicate your plans for the business for the next five years.

26. In your type of business what factors do you think are necessary or have been necessary for success.

27. Please make any other relevant observation which will assist this researcher in understanding Muslim businesses.

28. If an Islamic financial institution (bank) were established in Singapore, how successful do you think it would be.

29. *Final Question:* May I call on you personally to seek clarification if necessary?

Thank you.

Name of respondent: ______________________________

Designation: ______________________________

NOTES

The author would like to thank Dr Mohamed Ariff, the discussant of this paper and other participants of the 26–27 September 1988 Workshop on Islam and Economic Development in Southeast Asia: The Role of the Private Sector, held at ISEAS Singapore for helpful comments.

1 Richard V. Weekes, ed., *Muslim Peoples: A World Ethnographic Survey* (Westport, Conn: Greenwood Press, 1984), Volume I, p. 432.

2 *Straits Times*, 6 May 1988.

3 Margaret Sullivan, *Can Survive La! Cottage Industries in High Rise Singapore* (Singapore: Graham Brash, 1985), p. 72 and p. 108.

4 S. Siddique and N. Purushotam, *Singapore's Little India* (Singapore: Institute of Southeast Asian Studies, 1982) mention the Indian Muslim domination of the cattle trade prior to the 1930s. See p. 77.

5 Such a management culture was practised by Chinese businesses as well. See for example, Teo Soo Hong, "The Chinese Family Firms and Economic Development in Singapore", unpublished Academic Exercise, Department of Economics and Statistics, National University of Singapore, 1987/88.

6 Syed Mohamed Baquir bin Mohamed Ibrahim, "The Tamil Muslim Community in Singapore", unpublished Academic Exercise, Department of Social Work, University of Singapore, 1974, p. 111.

7 Loc. cit.

8 *Census of Population 1980 Singapore*, Release No. 2, Demographic Characteristics, (Singapore: Department of Statistics, 1981), p. 2.

9 Calculated from Census of Population 1980 Singapore, Release No. 2, Demographic Characteristics, op. cit.

10 Weekes, ed., op. cit., p. 295.

11 The early Arab businesses shared some characteristics with Indian Muslim businesses in that they employed their own countrymen and others, especially Indian Muslims. They also probably assisted the migration of Arab employees. See Nurzan binte Mohammad Wahlie, "The Arabs in Singapore", unpublished Academic Exercise, Department of Social Studies, University of Malaya (in Singapore) 1960, p. 47–48.

12 Song Ong Siang, *One Hundred Years' History of The Chinese in Singapore*, (London: J. Murray, 1923), p. 41.

13 They figured prominently in the establishment of Wakafs. See Amina Tyabji, "The Management of Muslim Funds in Singapore", in *Islam and Economic Development in Southeast Asia: The Islamic Voluntary Sector in Southeast Asia*, edited by Mohamed Ariff (Singapore: Institute of Southeast Asian Studies, 1992).

14 Nurzan binte Muhammad Wahlie, op. cit., p. 43.

15 See *Geylang Serai—Down Memory Lane*, (Singapore: National Archives, 1986), p. 18.

16 Ibid., pp. 36–37.

17 *Pioneers of Singapore*. A Catalogue of Oral History Interviews, (Singapore: Archives and Oral History Department, 1984), p. 170.

18 This account is drawn from Reza Namazie, "The Persian Community in Singapore", paper presented at the Singapore Heritage Society's Workshop on Singapore's Minorities, 6 March 1988.

19 Ibid. for an account of a successful Persian trader.

20 *Survey of Wholesale and Retail Trade, Restaurants and Hotels 1985* (Singapore: Department of Statistics, 1987), p. 29.

21 For details, see Lim Chong Yah et al., *Policy Options for the Singapore Economy* (Singapore: McGraw-Hill, 1988), p. 267.

22 The questionnaire is appended.

23 One study indicates that in 1982, Singapore's imports from and exports to India were dominated by SITC3—mineral fuels. None of the MMBs, not unexpectedly, is involved in this trade. See Mukul G. Asher, "Economic Relations between Singapore and South Asia", in *ASEAN—South Asia Economic Relations*, edited by Charan D. Wadhwa and Mukul G. Asher, (Singapore: Institute of Southeast Asian Studies, 1985), especially Tables 10 and 11, pp. 152–53.

24 For a discussion of the involvement of "Overseas Indian Firms" in India's trade, see K.N. Varai, *The Overseas Indian Community in Hong Kong* (Hong Kong: Centre for Asian Studies, University of Hong Kong, 1972), Chapter 4.

25 I am indebted to Dr Mohamed Ariff, the discussant of this paper for this point.

26 See Mike G. Gray, "Financial Planning and Management", in Proceedings of a Seminar on Finance for Small Business, Heller Centre for the Advancement of Small Business, 26 July 1984, mimeo.

27 D.J. Storey, ed., *The Small Firm: An International Survey* (London: Croom Helm, 1983); G. Bannock, *The Economics of Small Firms* (Oxford: Basil Blackwell, 1981).

28 *Census of Wholesale and Retail Trade, Restaurants and Hotels, 1985* (Singapore: Department of Statistics, 1986).

29 See for example, *Small Firms*, Report of the Committee of Inquiry on Small Firms, Chairman J. E. Bolton, (London: HMSO, 1971), para. 2.49.

30 See Amina Tyabji, "The Management of Muslim Funds in Singapore", op. cit.

31 Ibid.

32 Singapore Indian Chamber of Commerce, *Sixtieth Anniversary Momento*, 1984, p. 2. The predecessor of the Indian Chamber was the Indian Merchants Association established in 1924. Some of its Presidents were Muslims.

33 *Straits Times*, 6 May 1988.

34 *Singapore Business* 12, no. 7 (July 1988): 69–70 for findings of a recent survey on retailers.

35 *Mirror* 21, no. 17 (1 September 1985): 4.

36 For example, Ch'ng Hak Kee et al., "Financing of Small and Medium Businesses in Singapore", in *Small and Medium Business Improvement in the ASEAN Region: Financial Factors*, edited by Kenneth James and Narongchai Akrasanee (Singapore: Institute of Southeast Asian Studies Field Report Series, No. 16, 1986); Chew Soon Beng, *Small Firms in Singapore* (Kuala Lumpur: Oxford University Press, 1988).

37 See *Straits Times*, 23 January 1988; *Singapore Business* 11, no. 12 (December 1987): 82–83.

38 For a fuller discussion see Lim Chong Yah et al., op. cit., pp. 438–40; *Report of the Subcommittee on Local Business* (Singapore: Singapore Federation of Chambers of Commerce and Industry, August 1985).

39 *Far Eastern Economic Review*, no. 47, 23 November 1979, pp. 35–42.

References

Arasaratnam, S. *Indians in Malaysia and Singapore*. Kuala Lumpur: Oxford University Press, 1979.

Bannock, G. *The Economics of Small Firms*. Oxford: Basil Blackwell, 1981.

Bolton, J.E. (Chairman). *Small Firms*. Report of the Committee on Inquiry on Small Firms. London: HMSO, 1971.

Business Times, various years.

Census of Population 1980 Singapore, Release No. 2: Demographic Characteristics and Release No. 9: Religion and Fertility. Singapore: Department of Statistics, 1981.

Chew Soon Beng. *Small Firms in Singapore*. Singapore: Oxford University Press, 1988.

Curran, James, John Stanworth and David Watkins, eds. *The Survival of the Small Firm*. 2 Volumes. Aldershot: Gower, 1986.

Gray, Mike G. "Financial Planning and Management", in Proceedings of a Seminar on Finance for Small Business, Heller Centre for the Advancement of Small Business, 26 July 1984. Mimeo.

James, Kenneth and Narongchai Akrasanee, eds. *Small and Medium Business Improvement in the ASEAN Region: Financial Factors*. Singapore: Institute of Southeast Asian Studies Field Reports Series No. 16, 1986.

Lim Chong Yah et al. *Policy Options for the Singapore Economy*. Singapore: McGraw Hill, 1988.

Namazie, Reza. "The Persian Community in Singapore". Paper presented at the Singapore Heritage Society's Workshop on Singapore's Minorities, 6 March 1988. Mimeo.

Nurzan bte Muhammad Wahlie. "The Arabs in Singapore". Unpublished Academic Exercise, Department of Social Studies, University of Malaya (in Singapore), 1960.

Pioneers of Singapore: A Catalogue of Oral History Interviews. Singapore: Archives and Oral History Department, 1984.

Report of the Subcommittee on Local Business. Singapore: Singapore Federation of Chambers of Commerce and Industry, August 1985.

Sandhu, K.S. *Indians in Malaya: Some Aspects of their Immigration and Settlement*. Cambridge: Cambridge University Press, 1969.

Shaw, K.E., et al. *Elites and National Development in Singapore*. Tokyo: Institute of Developing Economies, 1977.

Siddique, S. and N. Purushotam. *Singapore's Little India: Past, Present and Future*. Singapore: Institute of Southeast Asian Studies, 1982.

Singapore. *Geylang Serai—Down Memory Lane*. Singapore: National Archives, 1986.

Singapore Indian Chamber of Commerce. *Annual Report 1986*. Singapore: SICC, 1987.

——. *Sixtieth Anniversary Momento*. Singapore: SICC, 1984.

Song Ong Siang. *One Hundred Years' History of Singapore*. London: J. Murray, 1923.

Storey, D.J. *Entrepreneurship and the New Firm*. London: Croom Helm, 1982.

——, ed. *The Small Firm: An International Survey*. London: Croom Helm, 1983.

Straits Times, various years.

Sullivan, Margaret. *Can Survive La! Cottage Industries in High Rise Singapore*. Singapore: Graham Brash, 1985.

Survey of Wholesale and Retail Trade, Restaurants and Hotels 1985. Singapore: Department of Statistics, 1987.

Syed Mohamed Baquir bin Mohamed Ibrahim. "The Tamil Muslim Community in Singapore". Unpublished Academic Exercise, Department of Social Work, University of Singapore, 1974.

Teo Soo Hong. "The Chinese Family Firms and Economic Development in Singapore". Unpublished Academic Exercise, Department of Economics and Statistics, National University of Singapore, 1987/88.

Tyabji Amina. "The Management of Muslim Funds in Singapore". In *Islam and Economic Development in Southeast Asia: The Islamic Voluntary Sector in Southeast Asia*, edited by Mohamed Ariff. Singapore: Institute of Southeast Asian Studies, 1992.

Vaid, K.N. *The Overseas Indian Community in Hong Kong*. Hong Kong: Centre for Asian Studies, University of Hong Kong, 1972.

Wadhwa, Charan D. and M.G. Asher, eds. *ASEAN-South Asia Economic Relations*. Singapore: Institute of Southeast Asian Studies, 1985.

Weekes, Richard V., ed. *Muslim Peoples: A World Ethnographic Survey*. Westport, Conn.: Greenwood Press, 1984. 2 volumes.

5 BANGKOK MUSLIMS AND THE TOURIST TRADE

Chaiwat Satha-Anand

Introduction

The biggest contributor to the high growth rates of the Thai economy in recent years is tourism.[1] In 1987, there were 3.48 million visitors to Thailand and through them the country earned some 50 billion baht (approximately US$1.96 billion).[2] These figures exceeded the official projections for 1987 which had put the tourist arrival at 2.83 million and the earnings at 42 billion baht.

Contemporary discussion on Thailand's tourist trade concentrates on the socio-economic factors behind the country's remarkable success in attracting foreigners and the social impact of tourism. The people involved in this industry are not given due attention in such discussions.

This study chooses to focus on the Muslims who constitute a sizeable minority group in the heterogeneous Thai society,[3] and seeks to portray their roles in Thailand's booming tourist trade. By virtue of their faith, the Muslims in the tourist trade seem to face a high degree of ethical dilemma. It is this conflict and how they live through it which constitute the subject matter of this study. Bangkok is chosen not only because it remains the most important gateway for international arrivals, but also because the tourism industry in a big city can sharpen the kind of conflict "devout" Muslims will encounter. Wherever possible, the portraits of problems and conflicts will be "described" from the point of view of the "actors" themselves. Documentary research is supplemented by intensive interviews with these social actors.

This study begins with a general picture of tourism in Thailand and its contribution, both positive and negative, to Thai society. It then raises the question of the role of Bangkok Muslims in this tourist trade. In the process, facts and figures about Muslims in Bangkok and their economic role in Thai society are discussed. The lives of Bangkok Muslims in the tourist trade and the pattern of conflict resulting from their identity as Muslims engaged in the tourist trade are also highlighted. This study concludes by raising some fundamental questions on the compatibility of Islam as a religion and a way of life with the modern world characterized by capitalism, which is basically responsible for the lives of paradox many Bangkok Muslims lead.

Tourism in Thailand: A General Portrait

The success story of the tourism industry in Thailand cannot be construed independently of the global trends in tourism. The World Tourism Organization reports that there were 215 million international tourists in 1973. Seven years later, there were 285.5 million tourists, an increase of 32 per cent. More importantly, there have been more and more tourists coming to Asia and the Pacific. In 1977, this region played host to some 8.3 million international tourists. In 1980, there was an 80 per cent increase in this figure, as there were 15 million tourists visiting the region.[4]

Thailand has much to offer its visitors: magnificent beaches, natural beauty, superb architecture, rich collections of arts, excellent cuisine, and good tourist facilities at affordable prices. In 1957, there were 44,375 visitors from overseas. Within 23 years, there has been a more than 4,000 per cent increase in the number of foreign visitors. During the Vietnam War period, there were American troops coming to Thailand for recreational purposes. The number of R & R personnel peaked in 1969, with some 70,000 American soldiers. Number of visitors from neighbouring countries also increased by 738 per cent from 1963 to 1980 (Table 5.1).

From 1981 to 1986, there has been a continuous increase in the number of tourists coming to Thailand, except for 1983 when there was a 1.2 per cent decrease. International tourist arrivals to Thailand increased by 15.6 per cent in 1986 and by 23.6 per cent in 1987 (Table 5.2).

Tourists from Asia possess a major market share, with Malaysians heading the list and the Japanese trailing behind since 1981. From 1981 to 1983, tourists from the United Kingdom and the United States ranked third and fourth in terms of market share, but this began to change in 1984 when the Americans and the Singaporeans became the third and fourth largest groups of tourists coming to Thailand. In 1986 and 1987, Singapore came third and the United States dropped to fourth.[5]

The figures provided in Table 5.3 are significant because tourism revenue is a result of three basic factors: number of tourists, their average length of stay in the country and their daily expenditure.

TABLE 5.1
Number of Visitors to Thailand, 1957–80

Year	Visitors from Overseas	Visitors from Neighbouring Countries	Total	R & R Personnel	Total
1957	44,375	–	44,375	–	44,375
1958	55,210	–	55,210	–	55,210
1959	61,527	–	61,517	–	61,517
1960	81,340	–	81,340	–	81,340
1961	107,754	–	107,754	–	107,754
1962	130,809	–	130,809	–	130,809
1963	134,271	60,805	195,076	–	195,076
1964	158,588	53,336	211,924	–	211,924
1965	189,620	35,405	225,025	–	225,025
1966	207,111	78,006	285,117	33,000	318,117
1967	244,283	91,562	335,845	54,000	389,845
1968	297,856	79,406	377,262	69,070	446,332
1969	378,315	91,469	469,784	70,737	540,521
1970	485,366	143,305	628,671	44,287	672,958
1971	465,992	172,746	638,738	26,614	665,352
1972	594,348	226,410	820,758	7,707	828,465
1973	763,189	274,548	1,037,737	1,447	1,039,184
1974	806,447	300,945	1,107,392	3,530	1,110,922
1975	850,459	329,616	1,180,075	–	1,180,075
1976	877,528	220,914	1,098,442	–	1,098,442
1977	923,046	297,626	1,220,672	–	1,220,672
1978	1,122,518	331,321	1,453,839	21,525	1,475,364
1979	1,230,820	360,635	1,591,455	–	1,591,455
1980	1,348,919	509,882	1,858,801	–	1,858,801

SOURCE: Constance M. Wilson, *Thailand: A Handbook of Historical Statistics* (Boston, Mass.: G.K. Hall, 1983), p. 233.

In the past, rice used to be Thailand's major export which brought in more revenue than other products. Now this is not the case because revenue from tourism has superseded those from other major exports since 1982 (Table 5.4).

The Thai Government anticipated that revenue from tourism would reach 90,000 million baht with approximately 4.8 million tourists in 1989.[6] It is thus interesting to briefly note who these tourists are.

TABLE 5.2
Number of Tourists Coming to Thailand, 1981–88

Year	International Tourist Arrivals
1981	2,015,615
1982	2,218,429
1983	2,191,003
1984	2,346,709
1985	2,438,270
1986	2,818,092
1987	3,482,958
1988	4,300,000

SOURCES: *Annual Statistical Report on Tourism in Thailand 1985, 1986; 1988 Mid-Year Economic Review and 1988 Year-End Economic Review.*

TABLE 5.3
Revenue from International Tourism, 1981–88

Year	No. of Tourists	Average Length of Stay (Days)	Average Expenditure Person/Day (Baht)	Revenue (Million Baht)
1981	2,015,615	4.96	2,146	21,455
1982	2,218,429	4.79	2,248.11	23,879
1983	2,191,003	4.91	2,328.56	25,050
1984	2,346,709	5.47	2,128	27,317
1985	2,438,270	5.58	2,334.92	31,767.86
1986	2,818,092	5.93	2,233	37,321
1987	3,482,958	6.06	2,370	50,024
1988	4,300,000	6.10	2,478	65,000*

* Figures for 1987 are from *1988 Mid-Year Economic Review*, and for 1988 are estimates from *1988 Year-End Economic Review, Bangkok Post Supplement* (December 1988). These figures, though accurate, are not as precise as those obtained from the Tourism Authority of Thailand. In addition, total revenue for 1987 and average expenditures per day per person for 1988 are based on my own calculation.

SOURCES: Wuthithep Intapanya and Chamlong Atikul, *Economic Consequences of Tourism Industry in Thailand*, pp. 16, 20, 24, 28; *Annual Statistical Report on Tourism in Thailand 1985*, pp. 56–57; *Annual Statistical Report on Tourism in Thailand 1986*, pp. 10, 12, 58; *1988 Mid-Year Economic Review*, pp. 9, 36; and *1988 Year-End Economic Review*, p. 11.

TABLE 5.4
Comparison of Revenue from International Tourism and Other Major Exports of Thailand, 1981–87
(In million baht)

Rank	1981	1982	1983	1984	1985	1986	1987
1	Rice 26,367	Tourism 23,879	Tourism 25,050	Tourism 27,317	Tourism 31,768	Tourism 37,321	Tourism 48,500
2	Tourism 21,455	Rice 22,505	Rice 20,157	Rice 25,932	Textile 23,578	Textile 31,268	Textile 35,899
3	Tapioca 16,446	Tapioca 19,869	Tapioca 15,387	Textile 19,155	Rice 22,524	Rice 20,315	Rice 22,668
4	Textile 12,531	Textile 14,049	Textile 14,351	Tapioca 16,600	Tapioca 14,969	Tapioca 19,086	Tapioca 20,719

SOURCES: Sources for data from 1981 to 1986 and tourism revenue in 1987 are the same as in Table 5.3. But for other export goods in 1987, see *1988 Mid-Year Economic Review*, p. 13.

In 1986, about 63 per cent of all the tourists coming to Thailand came independently. Male tourists made up approximately 68 per cent of the total. A little more than half of them were in the age bracket of 25 to 44. More than 80 per cent of the visitors came to Thailand for travel and holiday reasons. In terms of occupation, 20.89 per cent were administrators and managers, 17.22 per cent were labourers, production and service workers, and 14.63 per cent were professionals. First time tourists accounted for 46.58 per cent of the total international tourists to Thailand. More than 90 per cent of the tourists found accommodation in Thailand's hotels while some 5 per cent stayed at their friends' places, youth hostels or guesthouses.[7]

It is also interesting to note that tourists from Saudi Arabia constituted only 0.85 per cent to 1.46 per cent of the total international tourists during 1981–83. Between 1984 and 1986, Middle Eastern tourists accounted for 4 to 5 per cent of the total. In 1983, visitors from the Middle East ranked first as the biggest spenders (4,855 baht per day) per person, double the overall average (2,328 baht per day). In addition, while the average length of stay for international tourists in Thailand was less than five days in 1983, an average Middle Eastern tourist stayed in Thailand for 7.93 days. An average Saudi Arabian tourist, in particular, stayed in Thailand more than nine days at a time.[8]

Middle Eastern tourists are highlighted here because the majority of them are Muslims and they tend to spend more than any other group of tourists. In

TABLE 5.5
Revenue from Middle Eastern Tourists, 1984–86

Year	No. of Arrivals	% of Total Tourists	Average Length of Stay (days)	Average Expenditures per person/day (baht)
1984	127,081	5.41	7.06	4,055
1985	127,441	5.22	9.26	4,222.86
1986	113,004	4.00	7.58	2,759.54

SOURCES: *Annual Statistical Report on Tourism in Thailand 1985*, p. 56 and *Annual Statistical Report on Tourism in Thailand 1986*, pp. 56–57.

addition, they have been staying in Thailand longer than most other groups. Moreover, it is widely known that their behaviour as tourists in Thailand does not reflect the tenets of Islam. However, due to deteriorating economic conditions in the Middle East, the numbers, length of stay and amount of expenditure of these tourists have been declining (Table 5.5).

Literature on Tourism in Thailand: Pros and Cons

Many of the studies on tourism have concentrated on forecasting either the number of tourists visiting Thailand[9] or the revenue from tourism vis-à-vis the four main exports of the country.[10] One study found that for the period 1963–80, tourists' income and political instability emerge as the most important factors affecting tourist arrivals, and that the prices of goods and services in the host country did not have any significant influence.[11]

A different set of studies has concentrated on the impact of tourism on the Thai economy. Focusing on the multiplier effect of tourists' expenditures and the balance of payments during 1962–75, a study has concluded that tourism was quite beneficial to the Thai economy.[12] Another study has indicated that a decrease in the flow of foreign tourists can cause a considerable loss of revenue and employment. It has shown that a decrease of 1 foreign tourist will result in income loss of 9,400.04 baht and employment decline of .11 person. It was found that the service sector was most vulnerable to this danger followed by manufacturing and transport/communication sectors respectively.[13] Another study has cautioned that focusing on revenue earned from tourism may be misleading as it may lead to more imports while tourism itself cannot provide a strong basis for national development.[14]

It cannot be denied that it is because of tourism that arts, crafts and classical dance are preserved and revived,[15] but at the same time there is the danger of local values of adherence to familial ties and social discipline giving way to money culture.[16] It is argued that tourism serves merely as a catalyst in the proliferation of crimes and prostitution but is not its cause. The development of tourism in Chiengmai has resulted in the decline of the local people's participation in religious activities and festivals. There is also evidence of the northern languages being affected. However, changes in diet patterns, dress styles and traditional values seem to result more from media exposure and proximity to the urban areas than directly from tourism.[17] One study points out that, more often than not, the Thai authorities tend to overemphasize the economic impact of tourism at the risk of overlooking the adverse impact on spiritual values and traditional virtues.[18] Another study has shown that tourism tends to impact negatively on nature (e.g. deforestation and pollution), architecture (e.g. ignorant destruction of traditional architecture), local cultures (e.g. standardization of art forms and commercialization of traditions) and on the very lives of those residing in tourist locations (e.g. migration and prostitution).[19]

Since contrived adventure, fake liberty and unauthentic romanticism constitute the ideal of modern tourism, there tends to be a confrontation between tourism culture and local culture. An inevitable result is that local culture has to adapt itself to suit the rhythm of tourism culture backed by wealth and bureaucratic power. Such adaptation for the sake of commercial value tends to bring about the destruction of traditional values which are integral to the Thai way of life.[20]

In most of the literature under review, only scant attention has been paid to religion. One study made reference to unIslamic activities such as the selling of prohibited food and beverages, Ram-Wong (Thai popular folk dance) with dancing girls provocatively dressed and some forms of gambling in the annual fairs organized in the province of Pattani in conjunction with the Eid-ul-Fitr celebrations. This fair, which has become a tourist object, can be considered an affront to the Muslims' cultural identity. This has widened the rift between the Muslims and the non-Muslim bureaucrats who lack cultural sensitivity and knowledge.[21]

As a Thai Roman Catholic Cardinal in Thailand has pointed out, modern tourism is basically for pleasure and vacation unlike travelling in the Bible such as Abraham's voyage, Moses's exodus or Jesus's journey. Tourists do not travel in order to share what they have or to learn from others. The result is exploitation and cultural destruction. He concludes: "Forms of travel aiming at victory, exploitation or cheap women do not have a right to exist. Any country which chooses to promote such activities is betraying its own people".[22]

It is clear from the above discussion that Islam has not come up as a point of focus in studies related to tourism. The voice of the Muslims with respect to tourism from a religious perspective has not entered public discourse.[23] It is therefore interesting to discuss how the Muslims stand in relation to the fast moving world of tourism industry especially in Bangkok where approximately 70 per cent of all visitors to Thailand pass through.[24] However, it is instructive to first briefly sketch the role of Muslims in the Thai economy.

Muslims in Thailand: Figures, Facts and Economy

Based on information about Thailand published by the Ministry of Foreign Affairs, Muslims account for 4.05 per cent of the population of the country. However, according to the National Statistical Office, the number of Muslims in Thailand had declined from 2.24 million in 1984 to 2.01 million in 1985. Common wisdom suggests that this decline is plainly impossible. According to an independent estimate, there were approximately 2.6 million Muslims in Thailand in 1986.[25] A Muslim academician notes that there are approximately 2.2 million Muslims in a country of 52 million.[26]

There are 2,573 mosques in Thailand, and it has been estimated that there are 183 Muslim households per mosque and eight members per household.[27] The Muslim population, according to this calculation, numbers 3.77 million. A member of the Islamic Council of Bangkok recently indicated that Muslims in Thailand number 5.2 million. This figure is based upon the number of mosques, which was just at 2,600 and a rough estimate of 2,000 Muslims per mosque.[28]

All these estimates suffer from some weaknesses. The official figure of slightly more than 2 million Muslims in Thailand does not seem to take into account the fact that family planning is least effective among the Muslims. For the purpose of this study, an estimate of 8 members per household may be questionable in the case of Bangkok Muslims, while a flat estimation of 2,000 Muslims per mosque seems rather unrealistic. All this is mentioned to suggest the following. First, it is still difficult to prove or disprove most of these figures. Second, if it is already difficult to provide an exact figure of the number of Muslims in Thailand, obviously other data concerning this particular group of people will not be easily forthcoming. Be that as it may, it is sometimes argued that the number of Muslim population in Thailand is not a matter of statistics alone. It depends of whose figures one is using. It is safe to suggest that official figures or figures from institutions close to Thai officialdom will always be lower than figures given by Muslim writers, especially those who do not consider themselves a part of the Thai official domain for the obvious political reason. In this sense, the number of Muslim population in Thailand is basically political.

The economic role of Muslims in Thailand began during the Ayudhaya period when Persian, Malay, Indian, Arab and Cambodian Muslims interacted with the Siamese for commercial purposes. Because of their wealth, they began to gain political power, which in turn was used to secure more wealth for themselves and other Muslims, as evident during the reign of King Narai.[29]

During the first three decades of the Chakkri dynasty, Muslims around Bangkok were not very active in their business because many paid more attention to agriculture. But after the Bowring Treaty in 1855, they concentrated more on business. Those who were well established excelled as exporters and importers. Those who were not, travelled to four corners of the land as retailers taking with them all kinds of clothes, salt, sugar and onions. On their way back, their boats were loaded with rice, black pepper, fruits, teak and sometimes cattle. As middlemen, their business became quite profitable. It is believed that many Muslims in Bangkok had always been fairly well-to-do. Those who lived in the centre of Bangkok excelled in the field of commerce, while those who dwelled in the suburbs possessed large pieces of land for farming. Later, they also enjoyed the fruits of rising land prices.[30]

Although Muslims in Thailand have been the focus of attention among academics and journalists alike for quite some time, most of the literature on them seems to focus on politics, especially problems in the South.[31] In a recent article on Islam and Development in ASEAN, economic development was mentioned only in the context of ethnicity and state relationship.[32] It seems safe to conclude that very little has been done with respect to the economy of Muslims in Thailand in general and those in Bangkok in particular.

Surin Pitsuwan has pointed out that, through commercial pursuits, Muslim merchants of Indian or South Asian extraction in Bangkok are among the wealthiest Thai nationals.[33] However, Preeda Prapertchob has observed that Bangkok Muslims are not that well to do, adding that a large number of Muslims still live in slum areas.[34] Muslim residents of Ban Krua, descendants of the early Cambodian Muslims, live in slum conditions. In addition, as pointed out by Preeda, many Bangkok Muslims had sold their land and spent their money without moderation, ending up as have-nots. To be sure, exceptions do exist.

As a people, Bangkok Muslims are not dissimilar to other residents of the capital city. There are those poorer ones who constitute the majority of Bangkok Muslims. There are rich Muslims engaging in commercial pursuits of all sorts. In their own ways, they live and work as part of the fast moving city.

There are approximately 276,520 Muslims in Bangkok, a city of 6 million people, accounting for 4.6 per cent of the total.[35] It is interesting to ask how many are involved in the lucrative tourist business in Thailand at present. But more significant than mere numbers are the ways in which the Muslims of the tourist trade conduct their lives. The portrait that emerges from a description of the process of claiming to be Muslims on the one hand and working in the tourist trade in a modern non-Muslim city may perhaps shed a meaningful light on the destiny of Muslims in a rapidly changing economy.

Myriads of Muslims in the Tourist Trade

According to the International Union of Official Travel, tourists are "temporary visitors staying at least twenty-four hours in the country visited and the purpose of whose journey can be classified under one of the following headings: (a) leisure (recreation, holiday, health, study, religion and sport); (b) business (family mission, meeting)".[36] Be that as it may, an ordinary tourist has to have a place to stay, food to eat, transportation facilities to move from place to place, some form of entertainment to relax themselves and some souvenirs to take home. In order to construe the economic locus of a people in relation to the tourist trade, it may be wise to approach it from the actual expenditure of the tourists while in the host country.

Except for shopping and local tour/transportation, tourists' expenditures in Thailand seem to follow an identifiable pattern. They spend most on accommodation, which accounts for a little more than a quarter of total expenditure. In 1986, there were 97 hotels with 22,576 rooms in Bangkok alone. Accommodation in these hotels can cost anywhere from some 500 baht a room per day to more than 3,000 baht for a night in a standard room of a five-star hotel. Food and drink amount to one-fifth, while entertainment takes up approximately one-tenth of the total expenditures (Table 5.6). The share of shopping had fallen in 1986–87.[37]

If modern tourism can be considered as "commercialized hospitality",[38] the pattern of tourists' expenditures can be used as points of contact between the tourists and the local people where the latter's self understanding, whether a Muslim or not, will be manifested. However, not all these points of contact are relevant to

TABLE 5.6
Distribution of Tourist Consumption Expenditure, 1984–86
(In percentage)

Type of Expenditures	1984	1985	1986
Accommodation	28.12	25.62	26.63
Food and Drink	20.53	19.14	16.93
Entertainment	10.43	11.64	10.02
Shopping	30.16	33.66	27.39
Local Transport/Tour	8.48	7.82	15.59
Miscellaneous	2.28	2.12	3.44
Total	100.00	100.00	100.00

SOURCE: *Annual Statistical Report on Tourism in Thailand 1986*, p. 58.

this study of Muslims in Bangkok and the tourist trade. For example, of all the existing 97 hotels in Bangkok, none is owned by a Muslim. Although there are approximately 190 small-sized guesthouses, (some of them using Arabic names advertising halal Indian/Pakistani food and decent accommodation), the owners of some of these establishments turn out to be Christian Indians or Sikhs. As such, it may be more fruitful to focus on points of contact other than in the field of accommodation.

Before discussing the lives of Muslims in Bangkok and the tourist trade, a note on some problems encountered in the process of conducting research is called for so that the data presented here can be better construed. In the course of this research, government institutions, the official Muslim institution (i.e. the Shaikh ul Islam Office) and a local business paper were approached for relevant data without success. It seems that either they are not interested in systematic collection of data because of a lack of understanding of its significance or they are too unorganized to handle this task. In addition, there is no way to identify a Muslim tour company, restaurant, or souvenir establishment if Arabic names are not used. Even when such names are used, the owners may not be Bangkok Muslims. As a result, unless one knows from other sources of information, names like Put-taan Tour or Plublueng Restaurant do not reveal their Muslim identities. Such difficulty in identifying Muslims in the tourist trade together with a rather small number of Muslims in Bangkok curtailed the scope of this survey. More importantly, intensive interviews and candid dialogues with some of those involved in the tourist trade can better cope with the basic question crucial to this research, i.e. the Islamic ethical constraint that Muslims face or overcome in their tourist trade. It was through these dialogues that we were able to gain an insight into the ethical dilemma and tensions that confront the "actors" in the arena.

The form of presentation which will follow will be narrative. Data reported will come from both observation and dialogues. Wherever possible, the stories will be told from the subjects' perspectives in order that "their" process of overcoming the tension of being a Muslim on the one hand and involvement in the tourist trade on the other can be highlighted.

Muslim Restaurants: Differing Shades

There are several Muslim restaurants in Bangkok. *The Muslim Telephone Directory* published in 1987 listed 32 of them. The list is not complete, however. An average Muslim restaurant is no more than a small shop with five to six tables. Many are close to mosques surrounded by Muslim communities in the neighbourhood. Most of them are not directly linked to the tourist trade. Therefore only restaurants that are either famous or close to a hotel have been targeted for interviews. Fame is important in this case, because tour groups will sometimes drop by to experience particular dishes even if the restaurant is far from a hotel.

"Remote" Restaurants

There is only one Muslim restaurant in Bangkok whose name is a combination of a Japanese dish and a fabled Indian Muslim Queen. The restaurant is in Nonthaburi, North of Bangkok. Because of its location, the chance is slim for a tourist to just walk in. It is beautifully built, clean and well kept. There are 16 tables which can accommodate up to 82 customers at a time. The owner, a Muslim butcher from Ayudhaya, invested about 5 million baht in this two-year-old restaurant. It is making around 3,000 baht a day.

There have been few foreign guests. Those who did come were brought here on purpose. Most of them were business people. Many of them were Saudis, Malaysians and Bangladeshis. There have been no tour group coming to this restaurant. "Some tour agents approached us but we did not take it because they wanted us to charge the tourists more. We could not do that. We do our business with *ikhlas* (sincerity)," so said the proprietor.

When asked about his staff, the proprietor said, "We do not use a Muslim cook. We serve Thai and Chinese/Japanese-styled food. Muslim cooks only know how to cook *biryani* and there is no need for that here. In addition, we cannot afford to have all Muslim waitresses because the Muslims have too many relatives. They always find reasons to leave their work for a day or two. That is not good for business. I spent two years working in a famous Chinese noodle restaurant in downtown Bangkok and those experiences were extremely useful. I can only summarize it this way: For the Thais, when they are rich from business, they quit. For the Muslims, they do business just to survive. For the Chinese, they will always try to improve their businesses. Yet, we are proud to prove that Muslims can do business too."

There are two clear signs on the wall: "No beer or liquor allowed in this restaurant" and "If you wish to pray, please go upstairs". One can find a bathroom for ablution and a nice room for prayer there. "This restaurant is an 'on-the-way mosque'. There are people who will just come here for prayers and they leave without eating." It was easy to sense a trace of quiet religious content in his last remark.

Although far from the tourist district, "J Fried Chicken" occasionally entertained tour groups. Most of the tourists who visited the restaurant were from Malaysia. They came in groups of 30 at a time. "They added us on their list of restaurants simply to allow the tourists to taste Muslim food at least once. I don't think that they are doing it for religious reasons," the female proprietor remarked.

The restaurant is not new. It first opened for business in the Phra Kanong area 30 years ago, and has been in Klong Tan since 1983. There are 18 four-seat tables with one two-seat table. At its peak, the restaurant can make around 10,000 baht per day, while the lowest take per day is 3,000 baht. All the workers including the cook in this restaurant are Muslims. "Because they are clean," reasoned the owner.

Three highly visible signs reveal the character of this restaurant. The first is "Liquor and beer are not available here. Please do not bring them in. Thank You". The second is a huge picture of the Baitullah (the Grand Mosque in Mecca). The third is presumably the restaurant's motto taken from the Hadith, "Earn your living as if you are immortal. Do your Ibadat as if you will die tomorrow". This restaurant made its choice known clearly. Unfortunately, it ran out of business recently.

In contrast, two other famous restaurants seem to manifest their Muslim colour less visibly. "E" is a famous restaurant in the Thonburi area, approximately 5 to 10 minutes from Sanam Luang and the Grand Palace. It specializes in North-eastern dishes popular among those who love to drink. There are 27 four-seat tables and can accommodate up to 112 customers. One of the managers mentioned that in the previous month there were three small tour groups, ten at a time, which came to this restaurant. Most of the tourists were from Malaysia. With six waitresses and non-Muslim cooks, the restaurant earns from 10,000 to 30,000 baht a month. Liquor and beer are served.

There is nothing to indicate that this is a Muslim restaurant except for a frame of Qur'anic verses hanging decoratively on the wall and the conspicuous absence of pork dishes on the menu. Two of the four shareholders of this restaurant are Muslims. One of them is a very popular television personality and budding business tycoon.[39] "We do not advertise this place as a Muslim restaurant. But in the beginning, we started it because it was so difficult for the Muslims to find a good place to eat. So we do have the Muslims in mind," the night manager concluded. To my knowledge, except for a number of Muslim food vendors with similar dishes, this is the only restaurant where Muslims can come in and taste the halal Northeastern dishes.

"L" is a fancy restaurant far away from the main Ramkamhaeng Road. It was established in 1934 with some five to six million baht investment. With 30 waiters and waitresses, wearing their uniforms of Thai semi-formal dresses, serving up to 250 customers a day it is making 25,000 baht daily on the average.

Liquor and beer are served liberally. Against beautiful popular Thai and international songs performed by professional singers including one Filipino, there is no sign of any "Muslimness" in that restaurant except for the absence of pork dishes on the menu.

"We did not intend to start a restaurant," said the night manager (who occasionally serves as the Imam in a local mosque in numerous religious functions). "We had to entertain soccer teams coming to play in Thailand because the owner's father is involved in professional soccer sport. Now there are few tourists coming this way."

This restaurant does not describe or advertise itself as a Muslim restaurant, although during the month of Ramadan it uses the Muslim radio programmes which go on air every night as a channel for advertising. While all the food are definitely *halal* because the one who purchases the ingredients at the market is a family member, the cooks are non-Muslims. They are Chinese and non-Muslim Thais. Most of the waiters and waitresses are not Muslims either. "The Muslim workers lack perseverance," said the night manager. It seems that the business has been doing so well that this restaurant has to open even on the Eid days.

Muslim Restaurants in the Tourist Area

There are a number of Muslim restaurants in the Silom/Suriwong areas. Three restaurants are of particular interest to the present study. They are restaurants specializing in Thai dishes, Chinese cuisines and roti-styled dishes, respectively. These restaurants share two things in common. First, they describe themselves as Muslim restaurants. Second, a sizeable number of their customers are tourists.

"D" is not a very big restaurant. With 11 tables, it can serve up to 40 guests at a time. There are four waitresses, three of them wearing Pakistani dress. While none of the waitresses cover their heads, the woman manager does. In addition to food, the restaurant also sells Muslim newspapers, cigarettes, handmade artificial flowers, prayer mats and ladies' *talakong* (prayer outfit). Qur'anic verses are hung on the wall for decorative purposes. Everything looks Islamic. However, popular songs are played in the restaurant.

The manager said, "A group of friends joined hands to start a restaurant. We wanted a place to meet after graduation from the university so we started an ice-cream parlour. Five years ago we moved from Siam Center to Silom and started a restaurant. We decided from the very beginning that this was to be a Muslim restaurant and hence, the name of this restaurant which means 'religion' or 'way of life'. More than 70 per cent of our customers are Muslims. Many of them are tourists, mostly from Malaysia and a few from Brunei."

Tourist customers, mostly from ASEAN countries, can be classified into three groups: businessmen who frequent the place during their stay, tour groups which drop in for only a meal while in Thailand for a couple of days, and sportsmen who are participating in international tournaments in Bangkok. Occasionally, Muslim diplomats would order food from this restaurant for their national day celebrations.

Fifty per cent of the customers are tourists. Most of them are from the Victory and Narai hotels. "As long as the food is good and the customers are treated well, we will have good business," the manager indicated. For a given month they are making 25 to 30 per cent profit, but monthly expenditure ranges from 90,000 to 100,000 baht. Although the head cook is a Muslim, assistant cooks are not. While the restaurant wants to hire Muslims to work, it was difficult because "the Muslims are not interested in this kind of job".

When asked about business constraints, the manager and her husband who joined in the conversation later gave the following details. "It is not easy to operate a Muslim restaurant. We have to understand that we cannot get rich by being a restaurant operator because we cannot think only of profit. We are serving the

Muslims who need us. It is even difficult if we want to close the restaurant for a day because our customers may not be able to find other dining places. It is indeed a sin to do so. Problems facing us are numerous. For example, Muslims from South Asia would not eat squids and some other scaleless fish. When some ordered American fried rice and two slices of sausages were served with that dish, they would not eat it. It was useless to explain to them that the sausages served here are made from *halal* beef. Once a person came in and 'informed' me that oyster sauce cannot be consumed because it is mixed with lard. Then someone would prohibit the serving of Lipton tea accusing it of being mixed with gelatin. And gelatin, as you are aware of, is made from animals' bones. In the past, we used to serve jelly ice-cream. When jelly was prohibited because of its gelatin content, we dropped it from our menu. We had to inform our customers that we had stopped making it because it had become less and less popular. It was difficult to explain the truth of the story to non-Muslim customers. But if we are serious with everything, we will lose our sanity. We have to make up our minds in the end."

Coming from a Muslim family with backgrounds in agriculture and fishery, the owner of "D" tried hard to observe religious values. However, in terms of the relationship between the restaurant and the present capitalist economic system, the owners' solution is more compromising than their practice of serving *halal* food. The manager concluded: "In the capitalist system, the Muslims have to walk a difficult path. It is not possible to avoid all the sins in a society where the Muslims constitute but a portion. But even in a Muslim society, it is not that pure either."

"CJ" is a Chinese Muslim restaurant a few blocks from Narai hotel. Managed by a husband and wife team, the restaurant has 10 tables and can serve up to 40 customers. The husband, who is also a cook, came from Yunan in mainland China while the wife is a Chinese Thai. They started this restaurant some thirty years ago. Most of the customers are local Muslims hungry for the taste of authentic Chinese food. Foreign customers constitute only 5 per cent of the total because "people in this restaurant do not speak English ... But there are some Chinese Muslim tourists coming from Hong Kong. There are not many of them, however".

With drawings from Islamic history depicting Muslim seafarers in the past and Qur'anic verses hanging on the wall, this restaurant is currently the only one of its kind serving *halal* and authentic Chinese food in Bangkok. Most of the waitresses and the present cook are not Muslims. Similar to other restaurants, the owner's reason was: "The Muslims are lazy. They cannot match the Thai or Chinese waitresses."

"CJ" faces a number of problems. The sale of Chinese Muslim food has been dropping. Each month "CJ" has to spend some 25,000 baht while profit is nominal. One of the reasons for this is, according to the owner, the decline of faith among the Muslims themselves. The customers are no longer as strict as those in the past. They do not feel that it is necessary to eat in a Muslim restaurant. In addition, when the husband stopped serving liquor and beer to customers, his business suffered a significant decline.

His wife tried to reintroduce beer by arguing that it was strictly business. In addition, even most Muslims ordered and drank beer. She was also "informed" that beer is different from other kinds of liquor because it is milder and therefore it is easier for a Muslim restaurant to "tolerate" this kind of drink.

"B" is a unique restaurant in Bangkok. It is a really small restaurant with only five tables and cannot accommodate more than 20 customers at a time. It specializes in *roti* with sugar or curry. Many of its customers are either Westerners or Bangladeshis because it is quite close to various guesthouses in the Banglampoo area. More than three-quarters of the total customers are Muslims. Due to the nature of food this restaurant serves, the best time for its business is early morning serving breakfast.

"B" is clearly a Muslim restaurant. It does not serve beer or liquor. It started more than 45 years ago as a food stall near Thammasat University. The owner still retains his old stall which is doing better than "B" because of its location. The lack of manpower also contributes to the restaurant's problems. The owner tried to hire Muslim workers whenever possible.

Muslim Restaurants: Non-Thai Owners

There are Muslim restaurants whose owners not Bangkok Muslims because they are not Thais. One of these is Bagh, a restaurant serving Arabic and Indian/ Pakistani food. It opens from breakfast time until 3 a.m. Its peculiar dining hours can be explained by its location which is close to Grace Hotel where many Arab tourists choose as their lodging place for "entertainment" reasons. The restaurant, however, can be considered a strict Muslim restaurant. Liquor and beer are not served. All four waitresses dress politely. All the meat used in this restaurant is *halal*. It has been here for more than four years. For the capacity to accommodate about 50 customers, the owner, an Iraqi, has to pay a very high rent of above 50,000 baht a month.

"S" is perhaps the most Islamic of all restaurants in Bangkok. Signs of Islam are everywhere. It can serve up to 30 customers at a time. Most of its customers are Indians or Pakistanis. Despite the fact that the cook is a Northeastern Thai, it specializes in Pakistani and North Indian cuisine. Laundry service is also available in this "restaurant". The owner is a Pakistani from Karachi.

Taken together, the preceding sections present a diverse pattern of Muslim restaurant businesses operating in a modern capitalist system. Some are able to practise their faith better than others especially in terms of services made available to their customers. Aspects of services such as serving liquor, dresses of the waitresses, omission of some kinds of food, or conspicuous display of their "Muslimness" are matters of choice for the Muslim proprietors. However, with regard to those aspects of business which deal with a larger economic system, especially banking, they seem to have no control. Suffice it to say here on this issue, that the smaller the business, the easier the adoption of Islamic values.

Entertainment: Extreme Environment

If there is to be an economic locus where participating Muslims are facing an environment that is basically contrary to the tenets of Islam, it is the field of entertainment. It goes without saying that the kind of entertainment which Bangkok is famous (or rather infamous) for is the exploitation of women. However, in describing the lives of Muslims participating in tourist-related entertainment, activities other than sexual entertainment will also be included, namely Thai classical dance performances for tourists. It is important to note here that unlike the discussion concerning Muslim restaurants (since I cannot find a single Muslim owner of this kind of business) the focus will be on the lives of those Muslims who earn their living from tourist-related entertainment.

The Case of a Thai Classical Dancer

"J" is an attractive 37-year-old ex-Buddhist woman now happily married into a devout Muslim family. She is no longer a Thai classical dancer, but at present she teaches classical dancing at a local college. When asked whether performing arts is acceptable for a Muslim woman, she answered that her husband was not pleased with it. She decided to quit when she had a baby. To her, dancing was for fun and it had nothing to do with religion.

Thai classical dancing has to follow rituals based upon Hindu traditions. The classical dancers can only perform their dances after going through a ceremony paying homage to the Hindu deities. The ceremony requires the dancer to present a water bowl, a cone of banana leaf, money (16 baht), and some flowers to the teacher who will then place different classical dancing masks on the student's head.

"J" has been through all this although she underwent this ceremony before she became a Muslim. Though now a Muslim, everytime before she begins to dance she will still pay her respect to her teachers and the shining head gear she is about to wear by pressing both palms of her hands together in a respectful manner. She believes that all this has nothing to do with religion, given her intention to pay her respect to her teachers.

Muslim Girls in the Pleasure Business

An authoritative study on prostitutes maintained that there were 500,000 to one million women engaging in the sex industry all over Thailand. In Bangkok alone, their number is estimated at about 200,000 to 300,000.[40] Child prostitutes number around 20,000.[41] Prostitution is closely related to the tourism industry because foreigners constitute about half of their clients, especially in massage parlours.[42] Given such figures, one cannot help but wonder about the role of "Muslim" prostitutes in Thailand in general and in Bangkok in particular.

It seems that Muslims are perhaps most unlikely to participate in this unholy business. A survey research on Bangkok masseuses conducted in 1979 found that from 1,000 service girls in 13 massage parlours in the city, only 0.81 per cent had claimed to be Muslims.[43] It appears that there are quite a few "Muslim" girls working in a-go-go bars and cocktail lounges, places considered havens for prostitutes.

In an a-go-go bar, girls have to dance on the counter wearing very little to attract male customers. Ms A is one of them. She said she was 16 years old and had been in this business for more than a year.

She had this to say:

> I believed in heaven and hell because I have listened to a famous tape by a Buddhist colonel who was dead and came back to life and revealed all about afterlife. Yes, I consider myself a Muslim although I do not know how to pray. But I do not eat pork. I am sure I will go to hell when I die.

Ms S and Ms N have been friends for a long time. They went to Assala-fiya school together when they were younger. S is from Thonburi while N's family lives in the *kampong* of Maebaeng Mosque. While the father of S is a convert, both N's parents are Muslims. Both S and N have "studied" the Qur'an but found it difficult and incomprehensible. Both of them had fasted occasionally during the month of Ramadan in the past but now they have stopped this practice. N said she was making up to 30,000 baht a month, and spent it all on gambling.

S was unsure about her identity. She went with friends to Buddhist temples and sometimes paid respect to the monks. She knew what she was doing is sinful but,

> I am not sure what will happen after death. Perhaps, we will all forget what has happened in the past. When we are brought back to life, we will no longer remember our past lives. Therefore, it may not be too painful.

While Sainub works in an a-go-go bar, Naya works in one of those where profane shows are performed nightly. Describing her first pork eating experience, she said,

> I felt as though my tongue was swollen. But I thought pork was tasty so the next day I tried again. You see, when you are with friends, you have to eat whatever is available. You do not have much choice. After eating pork for some time, I felt bad about it. So I decided to refrain from eating another kind of meat as a compensation. I stopped eating beef as a substitute for pork. However, it did not last long.
>
> I try not to think about Islam. At the bar there are a Buddha image and "Grandpa and Grandma" (animistic objects depicting sexual acts) dolls which

> every nude performer has to pay homage to before beginning her act. I also do it. Once in a while I visit my folks and that's where I think about religion. My mother taught me to make merit by killing a lizard everyday. And I try to do so to lessen my sin. When I die, I want to be buried in an Islamic way because I consider myself a Muslim. I also think that the Muslim funeral is the best because it saves a lot of money and trouble.[44]

What I found in this brief encounter with these "Muslim" girls contradicts what an American anthropologist has suggested more than three decades ago that tourism-oriented prostitution in Thailand is incompletely commercialized.[45] The relationship between the girls and their clients is based on a clear understanding on both sides and sexual services are exchanged for money.[46] From the data obtained, it seems that the girls' identities as "Muslims" are subsumed under the new rules of the social environment. In fact, their Muslimness has already been undermined from the dynamics of diverse factors including family background, first sexual experience, friends and economic conditions. It is indeed amazing to see how they continue to call themselves "Muslims" and acknowledge their sin in such an unholy environment.

The Travel Business: Agency and Personnel

There seems to be a number of Muslims working in the travel business. Upon closer examination, most of the Thai Muslims are salary earners employed by airline and travel agencies. But rarely do they own the business themselves. In Bangkok, there are only two significant travel agencies owned by Thai citizens who are Muslims. One of them, "A1-K" is owned by a naturalized Thai citizen originally from Northern India. Most of the others are small agencies owned by Muslims who are Indian citizens. They start their businesses by sharing them with Thai citizens. For them, the travel business simply serves as a parallel with another more lucrative, business, namely foreign money exchanges. Even a relatively large travel agency such as "A1-K" did not occupy the main thrust of its owner's large business empire. Mr K himself told me that, "I started the A1-K travel agency for my own convenience because our people have to travel so much." When asked about the kind of profit his travel agency is yielding, he said, "It is negligible." From other sources of information, I understand that the travel wing of the A1-K business is not that significant.

"BL", another travel agency, began its business without any proper office space in 1974. At that time, Mr A was working with the East Asiatic Company. One day at a social gathering, the Pakistani Ambassador to Thailand asked whether there was any Muslim travel agency in Bangkok? The reply was negative. He then suggested that Mr A should start one, promising to give whatever assistance he could muster. With 50,000 baht, Mr A started the business with his wife, who was then working with Pakistan International Airlines. The business began to take off when the Americans left Indochina in 1975. Together with PIA, "BL" succeeded in securing contracts to transport refugees to Paris. Later on, with the emergence of the job market in the Middle East, "BL" continued to expand. Now located in Suriwong in a moderately spacious apartment, it has 11 full-time staff, one-half of whom are Muslims. Except for the workers going to the Middle East, 90 per cent of its customers, mostly Pakistanis and Bangladeshis, are Muslims. Another significant sector of his business is to serve people going for Hajj and Umrah. Each year these pilgrims account for some 10 million baht of business which amounts to some 40 per cent of the total business volume. It shows that "BL" is a travel agency dealing with some 25 million baht a year.

When asked about the secret of his success, Mr A answered in one word: Iman (faith). He said,

> Our name is very clean in terms of honesty. The prices of the tickets are reasonable and we try to help our customers in every way we can. Do you believe that I, as a managing director of this business, would go to an embassy and wait two hours for a Muslim consul and persuade him to grant visas to my clients? Even if you give me 10,000 baht, I will not waste my time like that. But I am doing it for Allah.
>
> I am not at a disadvantage being a Muslim businessman. Of course, there are the usual constraints in terms of social functions. For example, we cannot drink liquor with friends in the business, nor eat or enjoy ourselves as they do. I understand that if you are a minority in some countries, there will be a lot of obstacles for your business. But here in Thailand, things are fine for us and we can certainly compete with any travel agency of the same size and capital in Bangkok.
>
> In Thailand the only problem seems to be the authorities' lack of knowledge about Islam. While Muslims who go to Hajj are exempted from paying travel tax in the amount of 1,000 baht because it is considered a religious function, those who go for Umrah have to pay. Yet, Buddhists going to the Birthplace of the Buddha (which is not a religious requirement) are exempted from paying travel tax.
>
> As a Muslim businessman, there are times when these two identities (being a Muslim and a businessman) clash. Each year, there are several cases of Muslim customers running out of money. As a businessman, such is not my problem. But as a Muslim, I sometimes lend a helping hand.
>
> Another problem relates to the economic system we are in. There is no way that a travel business or any modern business in a non-Muslim society can avoid *riba* or bank interest. Even the *ulama* themselves are far from conclusive in their judgements. The guideline I am using is whether in so doing I am

> causing problems to others. If we take usury from people we are exploiting them and this is not acceptable. But taking bank interest does not seem to cause problems to anyone. If we really want to avoid using credit, then we have to have plenty of cash to engage in travel business which is not possible. My only solution is to seek repentance from God in whatever we do.

As in other cases, I asked about his Muslim staff. He expressed an intention to find good Muslims to work for his agency. But "the Muslims are slower and lazier. The Chinese are the best workers. They work as though this business is theirs." With his remark, one can't help but wonder where the good quality Muslim workers are. One answer is that there are many but they work for international airlines.

Ms V is the chief of the ticketing division of a Northern European Airline. She does not have any problem concerning her Muslim identity. When people in the business know that she is a Muslim, they treat her accordingly. Soft drinks will be available instead of wine whereas dishes other than pork-related food will be provided. It is up to her to choose *halal* food as opportunity avails itself. *Riba* does not present a problem to her, because "we simply pass the money from our clients to the cashier. We don't have to deal with the banks directly".

She also pointed out that there were four Muslim staff in the same company. In her division alone, there were two. Whenever there was an Eid holiday, there would be a problem because both of them had to be absent on the same day. This has sparked some dissension among her non-Muslim colleagues who sometimes pointed to Islam as the cause of disruption of normal life in the office.

When asked whether it was right, from an Islamic point of view, for a Muslim mother of three to work with men in such a secular environment, she answered: "We have got to survive. I have three children and they have to be brought up as best as possible. Working like this, however, religiously improper it may be, is indeed an unavoidable economic necessity."

"S" is an air hostess who has been working on international flights with Thai International for nine years. She became a Muslim after getting married to a Muslim pilot. Now, she is a working mother with two lovely children living with her husband's family.

She described her life as a Muslim hostess on the plane,

> In terms of my own eating, there is no problem. People know that I am very strict and I can simply get by with just bread and butter. But sometimes you have to serve pork dishes and wine to passengers on board. I consider it my duty to do so although I would prefer not to violate any Islamic precept. Some passengers may try to take advantage of the hostess. The Arabs are the worst when they are drunk. The hostess' uniform is plain and modest enough but you will have to be careful. What choice do I have? It is my career.

Her husband, a pilot with the same airline, did not think there was any serious problem as a Muslim that could not be overcome. Apart from the usual food and drink constraints which affect one's social function in a non-Muslim society, there are problems of performing obligatory duties. For example, a pilot's prayers, or for that matter an air hostess', may not be performed on the plane. He or she has to do the compensating prayers later. However, a pilot cannot fly with an empty stomach according to international airline regulations. This rule certainly affects fasting during Ramadan. Again, the pilot said he did not have a choice.

"D" is a 40 year old area manager of a Thai International office based in the Indian subcontinent. In his case, being a Muslim was an advantage.

> Whenever there is a position vacancy in Muslim countries, either in the Middle East or South Asia, Muslim staff will be thought of by the management first. They believe that we are able to do a better job than non-Muslims. So in this company of more than 10,000 staff, there are three Muslim country or area managers. However, it will be difficult for Muslims to reach the very top such as the position of a Vice President. One of the reasons for this is the VP of this airline has to perform a lot of rituals, most of which are not acceptable to Islam. We know it and they know it too.

In the airline services, there is a sizeable number of Muslim workers. For many women working in this tourist-related business, the question of whether they should even work in the first place is never raised. To raise a "good" family in a city such as Bangkok, one needs a stable job, and working with airlines is certainly an attractive proposition.

Souvenirs: Bronze and Brass

One of the most famous souvenirs from Thailand is a set of bronze spoons, forks and knives. In the country, there are only five factories making bronze tableware and one of them is owned by a Muslim family.

"SB" started its business some 30 years ago when a Muslim who was then working with an international airline saw the opportunity of selling Thai souvenirs to the Japanese tourists. He began by selling everything that was Thai, such as silk and gems, focusing solely on tourists. He then decided to venture into production, emphasizing the Thai character of the products and the uniqueness of handmade goods.

At present, Thailand is the only country in the world selling bronze tableware. Every piece in "SB" is handmade. There are some 40 workers mostly farmers from the Central plain and the Northeast whose skills in producing bronze items come from their family tradition. Most of the products are for export and produced on orders. Sale volume for a month is between 1 to 1.2 million baht. Walk-in customers contribute to some 20 per cent of total sales. Most of the products are sold to prestigious hotels in Bangkok or exported to Europe and North America.

These beautiful spoons and forks have three Thai patterns, two of them are Indra's three-headed elephant and a Hindu/Thai god. In "SB", there are other bronze and brass animal statues such as buffaloes, elephants and deers. Well designed semi-naked brass statues of women are also available.

I asked the daughter of SB owners whether producing souvenirs using images of Hindu deities or naked figures was appropriate for a Muslim business. She said it had nothing to do with religion. What she was doing, according to her, was strictly business, i.e. producing and selling bronze and brass sets based upon Thai culture. Bronze sets were seen as uniquely Thai, whose patterns were determined by market tastes.

Patterns of Overcoming Tension

In the study of tourism in general, there seems to be a tendency to overgeneralize, depicting a stereotyped model of participants in the tourist trade. A tourism researcher concludes that "Too much was imputed to the participants in the touristic process, tourists, entrepreneurs, and hosts alike; but their perceptions, evaluation and the bearing of these on their behaviour were too little investigated".[47] It is therefore imperative to analyse the patterns of how Muslim participants in the tourist trade perceive themselves within the web of tension characterized by religious beliefs and economic realities.

It is important to note first that the notion of "Muslim" itself is not unproblematic. The nude bar girl who pays homage to objects is a case in point. It is easy to argue that in so doing she ceases to be a Muslim. However, her self-understanding is such that she regards herself as a Muslim. Therefore, rather than passing judgment on the "Muslimness" of the subjects based upon their behaviour, their self-understanding is considered more relevant to this study.

Based upon the data collected, the following patterns of coming to terms with being Bangkok Muslims, on the one hand, and being practitioners in the tourist trade, on the other, emerges.

If tensions exist in the realm of private lives, then the kind of compromise which results tends to cluster around minor social behaviour. Compromise in the area of eating and drinking seems to be most common among participants who do not own the business but simply work either in the tour business or entertainment parlours. The degree to which they compromise their faith will depend on other factors influencing their lives such as background knowledge about Islam and family life. Those who come from secure homes tend to be in a better position to acquire more knowledge about Islam as well as better social positions which will, in turn, give them more confidence in their identities as Muslims. But the "Muslim" girls in the entertainment business hail from questionable family backgrounds which cannot provide them with a secure life and basic religious knowledge. Their confidence as Muslims easily gives way to the conventional night life enjoyed by their new-found friends. When this situation occurs in a context where money is the arbiter of living, it is not unusual for their Muslimness to fade into oblivion.

Where tensions exist in the economic sphere, two minor patterns can be discerned. First, for some, the tourist trade is nothing more than a business. For a business in the capitalist system, the prime objective is maximization of profit. Those who aim for profit will not choose to concern themselves with religious injunctions more than necessary. Hence, some Muslim restaurants which serve liquor liberally do exist. There are also some Muslim restaurants which proudly exhibit their Muslim character. True to their choice, religious injunctions in matters of food and drinks will be strictly observed. But despite being religious, quite a few Muslim tourist-related business owners do not want to tolerate the ineffectiveness of Muslim workers. This shows the extent to which they try to subscribe to the principle of Muslim brotherhood.

Muslim tourist businesses existing in Thailand's present economic system seem to have no choice but to succumb to the omnipotent capitalist system. In the domain of credit, it would be extremely difficult to avoid bank interest. The result is that the Muslim businessmen are forced by circumstances to make compromises of some sort.

There are also those who do not see any relation whatsoever between their work in the tourist business and Islam as their religion. The most common justification for ignoring religious injunctions in these cases is the assertion that whatever they do has nothing to do with religion.

Factors Explaining Patterns of Self-Explanation

In discussing some juristic aspects of Muslims living as minorities in non-Muslim states, a Muslim writer has suggested three guidelines. First, whatever is *haram* (forbidden) in Muslim states remains equally unlawful for Muslims in non-Muslim states. Second, whatever is *halal* (permissible) for Muslims where they are the majority remains equally lawful for Muslims in non-Muslim states. Third, the principles of *darurah* (necessity) would come into effect in the event of extreme compulsion.[48] These guidelines are not without problems, however.

The question of what is *halal* and *haram* is sometimes unclear. For example, there are a number of Muslim women working in the tourist business. Are their lives as career women, not to mention their dresses, *halal*? According to the very popular guide for the Muslim woman by Shaykh Muhammad Mutawalli al-Sha'rawi, the editor of *Minbar al-Islam* published in Egypt, the woman's place is in her home. He argues that when a woman stays at home she contributes through her labour far more to the economy of the family than when she works outside and has to pay for the expenses which accompany such a lifestyle. It is acceptable for a woman to work with her husband. But if she leaves home to work elsewhere, it is most problematic. He concludes that, "Such a course is acceptable only if there exists a true and established need for her to do so."[49] Although al-Sharawi's position can be reasonably argued against,[50] it is important, precisely because of its rigidity, which encapsulates a current stream of conservative Muslim thought. If this position is taken as final, then all the Muslim women working outside their homes without "a true and established need" are engaging in *haram* activities, not to mention the rather clear-cut *haram* cases such as prostitution.

In fact, one of the most important principles of Shari'ah about *halal* and *haram* is the *asl* or the basis of things created by Allah and the benefits derived from them which are useful for mankind. In other words, this principle points to what a Muslim author calls, "the natural permissibility of things".[51] This principle is based upon the following verse of Al-Qur'an, among others:

> Do you not see how Allah has subjected to you all that the heavens and the earth contain and lavished on you both His visible and unseen favours?[52]

It can indeed be argued that, as in other kinds of law, the number of prohibited things is smaller than those left out which are then considered permissible. Whatever is not mentioned as *haram* is consequently permissible. Prophet Muhammad (Peace be upon him) himself has said:

> Allah has prescribed certain obligations for you, so do not neglect them; He has defined certain limits, so do not transgress them; He has prohibited certain things, so do not do them; and He has kept silent concerning other things out of mercy for you and not because of forgetfulness, so do not ask questions concerning them.[53]

Another problem facing the above guidelines is the meaning of *darurah* or necessity. Many of the Bangkok Muslims in the tourist trade portrayed above look upon themselves as sinners. Some of them are even certain that they will go to hell after death. But they continue to work in the bars or engage in business transactions with commercial banks, and argue that they do so out of necessity and that they have no choice. The question then is what constitutes "necessity" which is acceptable to the canons of Islam.

In discussing women and work, Al-Sha'rawi points out that Islam's assessment of need involves the need itself and the rating of the need, among other things. To sustain life is a necessity, but it is luxury if a four-room apartment equipped with a refrigerator are "needed". He argues that, "Society lost its equilibrium when man forgot his natural worth and aspired to live beyond his level, which compelled him to steal or accept bribes or cheat."[54]

As is normally the case, the Qur'an is less specific than the *ulama*'s exegesis. A verse in Surah Al-Bagara reads:

> But whoever is constrained to eat any of these (forbidden food), not intending to sin or transgress, incurs no guilt. Allah is forgiving and merciful.[55]

For a situation to be considered "necessity", some conditions must be met. First, the person becomes so destitute due to either poverty or sickness that would endanger his life or his family's. Second, the person has absolutely no intention to break Islamic Law. Third, even under such circumstances, he does not partake of the unlawful more than necessary.[56] For example, facing starvation, one should only take a few morsels of *haram* food and not behave as a glutton.

If the Islamic guidelines suggested above are accepted, it seems that many Bangkok Muslims have transgressed the conditions of acceptable necessity judging from the kind of income some of them earn. It is important to note that what is needed here is not condemnation but explanation. It is always easier for some in a privileged profession, such as university academicians, to avoid things that are *haram* than those in other professions, especially tourist trade, in Bangkok. It is obvious that the former group are relatively cleaner not necessarily because they are "better" Muslims but presumably because their line of work seems less susceptible to the domain of *haram* things.

Three interrelated factors stand out as variables capable of significantly explaining the tensions discussed above. They are personal background, the city life, and the powerful capitalist system.

The extent to which a Muslim will maintain his or her posture as a sincere Muslim in the tourist trade depends largely on the Islamic knowledge one gains from his or her family background. One's knowledge about Islam as a way of life is largely shaped by the kind of family one has. A family where one of the parents is not a Muslim is clearly in a high risk category. A broken home will not be conducive to the process of Islamic upbringing of young children. A poor Muslim family may be hard pressed to make compromises because of economic necessity, while a rich Muslim family may easily fall prey to *haram* life-styles due to its social status. In a society where Islam is not understood as a way of life but as a religion of rituals, it is possible for a worldly educated person to separate Islam from his or her economic activities.

A modern city avails itself to the kind of life that seems to relegate religion to a marginal sphere. Approximately 13 per cent of the country's population live in the capital city. As a gateway to international tourists, temptations abound in Bangkok. Some tourists who had gone overboard were apprehended by the police. The files of the Bangkok Tourist Police shows that during the first six months in 1988, there were 126 arrests involving Muslim tourists. About 40 per cent of them were apprehended because they had caused social disturbance,[57] presumably due to drunkenness. Temptations are not confined to tourists only. The Bangkok city life is not conducive for the Muslim community. The community life of the Muslims is being eroded because of the advent of the nuclear family and the search for better living conditions. There are Muslim families that have become part of the city's slums. This transformation is accompanied by numerous social problems, drug addiction, sexual abuse and crime. Middle-class students are sent to good secular schools, usually quite a distance from their homes. By the time they return home, they are too tired to pay attention to Islamic lessons, if available. Their parents too suffer from fatigue resulting from work tensions and Bangkok traffic. It is obvious that all these do not contribute positively to the strengthening of Muslim family life. It is evident that for some Muslims, security in life is not sought in the holy setting of their homes but from friends in the streets to whom Islam may mean next to nothing.

Although it is still debatable whether Islam opposes capitalism *in toto* given its strong support for trade as well as its respect for private property, the Shari'ah is more explicit in its denunciation of exploitation, hoarding, usury, cheating, theft and unlawful dispossession.[58] In this sense, Islam is not congruent with capitalism where maximization of profit constitutes its main pillar and interest nurtured by the ubiquitous banking system serves as its artery. Tourist-related business, or for that matter any kind of business operating in the city (with the possible exception of small-scale self sufficient units) has little choice but to come to terms with the prevailing economic system. Does this mean that the Muslims cannot do business in a capitalist system without compromising their faith? One author points out that some *ulama* are of the opinion that there is no harm in giving (receiving) interest to (from) non-Muslims or non-Muslim banks. He is quick to add that the ideal thing for Muslim minorities living in non-Muslim states is to organize and support Islamic banking. But if such facilities are not available, there will be no harm "if business is transacted with interest involved in it on the basis of *darurah*".[59]

Perhaps it is safe to assert that doing business, especially tourist-related business, in a capitalist system leaves much to be desired from an Islamic point of view. But realistically, what is expected from a Muslim minority living in a non-Muslim country? Is the notion of *hijrah* still applicable in today's world firmly divided by the idea of the modern nation-state? It is therefore understandable why many Bangkok Muslims consider themselves sinners and seek repentance only from Allah, the most Forgiving, the Most Merciful.

Conclusion: Commercialization of Hospitality and Compromise of a Faith?

In the celebrated book *Islam and Capitalism*, Maxime Rodinson concluded two decades ago that the power of the capitalist economy has reduced other modes of production to secondary roles. None can stand up to the competition of a capitalist economy, especially inside a capitalist socio-economic formation. Although Rodinson recognized the specificity of Islam as a religion as well as that of the Muslim world, he emphasized that it was not exceptional.[60] If this is true, it means that in a world characterized by capitalism, Muslims do not have much choice but to lose themselves to the tide of this powerful economic system.

According to the late Faruqi, from an Islamic point of view, man is definable in terms of his economic pursuits. To him, man is *homo economicus* but he rejected the idea that man is subject to economic laws which dominate his activity. Faruqi maintained that the economic pattern to which man subjects his life is deliberately chosen.[61]

The case of Bangkok Muslims has to be understood in the context of Thai society as a social reality. In the capital city, Islam is relegated to a marginal position. In fact, religion itself seems to have become somewhat irrelevant. Many things that happen in Bangkok in the name of tourism is as unacceptable in Buddhism as it is in Islam. The corruption of life in such a surrounding blurs the line drawn between religions. Although the meaninglessness of modern life for a minority group in the midst of Islamic resurgence may propel the Muslims to search for meaning in the security of a more holistic life of a Muslim community, it is relatively easier for those privileged to be distanced from the centre of capitalism.

I would argue that the tourist-related business is now at the centre of capitalism. It is where the power of capitalism is at its zenith, because tourism itself is "commercialized hospitality", among other things.[62] The tourism process can be conceptualized as a commercialization of the traditional guest-host relationship in which strangers were given a temporary existence based much less on human relations than on monetary values. It is capitalism *par excellence* when even a smile and gentle courtesy can be bought. It proves conclusively the undeniable power of capital manifested in the form of money. The effect on participants of tourist-related business is the degeneration of decent human relations based on sincerity. If even sincerity is undermined in the process, how can a Muslim live fully in accordance with Islam and "choose the economic pattern" he or she may have once desired?

In conclusion, it seems that Bangkok Muslims participating in the tourist-related business are facing an extremely difficult situation. They are at a critical point where Islamic values are being undermined because of the secular city life. This is exacerbated by the fact that they constitute a religious minority in a non-Muslim state whose residences are scattered all over Bangkok because of historical circumstances. They are facing an uphill battle because tourism as a business, in the process of over-commercialization, highlights the power of capitalism, especially its dehumanizing effects on the participants.

In the century that saw the birth of the Prophet, the Syrian Monophysite Bishope Jacob of Saroug described a scene when Satan was lamenting its collapse of authority as a result of the recent disappearance of paganism. But finally the Devil exclaims, "I do not mind if the priest uses the interest he draws from his money to buy an axe with which to smash the temples of the gods! The love of gold is a greater idol than any idol of a god ..."[63] In Bangkok, while some Muslims are trying to lead their lives in accordance with Islamic teachings, many who are participating in tourist-related businesses are now facing this greater idol which, in some ways, contributes to the compromising of their faith.

NOTES

* The author gratefully acknowledges helpful comments from Dr Preeda Prapertchob and a stimulating discussion with Dr Yos Santasombat and Professor Erik Cohen during the preparation of this paper.

1 *1988 Mid-Year Economic Review, Bangkok Post Supplement* (June 1988), p. 7.

2 Ibid., p. 36.

3 Chavivun Prachuabmoh and Chaiwat Satha-Anand, "Thailand: A Mosaic of Ethnic Tensions Under Control". *Ethnic Studies Report* (Sri Lanka) 3, no. 1 (January 1985): 22–31.

4 Wuthithep Intapanya and Chamlong Atikul, *Economic Significance of Tourism in Thailand* (Bangkok: NIDA, 1985), pp. 13–14 (in Thai).

5 *Annual Statistical Report on Tourism in Thailand 1985* and *Annual Statistical Report on Tourism in Thailand 1986* (Bangkok: Tourism Authority of Thailand, 1986; 1987), pp. 26; 8; and *1988 Mid-Year Economic Review*, op. cit., p. 36.

6 *Siam Rath*, 4 April 1989 (in Thai).

7 *Annual Statistical Report on Tourism in Thailand* 1986, op. cit., p. 11.

8 Wuthithep Intapanya and Chamlong Atikul, op. cit., pp. 23–28.

9 Ubol Topinich, "The Forecasting of the Number of Tourists Visiting Thailand, 1975–1979" (Master of Commerce Thesis, Chulalongkorn University, 1975) (in Thai).

10 Chaleeporn Sangboonnum, "A Comparison of the Revenue from Tourism and that from Selected Main Exports" (Master of Commerce Thesis, Chulalongkorn University, 1975) (in Thai).

11 Bang-Ornrat Rojwannasin, "Determinants of International Tourist Flows to Thailand" (M.A. Thesis, Thammasat University, 1985).

12 Thai University Research Associates, *Tourism and Economic Development in Thailand* (Bangkok: NIDA, 1977) (in Thai); See also Prachom Suwatthee, *Job Creation in Tourism Industry* (Bangkok: Tourism Authority of Thailand, 1980) (in Thai).

13 Wuthithep Intapanya and Chamlong Atikul, op. cit.

14 Krikkiat Pipatseridham, "Economic Consequence of Tourism", in *Pu-Tai* (The Messiah), no. 2 (1987), pp. 23–30 (in Thai).

15 Wiriyabha Changrien, "Effects of Tourism on Forms of Arts, Customs and Classical Dancing," *Tourism Journal* 1, no. 3 (1982): 56 (in Thai). It is only fair to note that the author acknowledges the fact that such arts and culture have to be compromised in accordance with the tourists' demand.

16 Preecha Oopyokin and Suriya Weerawong, *Effects of International Tourism on Thai Society and Culture* (Bangkok: Social Research Institute, Chulalongkorn University, 1978) (in Thai); See also Nattaporn Sangpradab, "Socio-Cultural and Economic Changes Resulted from Tourism Development" (M.A. Thesis, Mahidol University, 1984) (in Thai).

17 Santad Sermsin, "Effects of Tourism on Society and Culture" (M.A. Thesis, Mahidol University, 1986) (in Thai).

18 Thai Khadi Research Institute, *Patterns of Preservation and Revivification of Tourism-Related Festivals and Traditions.* A Research Report submitted to the Tourism Authority of Thailand, Bangkok, September 1986 (in Thai).

19 Vinai Phunampol, "Negative Impacts of the Thai Tourism Industry," *Barn Mai Ru Roey,* 3, no. 6 (July 1987): 90–103 (in Thai).

20 Nidhi Eiosriwong, "Tourism Industry and its Cultural Impacts," *Arts and Culture* 8, no. 6 (April 1987). This article is reprinted in *Pu-Tai* (The Messiah), no. 2 (1987), pp. 15–21 (in Thai).

21 Thai Khadi Research Institute, Patterns of Preservation and Revivification, op. cit., pp. 137–41.

22 Cardinal Meechai Kijboonchu, "Theology of Tourism", in *Pu-Tai* (The Messiah), no. 2 (1987), pp. 4–7 (in Thai).

23 Dr Preeda Prapertchob has called my attention to various verses (e.g., 3:137; 40:21; 12:100; 27:69; 47:10; and 22:46) in the Holy Qur'an which encourage people to travel for reflection and knowledge but not for pleasure or entertainment. I have written a piece on tourism in Thailand which appeared in a monthly magazine. But it was not written from an Islamic perspective. See Chaiwat Satha-Anand, "Visit Thailand Year," *Hi-Class* (December 1987), pp. 68–69 (in Thai).

24 *Annual Statistical Report on Tourism in Thailand 1986*, op. cit., p. 11.

25 *Thailand and the Muslim World* (Bangkok: Islamic Center of Thailand, Institute of Middle Eastern and Muslim World Studies, Faculty of Political Science, Chulalongkorn University Under the Sponsorship of the Ministry of Foreign Affairs and the Information Division, Supreme Command, (n.d.), pp. 24, 26.

26 Surin Pitsuwan, "The Islamic Banking Option in Thailand," in *Islamic Banking in Southeast Asia*, edited by Mohamed Ariff (Singapore: Institute of Southeast Asian Studies, 1988).

27 Preeda Prapertchob, "Mobilization of Resources Through Waqf in Thailand". A paper presented at the Workshop on Islam and Economic Development in Southeast Asia Phase II, Institute of Southeast Asian Studies, Singapore, 24–25 August 1987.

28 Prayoonsak Chalayondecha, *Muslims in Thailand* (Bangkok: Tonson Mosque, 1988), p. 163 (in Thai).

29 Puangpetch Suratkavikul, "The Economic Role of Thai Muslims in the Past". *Journal of Social Science and Humanities* 10, no. 7 (May–June 1980): 28 (in Thai).

30 Ibid., p. 30.

31 See for example, Surin Pitsuwan, *Islam and Malay Nationalism* (Bangkok: Thai Khadi Research Institute, 1985); and Chaiwat Satha-Anand, *Islam and Violence: A Case Study of Violent Events in the Four Southern Provinces, Thailand*, 1976–1981 (Tampa, Florida: USF Monographs on Religion and Public Policy, 1987).

32 Howard M. Federspiel, "Islam and Development in the Nations of ASEAN". *Asian Survey* XXV, no. 8 (August 1985): 805–21.

33 Surin Pitsuwan, "The Islamic Banking Option in Thailand", op. cit.

34 Preeda Prapertchob, "Mobilization of Resources Through Waqf in Thailand", op. cit.

35 Calculated from ibid. According to Preeda Prapertchob, there are 155 mosques in

Bangkok and the average number of Muslim households per mosque in the Central plain is 223 while the average number of household members is eight.

36 International Union of Official Travel Organization (IUOTO), *The United Nations' Conference on International Travel and Tourism* (Geneva: IUOTO, 1963), p. 14. This definition is most widely accepted and approved by the World Tourist Organization in 1968.

37 *Bangkok Post*, 6 July 1988.

38 See Erik Cohen, "Who is a Tourist?: A Conceptual Clarification", *Sociological Review* 22, no. 4 (1974): 527–55.

39 I have tried desperately to interview him. All efforts were in vain due to his tight schedule abroad.

40 Pasuk Phongpaichit, "Bangkok Masseuses: Holding Up for the Family Sky". *Southeast Asia Chronicle*, no. 78 (1981): 14–15.

41 Charoen Kampeerapab, "Assisting the Thai Parliament in Human Rights Affairs". A Research Report Submitted to the House Affairs Committee, Bangkok, March 1988, p. 17.

42 Pasuk Phongpaichit, op. cit., p. 18.

43 Teppanom Muangmaen and Somsak Santa, "Knowledge, Attitude and Practices of Masseuses in Bangkok". A Research Report, Faculty of Public Health, Mahidol University, Bangkok, 1979, p. 25 (in Thai).

44 When asked whether she knew the meaning of her action, she replied in the negative. I have to relate to them a traditional tale about the incident during the Hijrah when the Prophet was leaving Mecca, a lizard signalled the Meccans who pursued him while the spider tried to mislead them. Hence, many Muslims are taught to hate the lizard and appreciate the spider. However, it was the first time I have heard that killing a lizard is a way of making merit.

45 John Embree, "Thailand: A Loosely Structured Social System", *American Anthropologist* 52, no. 2 (1950): 186.

46 Erik Cohen, "Thai Girls and Farang Men", *Annals of Tourism Research* 9, no. 2 (1982): 415.

47 Erik Cohen, "Rethinking the Sociology of Tourism", *Annals of Tourism Research* 6, no. 1 (January/March 1979): 30. [Emphasis in original].

48 Abdur Rehman Doi, "Duties and Responsibilities of Muslims in Non-Muslim States: A Point of View", *Journal Institute of Muslim Minority Affairs* 8, no. 1 (January 1987): 43.

49 Cited in detail in Barbara Freyer Stowasser, "Religious Ideology, Women and the Family: The Islamic Paradigm". In *The Islamic Impulses*, edited by Barbara Freyer Stowasser (London and Sydney: Croom Helm, 1987) pp. 268–69.

50 Ibid., pp. 286–89.

51 Abdur Rahman Doi, op. cit., p. 54.

52 Al-Qur'an 31:20. For translation of Qur'anic verses used here, see N.J. Dawood, *The Koran Translation* (New York: Penguin Books, 1985).

53 Quoted in Doi, op. cit., p. 54.

54 Quoted in Stowasser, op. cit., p. 270.

55 Al-Qur'an 2:173. See also Al-Qur'an 6:145.

56 See Doi, op. cit., pp. 43–44.

57 Data obtained from the Bangkok Tourist Police Division.

58 Isma'il Raja al'Faruqi, "Is the Muslim Definable in Terms of His Economic Pursuits?" In *Islamic Perspectives: Studies in Honour of Mawlana Sayyid Abu A'la Mawdudi*, edited by Khurshid Ahmad and Zafar Ishaq Ansari (London and Jeddah: The Islamic Foundation and Saudi Publishing House, 1979), p. 192.

59 The meaning of *darurah* is "necessity". See Doi, "Duties and Responsibilities, op. cit., pp. 50–51. He is cited in the *fatwah* given by Mufti Kifayatullah in 1938.

60 Maxime Rodinson, *Islam and Capitalism*, translation by Brian Pearce. (New York: Pantheon Books, 1973).

61 Faruqi, op. cit., p. 192.

62 Erik Cohen, "The Sociology of Tourism: Approaches, Issues and Findings", *Annual Review of Sociology* 10 (1984): 374.

63 Quoted in Rodinson, *Islam and Capitalism*, op. cit., p. 239.

6 THE ROLE OF MUSLIM WOMEN TRADERS IN KELANTAN

Nor Aini Haji Idris and Faridah Shahadan

Islamic Perspective on Women as Entrepreneurs

Islam regards all men and women as equals. In the eyes of Allah, faith is the factor that differentiates one from another. Islam had bestowed upon women special status, values and important roles that do not affect their femininity in this world (Siti Zulaikha 1981). Islam is not only a religion but also a way of life. The objective of human existence on this earth is to serve as a *khalifah*, or vicegerent of Allah on earth. This status applies to both men or women (Faizal Hj. Othman, *Berita Harian*, 12 July 1988). Women's role is normally categorized into three, i.e. as daughters, mothers and wives. Islam also allows women to work and be actively involved in activities that can contribute to the well-being of their households and society. As stated in Holy Qur'an (An-Nisa: 32), meaning

> Hence, do not covet the bounties which God has bestowed more abundantly on some of you than on others. Men shall have a benefit from what they earn, and women shall have a benefit from what they earn. Ask, therefore, God [to give you] out of His bounty: behold, God has indeed full knowledge of everything.

As stated above, the livelihood, earning and well-being of men and women are, therefore, based on their efforts. Work is an effort through which one can obtain earnings and work is based on one's talents, abilities, culture, environment.

Many Muslims have argued that Islam forbids women to work. However, such arguments were not based on the Qur'an, and were simply the result of cultural heritage (Faizal Hj. Othman, op. cit.).

In Islam, traders and entrepreneurs are highly respected, and in fact Prophet Muhammad (peace be unto him) himself was a trader. Khadijah, the wife of the Prophet, was a well-known, influential, respected and wealthy trader in the Meccan community before her marriage. On no occasion had the Prophet forbade women from trading. During the Prophet's time there were a few well-known women traders such as Umm al-Munzir binti Qays and Asmah binti Makhzamah bin Jandal. During the rule of Saidina Omar, a women trader by the name of Al-Shifa binti Muawiz was elected as a "commandant" of the Madinah market. Such was the honour given to women traders during the classical era.

In Malaysia, Muslim women work freely and voluntarily. Muslim women tend to look upon work as a Shariah requirement for earning a decent living. Women participation in business is particularly high in the state of Kelantan. The uniqueness of the Kelantanese Malay stems from strong female representation in all major economic activities. Kota Bharu's central market is a manifestation of this phenomenon with a heavy concentration of women traders. Kelantanese women traders are not confined to the informal sector or to petty trading at the market-place of Kota Bharu, but they are also actively involved in the formal business of wholesaling, retailing and manufacturing. Within the business sector, most of them are actively involved in retail business. According to the Manpower Survey 1980, 12.9 per cent of the female labour force were involved in the retailing business, compared with the 9.6 per cent male participation. On the whole, the retail sector is second only to agriculture in terms of female employment.

Kelantanese Malay Muslim women's active participation in business is not a recent phenomenon. Historical records had documented this phenomenon even as early as the seventeenth century. Travellers in the nineteenth century like Abdullah Munshi (1893), Norman (1894), Clifford (1897), and Skeat (1953) also made references to this phenomenon in most of their writings. Writings by Graham (1907), Swettenham (1927) and Firth (1966) provided further evidence.

It is this uniqueness that has prompted this study. Basically, this study is an attempt to examine the role of Malay Muslim women of Kelantan in the business sector. Three aspects of female participation in Kelantan will be discussed. This chapter will discuss the entrepreneurial role of women, the profile of their business and finally the problems relating to their activities.

The main source of the data used for this study is from a survey conducted amongst 200 Muslim women involved in trading. They were randomly selected from the shopping area within the Kota Bharu District Council, namely Pasar Besar Lama, MARA arcade, and Pasar Pusat Buluh Kubu. The fieldwork was carried out during the months of February and March 1988.

Kota Bharu was chosen because of the high percentage of women traders in the town. Being the capital city of Kelantan, Kota Bharu serves both as an economic and administrative centre, and offers a wide variety of economic activities that are not available elsewhere in the state. Besides, the number of Muslim women traders in Kota Bharu presumably exceeds that in any other Malaysian town.

Economic Development and Female Participation

Women have always been active participants in the economic development process, although their contribution have not been duly recognized. The lack of recognition may be attributed to the fact that female workers were unpaid or were supported by their families so that they were not included in the national accounts statistics (Nik Safiah 1982). However, it is significant to note that about one-third of the world's economicallly active population are women. Of the total women labour force, 40 per cent are economically active (Nik Safiah 1982: 6).

Traditionally, women's participation in wage employment was restricted, but their participation as unpaid labour especially in agricultural sectors and in cottage industry was high. Boserup's (1970) study had testified to the important role played by women especially in peasant communities. Besides accomplishing a host of domestic chores, women labour long hours in rice fields, rubber plantations and tin mines. The spread of Islam in Southeast Asia in the fifteenth century did not affect the participation of women in economic activities.

Economic development changed the structure of women's participation in economic activities resulting in more women joining the labour force. A study by the United Nations (1987) identified five factors that led to the increase in female employment in Asia and the Pacific, namely (1) socio-economic development in the country, (2) the increase in educational opportunities and awareness among women in the 1960s, (3) economic growth and industrialization in Southeast Asia in the 1970s that created unprecedented demand for female labour, (4) the development of the service sector, and (5) the reduction in fertility rate. However, not all women in employment are given fair rewards in all countries. In undeveloped countries, women still serve as unpaid agricultural labour in the subsistence sectors. Rural women continue to work in jobs with long hours which hardly pay for their basic daily needs. Women in the urban areas are concentrated in low-paid and marginal jobs.

In the case of Malaysia, one-half of the population consists of women. As in other developing countries, Malaysian women also play an active role in the economic development of the country. Women's participation, especially in the modern industrial and services sectors, has increased over the years.

There are three factors that can explain the increased participation of Malaysian women in wage employment in the modern sector: (1) the expansion of educational facilities and equal opportunity given to males and females, (2) rapid economic and industrial development, and (3) the introduction of the New Economic Policy (NEP). Major structural changes in the Malaysian economy have directly affected the pattern of women's participation in the labour force. In the early days of Independence (1957), the majority (68.7 per cent) of women workers were concentrated in the agricultural sector, 17.0 per cent in the service sector and only 5.8 per cent in the manufacturing sector.[1] Women's economic activities were basically confined to the subsistence rural agricultural sector. In the 1970s there was a sudden surge in women's participation in the modern industrial sectors.

The introduction of the NEP in 1970 and the shift in economic strategy from import substitution to export orientation provided more opportunities for women to participate in the labour market. One of the major strategies of the NEP was restructuring society through active participation of the *bumiputera* (indigenous Malaysians) in the more productive urban industrial sectors. Bumiputera were encouraged to migrate from the rural to the urban sector. Malaysia's export oriented strategy in the 1970s coincided with important changes in the international division of labour. This process was facilitated by the two most important forces operating in the economy: (1) the rise of transnational corporations, and (2) the application of new technology in all types of industries, especially electronics and textiles.

After the 1970s, industrialization in Malaysia took place within the context of a concerted political effort to restructure the ethnic division of labour in the country. The microchip revolution and the need to achieve the twin objectives of the NEP (poverty eradication and economic restructuring) led to increased labour mobility especially among women. These factors brought about an increase in demand for women workers especially in the urban industrial sectors.

Most of the manufacturing industries in Malaysia are located in the metropolitan areas of the Kelang Valley and the west coast of Peninsular Malaysia. The high concentration of industries in the west coast has attracted migrants from the more depressed regions in the east. As the result, in 1970s, rural-urban migration of women workers accelerated in response to the growth of industrial and other urban jobs. The proportion of rural women entering wage employment increased, and a majority of them were young, unmarried Malay women who came to cities to work as industrial workers (Jamilah Ariffin 1987). By 1980 the female share of the manufacturing workforce rose to 41 per cent, from 17 per cent in 1957, while their share in commerce increased from 19 per cent to 30 per cent. However, the female share in agriculture rose at a slower pace, from 32 per cent to 39 per cent (Chia 1987: 178).

Kelantan: A Historical Perspective

Geographically, Kelantan is situated on the east coast of Peninsular Malaysia, bordered by the states of Trengganu in the east, Pahang in the south, Perak and southern Thailand to the west. Administratively, the state is divided into eight administrative districts called *jajahan*, namely Kota Bharu, Ulu Kelantan, Pasir Mas, Pasir Putih, Bachok, Machang, Tumpat, Tanah Merah and Gua Musang.

Similar to the historical economic patterns of other states, Kelantan had traversed through three phases of development, from subsistence to barter and then to exchange economy where money was the medium of transaction. Historically, the Malay community was divided into two distinctive classes, the *sultans* as rulers and *rakyat* as subjects or masses. Sovereignty was the right of the ruler to command and those commanded (*rakyat*) had a duty to obey. A centralized system of government required a centralized system of administration. All economic activities, especially those pertaining to export and import taxes, were in the control of the *sultans*. Kelantan had a long history of successful trading activities with Singapore, Pahang and Johor. Tax structure in Kelantan had historically depended heavily on taxes on foreign trade, especially export taxes. The autocratic nature of the government permitted the sultans the right to the state treasury and the power to decide on land matters. The relationship between the rulers and the masses was one of "master and slave" where the loyalty of the subjects knew no bounds (Nik Hasnah 1977: 380). This unequal relationship was further accentuated by the practice of an "exploitative" economic system called kerah or corvee labour. Under this system, the rulers could secure labour from their subjects without any form of payment or fair compensation (Siti Hindun 1979: 23)

Retail outlets, petty traders and middlemen emerged with the introduction of trading activities in Kelantan. Most of these petty traders were women who had to travel far into the rural areas to market their products. For example, some of the women traders in the rural district of Salor (8 kilometres south of Kota Bharu) had to walk from as far as Pantai Cinta Berahi (10 kilometres north of Kota Bharu) to market their products (Zaidi 1982: 51). Petty traders and retail outlets abound throughout the region engaging in various sorts of trading activities. The proliferation of retail outlets and trading stalls especially in big towns led to the emergence of commercial centres in towns like Kota Bharu, Pasir Mas, Pasir Puteh and Kuala Krai (Zaidi 1982: 35).

During 1909–41, Kelantan was under direct British rule. Under the British, the economy of Kelantan underwent important changes. Foreign investors were encouraged to develop mining and plantations (Siti Hindun 1979: 32). However, foreign investments in the state remained comparatively low. Among the many factors accounting for the low level of investments in the state were lack of infrastructural facilities and the unwillingness of migrant workers to work in the state due to sheer geographical distance and lack of communications.

Women Traders in Kelantan

Kelantan is well-known for the high percentage of Malay participation in business in general and women's participation in particular. Within the business sector, the Malays are highly represented in wood processing (66 per cent), rice milling (50 per cent), printing (66.6 per cent), batik products (80.9 per cent), laundry (53 per cent), retailing (46.7 per cent) and rice selling (100 per cent) (Mohd Fauzi

1981:51). On the whole, about 49.7 per cent of the Malays are actively involved in all these sectors, and more than 70 per cent of them are thriving in Kota Bharu (Mohd Fauzi 1981: 51).

In the business sector, a sizeable number of Malays are concentrated in commerce (53 per cent), followed by services (21 per cent) and also manufacturing and industries (13 per cent). In manufacturing industries, Malays are mostly involved in batik production, gold and silverware making, and *songket* weaving. In the service sector, Malays are limited to managing food stores and tailoring shops. In the business sector, 54.2 per cent of the Malays are in retail business (Mohd Fauzi 1981: 54).

Nik Zainab (1985), in her study of women's role in Kelantanese Malay community, classified women's participation in business into three major categories:

1. Big businesses with capital amounting to more than M$30,000. These include businesses conducted either in shops belonging to the entrepreneurs or in rented premises. Household items are the major form of goods sold in this category. The size and nature of the business in this category usually require business owners to hire shop assistants.
2. Small businesses that usually require small amounts of capital. Food selling at the central market, hawking and petty trading are among the major economic activities in this category.
3. Manufacturing enterprises. Most businesses in this category belong to the *songket* and *batik* industry and the traditional medicine and food processing industries.

Business activities were conducted either in shophouses or at the market place. An empirical study by Nik Zainab (1985) showed that more than one-half of the 500 women respondents at Kota Bharu were actively involved in selling textiles, clothing, cosmetics, and jewellery, and also in the *songket* and *batik* trade.

The active participation of Kelantanese women in business is reflected in the number of women petty traders at the market-place. Most of the market-places in Kelantan are dominated by women traders. This situation is very obvious in Kota Bharu especially at the four major market-places, namely at the Pasar Besar Lama, Pasar Kubang Pasu, Pasar Padang Lido and at Pasar Buluh Kubu, where 90 per cent of the traders are women. What are the factors that account for this interesting phenomenon? To answer this question, it is not enough just to look at the current situation; it is also necessary to study Kelantan's rich history and the social and economic structure that characterizes the state.

Historically, Kelantan was ruled by a dynamic woman named Cik Siti Wan Kembang from 1610 to 1677. During this period, Islam had already spread. According to one source, Islam reached Kelantan even before twelfth century (Ismail Awang 1986) and Kelantan was known as "serambi Mekah" or corridor of Mecca, indicating that Islam had a strong influence on the Kelantanese. During the period in which Cik Siti Wan Kembang ruled, Kelantan emerged as a trading centre. Trading and other economic activities were encouraged and as a result Kelantan prospered. To a certain extent, she was a "source of inspiration" paving the way for modern Kelantanese women to follow (Alias 1975: 4).

Most Kelantanese men work and seek their fortune in other states in Malaysia and also in the neighbouring states of Thailand and Singapore (Nik Hasnah 1977: 55). The economic vacuum left by these men provided opportunities for those who stayed put, especially women, to participate actively in the local scene. Evidently, in the situation of migration, women were normally left behind.[2]

Kelantanese social attitudes toward working women have been positive. Participation of women in economic activities that contribute to household incomes is acceptable in the Kelantanese value system. Similar social norms also exist in Thailand and the Philippines. In these societies, it is not a "loss of face" for a man to let the female members in his family go out and earn a living (Pawadee 1987: 197).

It could be inferred from all this that the early placement of Islam in Kelantan, its traditional culture and values, and the economic history of that state have all been responsible for encouraging Kelantanese Muslim women to be economically active. However, many have argued that Kelantanese society is matriarchal rather than patriarchal and this is a subject of continuing debate among the anthropologists.

Some modern anthropologies regard matriarchy as pure conjecture, lacking any support from ethnographic or historical data. In Kelantan, women's dominance in certain types of economic activities may not be an indication of the existence of a matriarchal society.

Socio-Economic Profile of Women Traders in Kota Bharu

This section will discuss the socio-economic background of the survey respondents. The respondents were selected from a predetermined set of businesses. In other words, the respondents were chosen only from among selected business activities. More than 90 per cent of the women traders in the three selected places were Muslim women. Their businesses included petty trading, fish and vegetable selling, and retailing. Generally the traders are young women. As shown in Table 6.1, 44 per cent of the traders were young within the 18–30 age-group, and only 13.5 per cent of them were above 50 years of age. Mean age for all respondents was 33.6 years.

As shown in Table 6.2, out of the 200 respondents, 60.5 per cent or 121 traders were married, 32.5 per cent were single and 7 per cent were widows. A majority of the husbands of the married women were working as government servants, drivers, farmers and small business operators.

TABLE 6.1
Age Distribution of Women Traders

Age (in years)	No.	%
18–20	7	3.5
20–29	81	40.5
30–39	43	21.5
40–49	42	21.0
>49	27	13.5
Total	200	100.0

Almost one-half of the respondents (46 per cent) either did not have any formal education at all, or formal education if any was limited to religious or primary education. As shown in Table 6.3, 22.5 per cent of them had lower secondary education and 14 per cent of the total had received upper secondary education. Only one per cent of the respondents had college diplomas or university degrees. On the average, the respondents had 6–8 years of formal education.

As shown in Table 6.4, about 62 per cent of those in their fifties and beyond never received any formal education and 14.8 per cent received only religious education. In the 30–40 years age-group, 41 per cent received education up to the primary level, while 35 per cent up to lower secondary and 12 per cent up to upper secondary level of education. Among the young traders below 30 years of age, about 50 per cent had received formal education up to the upper secondary level.

Historical factors can explain why the older women traders never received any formal education. Traditionally, girls were deprived of formal education and

TABLE 6.2
Marital Status of Women Traders

Status	No.	%
Married	121	60.5
Single	65	32.5
Widow	14	7.0
Total	200	100.0

TABLE 6.3
Educational Level of Women Traders

Educational Level	No.	%
No formal education	22	11.0
Religious school	16	8.0
Primary education	54	27.0
Lower Secondary	51	25.5
Upper Secondary—O level	28	14.0
STPM/HSC—A level	24	12.0
Diploma/Degree holders	2	1.0
Others	3	1.5
Total	200	100.0

were encouraged to take up cooking, sewing, handicraft, etc. The girls were also given informal education in the form of religious education (Manderson 1981). Among the reasons accounting for the lack of response by Malays toward formal education was the fear that Malay children would be drawn into a Western-type

TABLE 6.4
Educational Level of Women Traders by Age

	Age (Years)									
	< 20		20–29		30–39		40–49		> 49	
	No.	%	No.	%	No.	%	No.	%	No.	%
No formal education	–	–	–	–	2	4.6	3	7.1	17	62.9
Religious school	–	–	2	2.5	2	4.6	8	19.0	4	14.8
Primary education	–	–	8	9.8	18	41.9	25	59.5	3	11.1
Lower Secondary	3	42.8	28	34.6	15	34.9	5	11.9	–	–
Upper Secondary—O level	2	28.6	20	24.7	5	11.6	1	2.4	–	–
STPM/HSC—A level	2	28.6	21	25.9	1	2.3	–	–	–	–
Diploma/Degree holders	–	–	2	2.5	–	–	–	–	–	–
Others	–	–	–	–	–	–	–	–	–	–
Total	7	100	81	100	43	100	42	99.9	24*	100

* In the above 50 age-group, there were a total of 27 respondents. Information on educational level of three respondents were not available.

of educational system. It was only in the 1950s that some of Malay girls began to receive a secular type of formal education (Manderson 1981).

Kelantan has always been a tourist destination to Malaysians especially during public and school holidays. Besides coming to enjoy the scenic beauty of Kelantan's villages and beaches, many local and foreign tourists also come to purchase local handicrafts and to buy cheaper goods from neighbouring Thailand. Being a popular tourist attraction, one would expect the traders to be able to communicate in more than one language, but only a few of the women traders had such ability. From a total of 200 respondents, only 42 respondents (21 per cent) could speak other languages besides Bahasa Malaysia, and out of these 29 respondents were conversant in English and 2 in Chinese.

Most of the respondents interviewed never had any formal business training. Only 18 respondents (19 per cent) had attended training or courses related to business management, tailoring, hairdressing or beauty salon. These courses were organized either by government institutions such as Institusi Usahawan Belia (Youth Training Institute), or by private institutions. Some had also benefited from training given by previous employers.

It is sometimes argued that the success of the Kelantanese women as traders and entrepreneurs was mainly due to the fact that they had inherited their businesses from their families. To test whether there is any element of truth in such statements, the respondents were asked about their family members' business involvements. Table 6.5 shows that, out of the 200 respondents interviewed, 74.5 per cent had at least one family member such as parent, sister, brother, uncle, aunt or husband who had business activities. It appears that this had indirectly influenced the women to be active in business or inspired them to be successful traders.

TABLE 6.5
Family Members who are Traders

Family Members	No.	%
None	51	25.5
Parents	28	14.0
Sisters or brothers	41	20.5
Husband	30	15.0
Mother/father-in-law	3	1.5
Uncles/aunties	35	17.5
Others	12	6.0
Total	200	100.0

Survey Findings

General Business Information

A majority of the Kelantanese women traders own their business. The result of the sample survey showed that 87 per cent of the respondents were owners or sole proprietors of their businesses while the rest were managers. In other words, most of them run their own businesses. About 36 per cent of the respondents had been in business for a period of one to three years, while 25 per cent had been at it for 10 to 20 years. On the average, women traders covered by the survey had been in business for seven years (Table 6.6).

There was a strong correlation between the age of the respondents and the number of years they were in the business. As shown in the cross tabulation of age of the respondents and the number of years in business (Table 6.7), those below 20 years of age had three-year old businesses. Of the total of respondents within 20–29 years of age, 52 per cent had been running their business for one to three years, 26 per pent had been in business for three to five years; and 21 per cent had been running their businesses for more than five years. About 57 per cent of those in the age-group of 40–49 years had been in business for more than 10 years. It thus appears that most of the women traders had started their businesses while they were young.

Reasons For Working

Women have their own reasons for going out to work. Several anthropologists and economists have attempted to establish the reasons, e.g. studies by Hoffman (1963), Morgan (1965), Oakley (1975), and Lindsay and Polly (1977). It may be surmised from all these studies that women go out to work to earn extra income and to avoid being lonely or bored.

TABLE 6.6
Number of Years Women Traders have been in Business

Number of Years	No.	%
< 1	3	1.5
1–3	72	36.0
3–5	33	16.5
5–10	35	17.5
10–20	50	25.0
> 20	7	3.5
Total	200	100.0

TABLE 6.7
Number of Years Women Traders have been in Business by Age

	Age (Years)									
	< 20		20–29		30–39		40–49		> 49	
Number of Years	No.	%	No.	%	No.	%	No.	%	No.	%
< 1	2	28.6	1	1.2	–	–	–	–	–	–
1–3	5	71.4	42	51.8	16	37.2	6	14.3	3	11.1
3–5	–	–	21	25.9	5	11.6	6	14.3	1	3.7
5–10	–	–	12	14.8	14	32.6	6	14.3	3	11.1
10–20	–	–	5	6.3	8	18.6	22	52.4	15	55.5
> 20	–	–	–	–	–	–	2	4.7	5	18.6
Total	7	100	81	100	43	100	42	100	27	100

Regardless of their marital status, about 73.5 per cent of the respondents in the survey cited their family economic situation or the need to improve family income as their main reason for going out to work (Table 6.8). About 79.3 per cent of the married women gave this reason for working. Only 10 per cent stated that they work merely to occupy their free time. It may be concluded that a wife's contribution is very important for improving family income. Business was chosen as an occupation mainly because there is no better or suitable jobs available to

TABLE 6.8
Distribution of Women Traders According to their Main Reason for Working and Marital Status

	Marital Status							
	Married		Single		Widow		Total	
Reason	No.	%	No.	%	No.	%	No.	%
To improve the family's income	96	79.3	39	60.0	12	85.7	147	73.5
To occupy free time	12	9.9	24	36.9	2	14.3	38	19.0
Encouraged by husband	12	9.9	–	–	–	–	12	6.0
Others	1	0.8	2	3.1	–	–	3	1.5
Total	121	100	65	100	14	100	200	100

them. Besides, self-employment represents an easy way out for these women, given the ease of entry and exit and the flexibilities that go with being one's own boss.

Types of Business

Basically, there were seven types of business in which the 200 respondents were engaged. The distribution of the respondents according to the types of business can be seen in Table 6.9. About 52.5 per cent of the respondents were in businesses selling ready-made dresses and clothes.

The answers given by most of the respondents to the query regarding their choice of particular types of business were: they inherited the business previously owned by their parents (25.5 per cent), they had the experience and skill in managing the business (22 per cent), they had opted for the business they considered easy to manage (10 per cent) or they were encouraged by their husbands (13 per cent). Therefore, in choosing a particular business, the women traders seem to prefer the type of business they had some knowledge of rather than the business which they felt was more profitable.

Ownership and Work Schedule

Most of the women traders surveyed were sole proprietors, while the rest only had a partnership status in their business.

An overwhelming majority of the respondents (96 per cent) are full-time traders and only a very few (4 per cent) considered their business as a part-time job. As shown in Table 6.10, a majority of the women traders worked for more than seven hours a day, the average working hours being 9.2 hours a day. And,

TABLE 6.9
Types of Business Women Traders are Involved in

Type of Business	No.	%
Clothing	105	52.5
Beauty Saloon	2	1.0
Tailoring	5	2.5
Souvenirs and gifts	20	10.0
Food Stall	9	4.5
Brass/Silverware	19	9.5
Others	40	20.0
Total	200	100.0

TABLE 6.10
Number of Hours Spent by Women Traders in Business/Store

Number of Hours	No.	%
< 6	5	2.5
6	3	1.5
7	4	2.0
8	80	40.0
9	30	15.0
10	39	19.5
11	1	0.5
12	34	17.0
14	4	2.0
Total	200	100.0

98 per cent of them worked six to seven days a week (Table 6.11). For traders in the services sector and retailers, this work pattern is normal as they tend to be busier during the weekends and during public holidays than during the weekdays.

Most women, who were burdened with the responsibilities of having babies, school-going children or family to look after, would only chose to work if they could be relieved of these responsibilities by helpers. Most of the married women in our survey sample were relieved of their burdens by their parents, other members of the family, such as sisters, and grown-up daughters. In other words, kinship provides the support system. This was mainly the reason why most of them (95.5 per cent) felt that their business did not interfere much with their family

TABLE 6.11
Number of Working Days Per Week

Number of Days	No.	%
3	1	0.5
4	1	0.5
5	2	1.0
6	132	66.0
7	64	32.0
Total	200	100.0

life. The strong commitment and responsibilities of women towards their families was reflected in the chores they attend to at home, after a hard day's work in business. Only 1.3 per cent out of 121 married women had paid domestic help. From all this, it may be concluded that either Kelantanese women have strong family ties or they could not afford to hire domestic help.

Business Planning and Promotion

Before setting up a business, proper business planning is called for and the viability of the business must be carefully considered and studied. A majority of the respondents (83.5 per cent) claimed to have carried out planning before entering business. Most of these businesses are either very small or of such nature that does not require much assistance. This study shows that 63.5 per cent of the respondents managed the business personally without hiring any workers or assistants, while 25 per cent of them had only one employee. The distribution of respondents according to the number of workers is shown in Table 6.12.

About 86.5 per cent of the women traders did not or had never advertised their businesses. The main reason for not advertising was budget constraints (48.5 per cent). The other reasons given were that they did not know much advertising techniques, and that the nature of their business does not require any advertisement. For 13.5 per cent of the respondents who advertised, the most common form of advertisement was through posters.

Due to space constraints, most traders did not make much effort to display their merchandise or undertake interior decorations. However, many of those surveyed exhibited business attributes that are often associated with good salesmanship. They are courteous, polite, friendly and knowledgeable about their products.

TABLE 6.12
Distribution of Women Traders According to their Number of Workers

Number of Workers	No.	%
0	127	63.5
1	50	25.0
2	18	9.0
3	3	1.5
4	1	0.5
6	1	0.5
Total	200	100.0

The women traders obtain their supplies from wholesalers and manufacturers. Most of the wholesalers are the cash-and-carry type who limit themselves to stocks of fast-moving items, and offer no credit or delivery services. About 33.2 per cent of the respondents who obtain their supplies from wholesalers had no delivery services while 50.2 per cent had to pay their supplies cash on delivery.

Financing and Financial Management

Respondents were asked about their initial capital investments in their business. Table 6.13 shows that about half (51 per cent) of the traders started their business with an initial capital of less than M$5,000 and only 29.5 per cent had put in initial capital of M$10,000–M$30,000. The average initial capital for all respondents was M$5,702.

The amounts of initial investments required vary according to the type and the size of business entities. For most retailers and traders in the services sector, the initial capital was in the form of stocks paid for in cash, and none of them had invested in fixed assets such as business premises. Table 6.14 gives the average amount of initial capital by type of business. Comparatively, traders in the clothing business registered the highest initial capital, followed by those in the brass and silverware business, reflecting the value of the merchandise stocked and traded.

Personal savings were the most important source of initial capital. Table 6.15 shows that three-quarters of the respondents started their business using their own personal savings. Since they had to raise the initial capital on their own, the amount they could raise was quite small. Another important source of initial capital was friends or relatives. Only eight traders managed to obtain loans from institutions; five from MARA[3] and three from bank or finance companies. Many small businesses do not resort to banks and other financial institutions for financial

TABLE 6.13
Distribution of the Amount of Initial Capital
(M$)

Initial Capitalization	No.	%
< $5,000	102	51.0
$5,000–$9,999	34	17.0
$10,000–$30,000	59	29.5
$30,000 and over	3	1.5
No response	2	1.0
Total	200	100.0

TABLE 6.14
Average of Initial Capital by Type of Business
(M$)

Type of Business	Amount ($)
Clothing	10,239
Beauty Salon	7,500
Tailoring	3,800
Souvenirs and Gifts	6,452
Food Stall	2,968
Brass/Silverware	7,677
Others	5,470

assistance. Lack of collateral, the inability to produce guarantors and ignorance about financial procedures are the main reasons for this.

It is interesting to note that most of the women traders kept records of their business transactions. More than three-quarters (77.5 per cent) of respondents had some sort of book keeping. Seventy-seven of them had their transaction entries or earning statements recorded daily, while 27 of them conducted such activities on a weekly basis (Table 6.16). Most of the respondents (67.5 per cent) recorded their business transactions personally; 7.5 per cent were assisted by their husbands; and 2.5 per cent by their children. The remaining 22.5 per cent felt that such accounting was not necessary.

TABLE 6.15
Main Source of Initial Capital

Source	No.	%
Own	151	75.5
Inherited	10	5.0
Friend	6	3.0
Relative	18	9.0
Bank/Finance Company	3	1.5
MARA	5	2.5
Profit from previous business	4	2.0
Others	3	1.5
Total	200	100.0

TABLE 6.16
The Frequency of Preparation of Financial Statements

Frequency	No.	%
Daily	77	38.5
Weekly	27	13.5
Monthly	40	20.0
Half-yearly	4	2.0
Annually	7	3.5
None	45	22.5
Total	200	100.0

Business Assets, Liabilities and Income

Given the size and nature of business, the current assets possessed by the traders consisted entirely of cash and stocks. There were no other forms of current or fixed assets. As depicted in Table 6.15, only 2.5 per cent obtained loans from MARA or finance companies. Account payable was the most popular form of business liabilities. Such liabilities arise mainly from supplies purchased on credit (in the case of 40 per cent of the respondents) and overdue rents on business premises (in the case of 36 per cent of the respondents).

The value of current business liabilities vary according to the type of business, as shown in Table 6.17. Thus, businesses that maintain large inventories usually incur higher liabilities. For example, current liabilities average $9,714 in

TABLE 6.17
Business Liabilities by Type of Business
(M$)

Type of Business	Current Liability ($)
Clothing	9,714
Beauty Salon	No response
Tailoring	1,000
Souvenirs and Gifts	2,855
Food Stall	167
Brass/Silverware	3,006
Others	1,113

TABLE 6.18
Monthly Business Income of Women Traders
(M$)

Amount ($)	No.	%
< 100	1	0.5
100–299	75	37.5
300–599	50	25.0
600–999	40	20.0
1,000–3,000	33	16.5
> 3,000	1	0.5
Total	200	100.0

the clothing business, compared to other businesses where the current liabilities are less than M$3,000 on the average.

There is no evidence to show that the Kelantanese women traders are engaged in activities that are very rewarding in monetary terms. As shown in Table 6.18, about 38 per cent had an average income of less than M$300 a month, while 17 per cent were within the income bracket of M$1,000–$3,000 a month. Only one respondent managed to earn an average monthly income of more than M$3,000. Variations in income earned between various types of businesses were small and insignificant, as shown in Table 6.19.

Despite their low income levels, 51.5 per cent of the respondents expressed satisfaction. Many felt that they lived moderately comfortable lives thanks to their

TABLE 6.19
Average Monthly Business Income by Type of Business
(M$)

Type of Business	Average Monthly Income ($)
Clothing	625.00
Beauty Salon	700.00
Tailoring	376.00
Souvenirs and Gifts	663.00
Food Stall	505.00
Brass/Silverware	668.00
Others	425.00

TABLE 6.20
Savings of Women Traders
(M$)

Amount ($)	No.	%
< 100	2	3.2
100–599	11	17.5
600–1,999	14	22.2
2,000–4,999	30	47.6
5,000–7,999	5	7.9
> 8,000	1	1.6
Total	63	100.0

business. However, some respondents (22 per cent) complained that their income was unstable, while others (17.5 per cent) had difficulties in making both ends meet.

Saving

Out of the 200 respondents surveyed, only 31.5 per cent had savings. Of these, about 9 per cent had started saving while they were at school and 18.5 per cent started saving upon entering business. The main reasons for savings were precautionary and speculative purposes. About 16.5 per cent of the respondents saved for their family's future, 6.5 per cent had the intention of expanding their business and only about 3 per cent saved as a precautionary measure. About 47.6 per cent of the respondents who saved had accumulated savings of M$2,000–

TABLE 6.21
Women Traders' Forms of Savings

Form	No.	%
Deposit in Bank	41	65.1
Tabung Haji	4	6.3
At Home	17	27.0
Gold/jewellery	–	–
Other	1	1.6
Total	63	100.0

$5,000, the average being M$2,064. Classification of respondents by their size of savings is shown in Table 6.20.

The forms of savings are shown in Table 6.21. About two-thirds of the respondents had savings deposited in banks, while 27 per cent kept their savings at home in the form of cash. A majority of the women interviewed displayed their jewellery. However, jewellery was never considered by them as a form of saving, although many of them had stated precautionary reasons for purchasing gold.

Investment

Only about 13 per cent of the respondents had investments. The average size of their investment was M$1,340. Amanah Saham Nasional (ASN)[4] was the main mode of investment as 84 per cent of the respondents had invested in ASN. It is of interest to note that 11.5 per cent of the respondents had resorted to other forms of investment such as stocks and corporate shares. The main reason for investing was concern for their families' future as stated by 57.6 per cent of the respondents. Business expansion was cited as the main reason. The amount or size of investment was small, as shown in Table 6.22. About 48 per cent of the traders had investments of less than M$500, while 31 per cent had investments in the range of M$2,000 to M$5,000.

Problems and Perceptions

Problems

The main problems faced by women traders in Kota Bharu were marketing and stiff competition especially among stores selling similar items. This is clearly reflected in the number of stores selling similar products, for example, at a popular shopping arcade at Pasar Pusat Buluh Kubu where there were about 100 stores selling similar merchandise. Some of them did not have the advantage of strategic

TABLE 6.22
Size of Investments of Women Traders
(M$)

Investments' Size ($)	No.	%
< 100	2	7.6
100–499	10	38.4
500–1,999	6	23.0
2,000–5,000	8	31.0
Total	26	100.0

TABLE 6.23
Problems Faced by Women Traders

Problems	%
Marketing and obtaining customers	55.0
Capital financing	31.5
Obtaining business premises	31.5
Obtaining supplies	10.0
Hiring worker or assistant	3.5

locations, which led to their stores being overlooked by potential customers. The daily average number of customers was quite small, usually between 15 and 20.

In addition, women traders were also confronted with other types of problems (Table 6.23). About 31.5 per cent of the respondents had difficulties in obtaining business premises due to the huge number of applicants vying for similar business locations. Moreover, most traders felt that the rent imposed on them was a little too high.

Less than one-third of the traders in the sample reported that they had inadequate capital. The general lack of capital was reflected in the number of rented premises, the cramped appearance, unattractive surroundings, limited range of products available. A majority of them (84.1 per cent) who had this problem stated that the lack of savings was the main reason for poor capital financing. Some respondents had tried to obtain loans from financial institutions but without much success. The main reasons why the traders could not obtain loans from the organized financial sector were their poor credit ratings and their inability to furnish collateral.

Securing regular supplies was cited as a problem in about 10 per cent of the sample. The difficulties were attributed mainly to the distance of business premises from their suppliers, failure on the part of the suppliers to meet order specifications, and slow delivery of goods. Small quantities had also disqualified them from obtaining credit facilities.

Only a small number of respondents were facing problems in hiring workers (3.5 per cent), and these were associated with high turnover of workers and demands for higher wages. As mentioned earlier, a majority of the traders managed their stores personally without any assistance from hired workers or family members. The small size of the stores (averaging about 300 square feet), makes it uneconomical to hire shop assistants. Therefore, it can be concluded that hiring of workers is the least important of all the problems faced by the women traders in Kota Bharu.

Future Plans

Despite facing numerous problems, the traders were very optimistic about their future. About 85.5 per cent of the respondents had the intention to expand their business in the near future, while 7.6 per cent of them were even planning to set up branches in other places. Only 5 per cent of the respondents were thinking of finding other jobs to supplement their incomes while at the same time still wanting to keep their business going.

Although business expansion was the main aim for most respondents, however, less than one half (45 per cent) of them will try it only if their business performance was encouraging, while 16 per cent of them admitted that they could expand their business only if they could obtain government assistance.

Perceptions

The success and sustainability of the Kelantanese women in business is often attributed to their positive response to what is perceived as an economic necessity. Besides, the Kelantanese women by nature are blessed with a blend of strong will and gentle character. The success of the Kelantanese women traders is evidenced by the sizeable number operating their own businesses for a long period of time. For example, 28.5 per cent of the respondents had already been in their current business for more than 10 years.

About 48 per cent of the respondents reported satisfactory business performance, while 30.5 per cent felt otherwise. Although a feeling of satisfaction is no measure of good business performance, it can explain why they continue to be and take pride in being traders. This is indicated by the fact that 73 per cent of the respondents wanted at least a member of their family to follow in their footsteps and venture into business. In fact, 20 per cent of the total even wanted everyone in their family to be traders.

To the majority of the respondents (84.5 per cent), the main ingredients for business success were hard work, perseverance and willpower to succeed, while 13 per cent of them ascribed their success to faith. Only 2.5 per cent stressed the importance of government assistance. It is clear from all this that the women traders were not fatalistic in their business behaviour.

Nearly all those interviewed (92 per cent) believed that they were as capable as men if not better in the handling of business. In fact, about 40 per cent of them were of the opinion that they were more capable than their male counterparts.

Women Traders: Islamic Perspectives

Islam recognizes the importance of traders and entrepreneurs as economic agents. The respondents were asked about their views on women's participation in business. A majority of the respondents believed that Islam permits women to participate in business on the basis of Qur'anic injunctions. Twenty-five per cent of the respondents conceded that women should only participate in business with the consent of their husbands. This is very much in line with the requirement in Islam that it is the rightful duty of the husband to provide sustenance for the family, while it is incumbent upon the wife to obey her spouse. About 16.5 per cent felt that women can be traders so long as they follow the basic tenets of Islam which requires women to be properly attired. Thus, most of the women traders were aware of the constraints imposed by Islam on their role as entrepreneurs.

Riba

In every respect, interest (*riba*) is forbidden in Islam. It is considered a taboo (*haram*) to receive or pay interest. The respondents were asked whether they would resort to borrowing from commercial banks in times of need with full knowledge that interest will be charged. Only 33 per cent of the respondents admitted they would resort to such sources of finance. Among those who had thought about it, only 30.6 per cent were Islamically motivated not to borrow on interest. For others, their unwillingness was basically due to lack of collateral and cumbersome bureaucratic procedures involved. In situations where the women traders or entrepreneurs were desperate and had no other option, they would grudgingly borrow from financial institutions although the credit offered by such institutions was obviously in conflict with Islamic principles.

Profit

About 67.7 per cent of the respondents interviewed had no knowledge of the profit margin on similar merchandise sold by other stores. It was normal for the selling price to be determined solely by the traders without much knowledge of prices charged by others. About 37 per cent of the respondents charged profit margins of 10 to 20 per cent while 3 per cent of the respondents priced their merchandise with a profit margin of 20 to 50 per cent. However, the majority of them (60 per cent) claimed that their profit margin was less than 10 per cent.

A question was also raised as to whether the narrow profit margin was in compliance with Islamic principles. Available evidence suggests that it was mainly the stiff competition that was responsible for the low profit margin.

Business Ethics

In business transactions, fraud, deception, exploitation, false statements, etc., are strictly prohibited by Islamic laws (Siddiqi 1972: 52). For example, it would be unIslamic to charge the tourists exorbitantly high prices, taking advantage of their ignorance about the local situation. Although a majority of the respondents declared that they did not practise any form of price discrimination, about 13.5 per cent of them had no qualms about charging higher prices if their customers were tourists.

The Prophet had been quoted as saying, "One Muslim is the brother of another Muslim. It is not permissible for a Muslim to sell a commodity to another in which there is some defect, and not to state that defect" (Siddiqi 1972: 53).

Bearing that statement in mind, almost all the respondents felt that it was their duty to inform their customers beforehand, if the merchandise purchased were found to be defective. Some of the respondents reported that they would reduce the price of the merchandise if the customer was willing to buy the defective merchandise.

Islam encourages its believers to work hard to solve whatever problems they face. When respondents were asked what their reactions would be, for example, in a situation where there was stiff competition for business premises which they desperately needed. About 44.0 per cent of them said that they would try to seek help from those in authority while the rest would just leave it to fate.

A question was asked regarding whether an Islamic business system could be implemented in Malaysia given the current economic and political situation. Only 53.5 per cent of the respondents had full confidence that such a system could emerge while 2.5 per cent were uncertain, and the rest expressed serious doubts.

Conclusion and Recommendations

Statistically, the Kelantanese women, compared to their counterparts in other states, are shown to be more actively involved in the business sector. Kelantan's unique economic phenomenon is often seen in terms of historical and socio-economic factors. The survey undertaken for this study reveals that most women traders view their business as a means of supplementing their household income, given the ease of market entry.

The high percentage of Malay female participation in business had always been the pride of Kelantan. Nevertheless, the scope and types of business activities are very limited. The question here is: can we categorize them as entrepreneurs? An entrepreneur is a person or small group of persons who start and manage a business and who stand to gain or lose depending upon the success or failure of that business (Abdul Aziz 1981: 5). To be successful, entrepreneurs should make efforts to expand their businesses through innovative changes, continuously aspiring to improve their economic position (Mohd Fauzi 1981). According to this definition, this study has dispelled the common belief that there is a high percentage of Muslim Malay women "entrepreneurs" in Kelantan. In reality, only very few of them could be qualified as "entrepreneurs", and the majority of them may be termed as small traders. Potter and Mohd Fauzi called these traders "chandlers" and this terminology was also used to describe their business practices. Although the traders may differ from "entrepreneurs", the fact remains that the Kelantanese Muslim women are highly self-motivated, industrious and emancipated.

Typical women traders in the survey lack formal educational qualifications, adequate initial capital and knowledge of proper accounting procedures. This study confirms that most of the businesses run by the Kelantanese women have not gone through much transformation since inception. The inability to change and adapt has resulted in the proliferation of similar business activities which consequently have led to stiff competition, price cutting and also low profit margins. Low profits have constrained expansion and reinvestments. It is interesting to note that only a small number of the respondents had carried out real investments, while a majority of them resorted to buying jewellery as a form of precautionary savings.

The informality of the business is manifested not only in the small size of its capital, simplicity of operation, ease of entry but also in unsound business practices. Lack of economic planning and accounting have resulted in poor pricing, marketing strategies and book-keeping procedures. Some do not even keep financial records. Put together, these factors have aggravated the problems of women traders, making them more vulnerable to business risks than they would otherwise have been.

For many, despite all odds and high risks, the business sector still holds much promise. The sector allows married women to have their own source of income without depending on their husbands. More often than not, it serves as a supplementary source of family income; and for those who are married to non-working husbands, income from these businesses are the main source of household income.

Obviously, trading represents one of the most important non-agricultural activities for women. In a developing country like Malaysia, where the importance of the role of private enterprise is acknowledged, the active participation of Kelantanese women in business is indeed a welcoming sign. Their contributions to economic growth can no longer be ignored and remain unaccounted for in the computation of national income. There is a need for a sound national policy on the role of women in the economic development of the country. As mentioned, most of the women are lacking in education and training. Although basic business training is being conducted by Kelantan's Ministry of Youth and Culture, the number of women involved in the programmes is limited. There is clearly a need to step up such efforts to ensure wider participation especially among the younger generation.

Another major problem confronting women traders in Kelantan is the lack of capital financing. Many of these women traders have little or no access to institutional credit and have to finance expansion or working capital requirements from internally generated funds or non-institutional sources. There is a need for the government to persuade the financial institutions to allocate more funds to small operators. Although the Kelantan state government had set up two programmes under its financial assistance programmes called Rancangan Belia Niaga (Youth in Business) and Rancangan Peniaga Kecil (Plans for Small Business), only a very few women traders have benefited from these schemes. As a matter of fact, none of the respondents in our survey had participated in any of those programmes.

The formation of woman's groups or business associations is a fundamental strategy in attempts to increase women's business capacity. Such an association would not only serve as a meeting place for women traders but also as a forum to share business knowledge, information and strategies. Reference may be made to Peniagawati, a (women trader's) association, whose main objective is to equip its members with business knowledge through activities such as seminars and training programmes. Peniagawati also helps its members obtain loans from financial institutions. Unfortunately, however the association is active only in the state of Selangor and the Federal Territory. Since its establishment in 1981, its registered members number only 150 (*Mingguan Wanita*, 28 October 1988).

Attempts should be made to reorient the national planning processes to increase female participation in business. A holistic approach is warranted based on the concept of women's development as an integrative process. This means that economic, social, political and personal aspects of life, the interaction among these, and the effect of changes in one aspect on other aspects must be taken into account as a whole.

NOTES

1 See G. Jones (1965), p. 62.

2 This is a more traditional pattern of migration where the men would migrate for periods of short duration while their wives took care of the rural households (Heyzer 1986: 36).

3 MARA (Majlis Amanah Rakyat) was set up in 1966 to motivate, guide, train and assist the Malay and other *bumiputera*, with emphasis on the rural population, to participate actively and progressively in commercial and industrial activities as part of economic and social development in line with the government economic policy.

4 ASN represents the National Investment Trust in which *bumiputera* can participate.

BIBLIOGRAPHY

Abdul Aziz Mahmud. "Malay Entrepreneurship: Problems in Development—A Comparative Empirical Analysis". Occasional Paper no. 7: November 1981, SERU, Kuala Lumpur.

Abdullah bin Abdul Kadir Munshi. *Kesah Pelayaran Abdullah*. Kuala Lumpur: Oxford University Press, 1968.

Alias Muhamad. *Kelantan: Politik dan Dilemma Pembangunan*. Kuala Lumpur: Utusan Melayu (M'sia) Berhad, 1975.

Boserup, Ester. *Women's Role in Economic Development*. London: G. Allen and Unwin Limited, 1970.

Chee, Peng Lim. *Financing the Development of Small Industry in Malaysia*. Occasional Papers on Malaysian Socio-Economic Affairs. Kuala Lumpur: University of Malaya, 1977.

Chia, Siow Yue. "Women, Economic Participation in Malaysia". In *Women's Economic Participation in Asia and The Pacific*. United Nations, Economic and Social Commission For Asia and The Pacific, 1987.

Clifford, H. "A Journey Through the Malay States of Trengganu and Kelantan". *The Geographical Journal* IX, no. 1. (1970).

Firth, R. *The Malay Fishermen: The Peasant Economy*. London: Routledge and Kegan Paul Ltd., 1966.

Graham, W.A. *Kelantan*. Glasgow, 1907.

Heyzer, N. *Working Women in South-East Asia—Development, Subordination and Emancipation*. Milton Keynes, Philadelphia: Open University Press, 1986.

Hoffman, L.W. "The Decision to Work". In *The Employed Mother in America*, edited by F.I. Nye and L.W. Hoffman. Chicago: Rand McNally, 1963.

Ismail Awang. "Sejarah Masuknya al-Quran ke Kelantan". In *Warisan Kelantan V*. Monograf Perbadanan Muzium Negeri Kelantan, Kota Bharu, 1986.

Jamilah Ariffin. "Female Rural-Urban Migration and Labour Force Participation Trend in Peninsular Malaysia". Paper presented at The Population Studies Unit Seminar on Changing Society and Economy: The Role of Population. Kuala Lumpur: November 1987.

Jones, G. "Female Participation in The Labour Force". *The Malayan Economic Review*, 1965.

Kanitta Meesook. "The Economic Role of Thai Women". In *Aspects of Thai Women Today*, a publication of the Thailand National Commission on Women's Affairs, 1980.

Khor, Kok Peng. *Ekonomi Malaysia dan Kemerosotan*. Translated by Toh Kin Woon. Pulau Pinang: Institut Masyarakat, 1983.

Lim, Chu Poh. 'Penyertaan Bumiputera dalam Bidang Perniagaan dan Perusahaan di Kelantan'. Final Report, 1976.

Mackie, Lindsay and Polly Pattulla. *Women at Work*. London: Tavistock Publication, 1977.

Manderson, L. *Wanita, Politik dan Perubahan: Pergeraken Kaum Ibu UMNO Malaysia, 1954–1972*. Translated by Samsudin Jaapar. Kuala Lumpur: Penerbit Fajar Bakti Sdn. Bhd., 1981.

Masitah Mohd. Yatim, "Employment of Women in Malaysia". National Family Planning Board, Malaysia: Prime Minister's Department, 1983.

Meier, G.M. *Leading Issues in Economic Development*. London: Oxford University Press, 1970.

—— and Baldwin. *Economic Development*. New York: John Wiley and Sons, 1957.

Mohd. Fauzi Hj. Yaacob. *Peniaga dan Perniagaaan Melayu*. Kuala Lumpur: Dewan Bahasa dan Pustaka, 1981.

Mohammad Nejatullah Siddiqi. *The Economic Enterprise in Islam*. Lahore: Islamic Publication Ltd, 1972.

Morgan, J. "Time, Work and Welfare". In *Patterns of Market Behaviour: Essays in Honor of Philip Taft*, by M.J. Brennan. Rhode Island: Brown University Press, 1965.

Muhamad Asad. *The Message of the Qur'an*. Gibraltar: Dar Al-Andalus Limited, 1980.

Nik Hasnah Nik Li. "Sejarah Bandar Kota Bharu 1900–1940". Thesis submitted to History Department, UKM, 1977.

Nik Safiah Karim. *Wanita Malaysia*. Kuala Lumpur: Pustaka Ilmu Raya Sdn. Bhd., 1982.

Nik Zainab Haji Karim. "Peranan dan Kedudukan Wanita dalam Masyarakat Melayu Kelantan". In *Kelantan Dalam Perspektif Sosio-ekonomi*, by Nik Safiah Karim and Wan Abdul Kadir Yusuf. Kuala Lumpur: Jabatan Pengajian Melayu, Universiti Malaya, 1985.

Oakley, Ann. *Women's Work: The Housewife, Past and Present*. New York: Panthean Books, 1975.

Osborn, Ruth H. *Developing New Horizons for Women*. New York: McGraw-Hill Book Company, 1977.

Pawadee Tonguthai, "Women and Work in Thailand and the Philippines". In *Women's Economic Participation in Asia and the Pacific*. United Nations Economic and Social Commission for Asia and the Pacific, 1987.

Siti Hindun Ahmad. "Sejarah Ekonomi Kelantan 1909–1945: Satu Kajian Awalan". Thesis submitted to History Department, UKM, 1979.

Siti Zulaikhah Mohd. Nor. "Kedudukan dan Peranan Wanita dalam Islam". Angkatan Belia Islam Malaysia, 1981.

Skeat, W.W. "The Cambridge University Expedition to The North-Eastern Malay States, and to Upper Perak 1899–1900". *JMBRAS* 26, no. 4 (1953).

Standing, Guy and Glen Sheehan. *Labour Force Participation In Low Income Countries*. International Labour Organization, 1978.

Todaro, M.P. *Economics for A Developing World*. London: Longman Group Limited, 1977.

United Nations. *Women's Economic Participation in Asia and the Pacific*. Economic and Social Commission for Asia and the Pacific, 1987.

Zaidi Saidi Ibrahim. "Aspek-aspek Budaya Ekonomi Masyarakat Kelantan sebelum 1909". In *Beberapa Aspek Warisan Kelantan*, edited by Khoo Kay Kim. Kuala Lumpur: United Selangor Press, 1982.

7 VENTURE CAPITAL: THE INDONESIAN EXPERIENCE

Bahauddin Darus

Introduction

Indonesia has the largest concentration of Muslims in Southeast Asia, and therefore Muslims are economically and politically a dominant force in Indonesia. It is well known that Islam prohibits interest and encourages equity participation, and there have been attempts to bypass interest payments through equity financing.

Some interesting experiments have been made by several financial institutions in promoting venture capital as a means of mobilizing funds for investment. This study will focus on one of these experiments. It will identify appropriate measures that may be undertaken by the Indonesian authorities to facilitate the growth and development of equity financing for small and medium-sized enterprises (SMEs), and to identify specific opportunities for the Islamic Development Bank (IDB) and the Asian Development Bank (ADB) to provide financial and/or technical assistance in promoting the growth and development of venture capital companies (VCCs) in Indonesia. The case in point is the progress of Bahana (Bahana Pembinaan Usaha Indonesia, or Indonesian Development Finance Institution) in its efforts to spawn new entrepreneurs through divestment which corresponds to *musharakah* (equity-based operations) in the Islamic concept of business entities.

In addition to evaluating the degree of success, the study will also discuss the problems and prospects of such operations in the Pancasila economy of Indonesia. This study focuses on the institutional sources of venture capital and other forms of equity financing for SMEs in Indonesia.

Venture Capital: Nature and Scope

Venture capital is becoming a world-wide phenomenon. From its modern beginnings some 30 years ago in the United States, it has begun to spread, first in Europe and now in the Pacific Rim. Except for the culture in which it exists, venture capital is the same around the world. It seeks to add value through investing in the equity of a company and working with its management. Venture capitalists do most of their work with a company after the investment is made. Such work adds value not only to the company, but also to the market and the economy it serves.

The international venture capitalist acts as catalyst, adding value to investments by drawing on an international network of others with the same objectives. International success stories, therefore, are infinitely repeatable. First, there is the fact that venture capitalists do not make money by investing. Rather, they make money by divesting, selling their investments at a gain. Second, in order to sell one's investment at a gain, one first must help the investee company grow and add value. Third, any company, particularly in high technology, must sell to the world market in order to reach its full potential.

Generally, there is a tendency in the developing countries to invest in high-technology projects similar to those found in Silicon Valley and Route 128 in the United States. Consequently, low-technology and "appropriate" technology areas for venture capital investments are often ignored.

In addition, there is virtually no capability to evaluate service ventures where the primary ways of gaining competitive advantage are through superior execution of marketing and distribution strategies. People are generally uncomfortable with venture projects, where a new market has to be created or where the foundation of competitive advantage will be an innovative distribution system or marketing strategy.

In terms of "appropriate" technology, agribusiness, aquaculture, and horticulture represent the major venture capital investment opportunities. Yet, there has been no organized venture capital effort to develop the expertise needed to identify and research new investments in such areas.

Another example of "appropriate" technology deals with packaging technology. Many agricultural products are perishable and a significant number of industrial products are fragile. There can be venture capital investment opportunities to provide existing packaging technology to other new ventures in the developing countries, or to pioneer the development of new packaging technology that will be appropriate for products sold to Asia-based consumers, rather than those in North America or Europe.

It appears that there are outstanding prospects for venture capital firms whose executives have the ability to spot uncovered investment areas and to finance the commercialization of proprietary technology. A similar sort of opportunity exists for superior thinkers in these firms who can assess trends and technologies, particularly those that are germane to the Asia-Pacific region. There is much market research available on the changing tastes of consumers in the United States, but there is very little available on how consumer tastes and life-styles are changing in Asia as personal affluence steadily increases. These changing life-styles can provide opportunities to venture capital.

Perhaps the most pervasive factor inhibiting the development of venture capital financing in Asian countries is the conservative, inward-looking business culture and practices that often prevail in these business communities. Asian entrepreneurs are very reluctant to share management control with outsiders. If left to their own devices, many Asian entrepreneurs would prefer to see the growth of their companies restricted to that size where most senior management positions are filled by direct family members.

Those Asian entrepreneurs with a more modern and professional perspective on management control often find the initial seed capital financing hard to come by. To my knowledge, there is no incubator fund operating in Asia at the present time, and the sources of seed capital financing from institutional venture capital firms are very few indeed.

Against this backdrop, there appear to be outstanding prospects for Asian venture capitalists who are willing to create their own deals. In fact, a key requirement for success in Asian venture capital may be the ability to originate one's own deals. In effect, this means turning the normal venture capital process on its head. A successful Asian venture capitalist will have to be able to originate the new investment idea, perform the market research, confirm the dimensions of the opportunity, prepare the business plan, secure the financing from the venture capital community, and put together the management team that will actually execute the business plan. By taking this approach, venture capitalists in Asia should be able to circumvent the problem of the Asian entrepreneur's reluctance to share management control with outsiders.

Entrepreneurs are always starting and building companies, whether in the Asian and Pacific region, Europe, or North America. A venture capitalist basically catalyses this process and accelerates the building of a company with the input of his time, money, and experience. Venture capital investing, therefore, systematizes something that occurs naturally. One might say that the venture capitalist energizes the entrepreneurial process and enhances its chances of success.

In Europe and North America, well-established venture capital communities help add value on a systematic basis to this process of building companies. In Asia, however, very few venture capital firms have been established. To understand why few venture capital firms have been set up and to formulate an overall Asian Development Bank (ADB) strategy for assistance to venture capital in the region, a review of venture capital financing in selected developing member countries was carried out under an ADB regional technical assistance study. This study was done in late 1986, covering Pakistan, Sri Lanka, Thailand, Malaysia, and Indonesia. It was found that venture capital activities in these five countries had not developed to any significant degree, particularly when contrasted with the substantial development of such activities in the developed countries of the region, such as Australia and Japan. However, the study also discovered the existence of a demand for institutional sources of equity capital for innovative new ventures. Moreover, the opportunities for establishing such ventures, based on downstream processing of domestic resources and new technologies, are increasing in these countries.

On the basis of all these, it may be surmised that the establishment of a strong venture capital industry can contribute significantly toward private risk-capital mobilization for investment in innovative projects undertaken by entrepreneurs with sound business plans but limited capital resources. Such a development would broaden the industrial base and generate much needed employment opportunities in the region.

Venture capital financing is commonly regarded as equity investment for a predetermined time period in small businesses with high growth potential. However, venture capitalists generally participate in a broad range of business development financing, from providing seed-financing to an entrepreneur (to develop a new business concept, idea or product) to financing leveraged/management buyouts (where entrepreneurs and managers acquire subsidiaries of major corporations or other businesses). Although venture capital financing over the past 15 years has been most successful in high-technology industries such as computers and genetic engineering, venture capital investments are generally drawn towards any industry that has strong prospects for rapid growth and substantial capital appreciation within five to 10 years. Furthermore, the venture capitalist typically attempts to spread his risks by diversifying investments across several industries as well as across the various stages of business development financing.

Given that the major thrust of venture capital financing is investment in small and medium sized businesses with high growth potential, three main characteristics of venture capital financing are:

1. Venture capital financing involves equity or equity-related participation in the form of a direct purchase of shares, or through warrants, options, or convertible securities.
2. Venture capitalists add value to investments by developing an active ongoing involvement in the strategic and operational management of the investee companies, often through working representation on the Board of Directors. In addition to adding value to the investment by providing advice and assistance, the venture capitalist's involvement in management is also an effective way of monitoring the investee company.
3. Venture capital financing is a medium-term investment discipline that often requires a period of seven to 10 years before receiving any significant return on investment.

The returns to the venture capitalist's investments are derived from substantial capital appreciation, and as such, prospects for future liquidity are evaluated before any investments are made. Investments are liquidated via an initial public offering, a sale to another company or a buy back agreement with the entrepreneur or the major shareholders.

The institutional approach to venture capital financing is embodied in the VCC, which usually exists as a fund managed by a professional venture capital management firm. The organizational form of the VCCs is determined by legal and tax considerations. For example, the predominant form of the VCCs in the United States is a limited partnership managed by general partners (the venture capitalists) who assume unlimited liability for the obligations of the partnership, and are funded by limited partners who have limited liability. The principal advantage of the limited partnership is that the partnership itself is not taxed, and tax attributes (income, losses, etc.) are extended to individual partners who may have differing tax preferences or tax-exempt status.

The sources of money may be individual investors, large corporations, pension funds, and insurance companies. The professionally managed VCC provides investors with the opportunity to invest in high growth industries without being directly exposed to the inherent risks and time demands of individual small business development investments. The investors in a VCC must be willing to commit their invested capital over a period between seven and 10 years, to expect to receive the bulk of the return on investment only at the end of that period, and to accept a passive role in the investment process. The current aggregate return on investment for most VCCs in the United States ranges between 25 per cent to 30 per cent compounded per annum, although exceptional returns of 40 per cent per annum or more have been achieved. From the perspective of the investor, venture capital financing is a long-term investment discipline with an open-ended upside potential for high returns and a downside limited to the total loss of the amount invested.

The venture capitalist has a broad range of specialized management skills, such as the ability to analyse the long-term potential of prospective investments, to appraise the quality of management, to negotiate the structure and closing of investment deals, and to develop a close working relationship with the entrepreneur. This unique combination of management skills typically cannot be taught, and is best acquired through apprenticeship. In particular, the long-term orientation required of the venture capitalist generally can be acquired only through experience, and it has been observed that because venture capital has such distinct characteristics, it has evolved into a profession *per se*. In early attempts to institutionalize venture capital financing in the United States, many investors such as financial institutions perceived venture investing as an extension of the traditional modes of financing and investments.

Venture capital financing can play an important role in providing financial assistance to entrepreneurs, particularly where the entrepreneur lacks adequate collateral to secure conventional credit facilities from financial institutions such as commercial banks and finance companies. Venture capital can also contribute towards increasing the availability of funds for entrepreneurs involved in innovative projects that carry a high degree of risk in addition to attractive growth prospects. The venture capitalist adds value to portfolio investments by providing assistance and support in areas such as general corporate and business strategy, financial planning, recruitment and training of key management personnel, and marketing.

Economically, venture capital encourages the development and growth of SMEs and the nation's industrial base by mobilizing capital resources, and can result in new businesses, additional employment, and an increase in national revenue.

The Indonesian Setting

In Indonesia, financial and economic infrastructures still remain underdeveloped. The traditional method of business financing from institutional sources in Indonesia follows the pattern established in most ASEAN (Association of South East Asian Nations) countries, i.e. short to medium term loans secured with collateral. A major criticism commonly directed towards the financial institutions in Indonesia is that the overall lending criteria are heavily biased towards security rather than project viability and entrepreneurial capability. As a result, more often than not, large businesses enjoy the benefits of bank financing while the SMEs may be deprived of such facilities. Partly to remedy this situation, the Indonesian Government has implemented several small credit schemes to assist the SMEs.

The more popular credit schemes are KIK (Small Investment Credit) and KMKP (Permanent Working Capital Credit). However, the aggregate bank lending to the SMEs under these schemes has been insignificant compared to the needs of the SMEs. As of 31 March 1988, credit figures show that only Rp1,254 million credit was extended to KIK and KMKP as opposed to a total of Rp35,194 billion outstanding bank credit (Tables 7.1 and 7.2).

Other efforts to assist the development of SMEs include equity participation schemes provided by several financial institutions. However, these equity participation schemes cannot be viewed as venture capital activities because there are no predetermined divestment periods, and investment decisions are based on socio-economic considerations rather than high levels of projected capital gains. Also, the extent of equity financing provided by these institutions is small and relatively insignificant (Table 7.3).

The dilemma facing the SMEs is not restricted to financing alone. The lack of management and technical skills represent another major problem of the SMEs. In fact, the failure of equity participation schemes experienced by most financial institutions generally has been caused by the lack of managerial and technical assistance and support for the SMEs.

TABLE 7.1
Credit for Small-Scale Entrepreneurs
(In million rupiahs)

Particulars	1983	1984	1985	1986	March 1987	March 1988
Small Investment Credit (KIK/Kredit Investasi Kecil)	0.414	0.387	0.356	0.326	0.311	0.311
Permanent Working Capital Credit (KMKP/Kredit Modal Kerja Permanen)	0.815	0.867	0.931	0.889	0.878	0.943
General Rural Development Credit (Kupedes/Kredit Umum Pedesaan)	0.104	0.099	0.166	0.273	0.384	–
Working Capital Credit Keppres 29/1984	–	–	0.036	0.067	0.046	–
Credit through - Rp. 75 million	–	0.009	0.079	0.185	0.324	–
House Ownership Credit (KPR/Kredit Pemilikan Rumah)	0.407	0.597	0.836	1.237	1.459	–
Credit for Petty Traders (KCK/Kredit Candak Kulak)	0.008	0.010	0.012	0.012	0.012	–
Credit for Teachers	0.056	0.051	0.058	0.112	0.287	–
Credit for Indonesian Students (KMI/Kredit-Mahasiswa Indonesia)	0.004	0.013	0.026	0.040	0.052	–
Credits for Cooperatives	0.241	0.278	0.271	0.300	0.275	–
Total	2.049	2.311	2.771	3.441	4.028	1.254

SOURCE: Bank Indonesia, *Annual Report* 1986/1987 Bank Indonesia, *Indonesian Financial Statistics*, October 1988.

TABLE 7.2
Loans/Credit Extended by Financial Institutions
(In billion rupiahs)

Particulars	1983	1984	1985	1986	March 1987	March 1988
Bank Indonesia	2.356	1.160	1.110	1.114	1.173	1.457
State Banks (2)	8.854	10.283	13.522	15.240	18.902	22.894
National Private Banks (2)	1.354	2.151	3.269	4.487	5.772	8.210
Local Development Banks	0.372	0.432	0.545	0.633	0.786	0.994
Foreign Banks	0.737	0.977	1.062	1.072	1.219	1.520
Agricultural & Rural Banks	0.012	0.016	0.019	PM	PM	0.0298
Development NBFI's	0.072	0.101	0.136	0.172	0.231	PM
Pawn Shops	0.055	0.062	0.065	0.070	PM	0.0891
Total	13.812	15.182	19.728	22.788	28.083	35.194

SOURCE: Bank Indonesia, *Indonesian Financial Statistics*, October 1988.

TABLE 7.3
Equity Participation at Year End Investment at Cost
(In billion rupiahs)

Particulars	1983	1984	1985	1986	March 1987
State Banks	91	74	81	84	93
National Private Banks	7	8	11	11	13
Local Development Banks	1	1	1	1	1
Foreign Banks	–	–	1	1	1
Development NBFI's	10	6	5	5	6
Investment NBFI's	7	8	8	9	11
Total	116	97	107	111	125

SOURCE: Bank Indonesia, *Annual Report* 1986/1987.

The ADB study reveals that venture capital financing can play a major role in the promotion and development of entrepreneurs and the SMEs in Indonesia, but only if the basic infrastructure exists. However, there are several impediments that would severely limit the probability of successfully establishing a VCC that would achieve the desired financial goals in Indonesia in the short to medium term. Several private sector businessmen interviewed during the course of this study indicated that a return on investment in excess of 25 per cent compounded per annum cannot be expected from most business ventures in Indonesia under the current economic conditions. In view of the availability of 16 to 20 per cent tax-exempt returns on time deposits that are virtually risk free, it is unlikely that a VCC will be successful in attracting local investors unless the VCC can offer a significantly higher return. Foreign investors, on the other hand are deterred from investing in Indonesia by the declining rupiah and the high cost of forward contract cover for foreign exchange devaluations and the 20 per cent withholding tax on remittances out of the country. In addition, foreign investment is heavily regulated by the government. Highly placed government officials have expressed unfavourable views on venture capital financing, and it is unlikely that a VCC would receive government sanction or support.

To successfully operate a VCC, there must exist not only investment opportunities with high growth potential, but also the ability to monitor investments effectively and the means to exit from the investment when it is brought to fruition. In Indonesia, the venture capitalist's ability to evaluate these investment opportunities is seriously handicapped because accounting standards and reporting practices are often not of a level that would be conducive for effective appraisal.

Monitoring investments effectively would be difficult in Indonesia due to poor accounting standards and reporting practices, and the shortage of adequate managerial and technical skills. The means of exiting from investments are also limited as a result of a virtually inaccessible and inactive stock market and restrictions on private placement of shares.

Be that as it may, the state-owned Development Finance Institution PT. Bahana Pembinaan Usaha Indonesia, established in 1973, was given the new task to function as a venture capital company in 1985. The 6 May 1986 policy package and a series of deregulatory actions since adopted by the government do indicate strong efforts by the government to encourage foreign investment.

A number of important deregulations took place recently. First, the highly regulated banking industry was shaken up on 27 October 1988 when the government unveiled sweeping reforms to curtail the power of state-owned banks and to increase competition in its financial system. Second, the government's 21 November 1988 package was aimed at enlarging job opportunities, encouraging investment related to the promotion of non-oil exports, smoothening distribution of goods and increasing efficiency of national production. Third, on 20 December 1988, the government issued another series of deregulation measures in the areas of stock market and financial institutions-financing and insurance agencies as a follow-up to similar finance, monetary and banking policies which were announced on 27 October 1988.

As the Indonesian Finance Minister indicated recently, investment today is mostly financed by the banking sector, and other sources of financing are needed. If the stock market develops, it will enlarge long-term fund sources as well as public participation in productive investments. Policies in the stock market cover the operation of security-stock by the private sector, the establishment of security stocks in various cities and the trading of security in the Jakarta Stock Exchange. In the new policy, the private sector is allowed to operate the security-stock market, besides the one operated by the government. The conditions to set up security stock include payment of standing capital of Rp500 million, while all shares must be owned by Indonesian citizens or companies with local share ownership.

Policies in financing agencies cover venture capital, leasing business, transfer of debt, security trading, credit card business, and consumer financing business. With those policies, the government resumed leasing ventures both in the form of national and joint-venture companies. This business could be run by bank and non-bank financial agencies. For venture capital and leasing, the operators (private and cooperative) would have to pay standing capital of Rp3 billion. In order to support public fund raising and development, the government issued policies covering national and joint-venture insurance businesses.

Structure

The rest of this chapter is structured as follows. The next section provides a history of business development in Indonesia and an overview of the Indonesian economy today. It focuses on the development of private sector entrepreneurs of both indigenous and Chinese backgrounds. The third section examines the financing environment with special reference to securities and the financial market as key areas in the mechanism of venture capital financing and as general sources of financing for SMEs. It discusses in detail the prospects of the Indonesian capital market and examines other sources of equity financing, such as the Islamic Development Bank (IDB) and the Asian Development Bank (ADB). The fourth section offers an evaluation of PT. Bahana Pembinaan Usaha Indonesia, established as the first Indonesian venture capital company in early 1985 as a case study.

The Indonesian Economy and the Role of the Private Sector

Macro Analysis

The Indonesian economy has been under considerable strain since 1982, when oil and other primary commodity prices started their downward trend. In previous years, an annual growth rate of seven per cent was fuelled by buoyant oil and commodity prices, foreign investments and international aid. At the same time, manufacturing industries grew at double-digit rates under the protectionist regime. The government accorded high priority to food production, and fertilizers were subsidized. The result was an impressive increase in food production, contributing to a healthy growth of the agricultural sector.

In the eighties, all these advantages came to an end. The growth rate of the economy started to decelerate and export proceeds began to shrink. Current account deficits began to swell, necessitating two substantial devaluations, in 1983 and again in 1986. At the same time the appreciation of the yen and European currencies *vis-à-vis* the dollar increased the Indonesian debt burden and its annual servicing. Inflation could not be fully controlled, also because of the two devaluations. (This inflation, however, was confined to upper single digit levels). The flow of foreign investments and the amount of oil exploration also were reduced, partly as a world-wide phenomenon, but partly because of bureaucratic obstacles and greater domestic economic uncertainty. The country has been suffering a "growth recession" since 1982, and is now slowly recovering thanks to major restructuring efforts.

There will be continuing resource constraints because oil prices are not expected to improve much, and the effect of new borrowings will be limited by a heavy debt service burden, already in the order of US$7 billion annually. New borrowing will probably only match the outflow of capital because of debt repayment. Hope is placed on continued strong showing of non-oil exports and continued advances of productivity in all sectors of the economy through mechanisms of further deregulations.

The Private Sector

The composition of the private sector and the problems today in many ways still reflect the legacy of the Dutch colonial system. Before World War II, the modern sector was dominated by the Dutch companies, with a number of medium-scale Chinese companies on the ascendancy. The Dutch companies were engaged primarily in plantation, mining, international trade, banking, shipping, manufacturing, and construction. After World War I, many Chinese companies entered medium scale manufacturing of consumer goods; their plants were often located in provincial towns in Java. Some Chinese business houses, however, also ventured in plantations, such as sugar, tea and coffee.

Native Indonesians living in rural areas in those days occupied the traditional sector of subsistence and smallholders' agriculture, petty trade, local transportation, handicraft, etc. In the cities, members of the Indonesian élite and educated class worked in the colonial administration. Although many Indonesians occupied middle level positions in the colonial administration, they were not in a position to play a significant role in the modern sector after independence. The swelling urban population drifted into trade, home industry and handicraft, such as textile weaving and batik, and became the nucleus of a nascent indigenous middle class. They became the "underdogs" in the colonial commercial hierarchy, below the Chinese merchant class.

The Chinese, representing some two to three per cent of the population, became the middlemen in the economy, linking the modern Dutch-controlled economy with the traditional sector.

The political stance for the past 20 years has been "pragmatism", which is a policy blend that respects old ideological commitments embedded in the 1945 Constitution and yet tries to accommodate these with the requirements of the growth of the economy under present day circumstances. Article 33 of the 1945 Constitution, for instance, contains the mandate that "branches of production important for the State and of dominating interest to the livelihood of the masses of people have to be controlled by the State". Such were the convictions of the founding fathers of the republic, many of whom were steeped in the socialist traditions of Western Europe before World War II.

The new regime which took over the administration in 1966 recognized that the country was severely capital deficient and that it also needed new technologies to develop the economy. The new government overcame the old prejudice against foreign investments and enacted a law to attract and to give guarantees to incoming foreign investments. This promulgated law (1967) was soon followed by another law extending the same incentives to domestic investments. Since many of the strong domestic private enterprises were Chinese-controlled, it meant that the new government wanted to extend its pragmatic approach to this part of the business community, whose growth had never been free from domestic socio-political controversy.

The Chinese have been regarded as alien by indigenous Indonesians, because of colonial history, and have often been the subject of some discrimination. However, the New Order government, recognizing that the domestic Chinese are part of the "national assets", deemed it opportune to utilize their capital and capabilities to develop the national economy rather than to leave them apart.

A prudent government, however, would still respect the strong historic predilections and steer a balanced course. That is why the new government did not abandon the old preference for a strong public sector. Such a sector can be appreciated as being part of the "indigenous" or "national" sector, especially when there is no strong indigenous private sector as yet. Hence, fuelled by the revenues from the oil boom, this public sector has also grown much during the present regime. Apart from the traditional public utilities sector, it has also ventured into heavy industries such as steel and shipbuilding, and chemical industries such as cement, paper, fertilizers, and petroleum refining.

The modern enterprise sector in Indonesia today, therefore, consists of three major elements, i.e. the public sector, the foreign sector and the domestic private sector. The public sector is very dominant in banking (75 per cent in terms of assets); this is true also in petrochemicals, and plantations. In downstream manufacturing industries as well as in trade, private interest, both foreign and local Chinese, have the upper hand. There are many interactions and interrelations between these three sectors, but their distinct politico-economic roles remain.

Within the domestic private sector, a relevant distinction should be made between the so-called strong and weak economic sectors. "Strong" and "weak" are political euphemisms for identifying the Chinese and the indigenous Indonesian entrepreneurs without sensitive racial connotations. The Indonesian Government remains, in terms of formal policy, non-racial in orientation, because this is one of the tenets of the independence movement. Nevertheless, it has to contend with strong underlying sensitivities. The indigenous Indonesian entrepreneurs are mostly in the weak category, while many of the foreign and Chinese enterprises are assumed to belong to the strong category. This categorization is a subjective matter, because good statistics do not exist. However, the larger foreign and Chinese enterprises have greater visibility, especially in big cities.

For the sake of long-term social and political stability, it is important that the gap between the weak and the strong economic groups be bridged and their disparities alleviated. Accordingly, there is a government programme to assist the growth of these small and weak enterprises by giving them preferential access to government credit and government contracts. State banks maintain a small business credit programme with subsidized interest rates, and small government contracts are reserved for the same category.

To foster linkages and interrelations between the social categories of enterprises, including the foreign sector, several policies are being promoted. Incoming foreign investments are required to associate themselves with domestic partners in joint ventures, where the local party is required to have a 20 per cent share at the start, with an opportunity to increase the stake to 51 per cent.

Since 1974, state banks can only lend long-term (investment) credit to domestic companies which have an "indigenous majority", meaning that (1) such domestic companies must be at least 51 per cent owned by indigenous Indonesians, or (2) when majority share ownership is held by non-indigenous (meaning Chinese) Indonesian citizens, the majority of directors and commissioners should be indigenous Indonesians. Commissioners are members of the supervisory board.

Official policy and practice, however, are not always congruent. In practice, the requirement that only so-called indigenous companies have access to investment loans from government banks is met only in a nominal sense, giving rise to so-called Ali-Baba companies where indigenous Indonesian parties (i.e. the Alis) fulfil the majority requirements, while in reality the original owners (i.e. the Chinese Babas) still control the operations. The state banks, cognizant of such facts, tacitly condone these arrangements. Last, too few indigenous companies would be able to meet the minimum capital requirements. For the government, these nominal accommodations are also sufficient for the time being because it isn't possible to force the development of certain preferred conditions.

On the Indonesian side, the supply of entrepreneurs grew fast during the boom period until 1902. Partly, this reflected the swelling numbers of graduates from secondary and tertiary educational institutions. Education has greatly improved during the last 15 years. As the government could not afford the additional workforce, the young educated Indonesians had to enter the private sector under the preference schemes. Besides, government pay scales were never as good as those offered in the private sector.

The negative side of the preference schemes, however, was that many new entrepreneurs have not had to work hard for their survival and growth, and this experience has not helped them to face the harder times since 1982. Some have found a comfortable niche because, even under adverse economic circumstances, there are still a considerable number of government projects and procurements, including those of the state-owned companies. In general, however, business conditions have become much more competitive since 1982, and fat profit margins have become largely a thing of the past.

The Chinese entrepreneurs were able to hold and even strengthen their positions because of their superior business acumen, much longer experience, and the advantage of their extensive national and international network. They also learned to accommodate and co-operate with the indigenous entrepreneurs when government business was at stake. Consequently, a symbiotic relationship is shaping up, especially among the younger generation. This is because they have shared the same national educational experience, unlike their predecessors.

The Indonesian Capital Market

The securities market in Indonesia was started in Jakarta on 14 December 1912 under the Dutch colonial government. The securities traded in this market were primarily shares of Dutch companies operating in Indonesia and bonds of the Dutch Government. The stock exchange was then closed in 1914. In 1925 stock exchanges were set up in two other cities, Surabaya and Semarang. However, in 1942, these two stock exchanges were also closed.

In 1952, the stock exchange was reopened. The management and operation of the stock exchange were assigned to the Association for Money and Securities Trading (PPUE), with the Central Bank as the advisory body. Through 1958, the stock exchange did not develop well because of the nationalization of Dutch businesses in that year, the ban on the trading of Dutch securities in 1960, and the high level of inflation, especially in 1965. In 1976, the Indonesian Government again reformed the securities market by establishing the Capital Market Executive Agency (BAPEPAM). Semen Cibinong, a joint venture cement producing firm, became the first listed company on 10 August 1977, which marked the start of the second phase of capital market development. As of October 1988, 31 companies have issued shares or bonds through the capital market. Twenty-four of these companies have issued 65,203,011 shares with a primary market value of Rp156.045 billion.

During 1981–83, capital market growth perked. This can be seen from the increase in the number of listed companies from eight, with the primary market value of Rp45,780.1 million in 1983. In terms of stock trading activities, there were also peaks in 1981, 1982, and 1983 with the average daily trading of Rp30.1 million, Rp50.7 million, and Rp40.4 million, respectively. However, from 1983 through 1987, growth in stock trading activities in the capital market tended to decline (although in 1987 the average trading increased slightly). From January through October 1988, the average daily trading volume increased to Rp32.3 million average which compares favourably with the 1986 Rp7.3 million. In terms of the share price index, the composite price index dropped from 100 (base index) in August 1982, down to 66.83 at the beginning of 1986. Since 1987, the composite share price index has rebounded with the highest composite index 82.43 in 1987 and 137.06 for first 10 months of 1988.

The decreasing activity of the capital market was caused primarily by the effect of the world recession and by high local interest rates. On 1 June 1983, Bank Indonesia (the Central Bank) announced a package of policies to deregulate various activities of the banking industry. One of these was to allow state commercial banks to determine freely the interest rates for their deposits and loans. Another aspect of this package was that Bank Indonesia would phase out its liquidity credits, except for a limited priority sector. Based on this package of policies, state commercial banks increased their interest rates on time deposits, from nine per cent to 18 or 19 per cent for one year deposits, with much higher rates for two-year time deposits. Compared with the share dividend rate, the interest rate for time deposits was higher. Moreover, tax postponement was granted to interest income on deposits, further depressing the capital market.

Meanwhile, bond activity has been rising. As of September 1988, six companies have been listed in the capital market with a total of 22 bond issues which raised Rp805.7 billion from the primary market, while two other companies, BPD Jatim and PT Papan Sejahtera, have been granted licences to issue bonds of Rp25 billion each.

In order to encourage greater dynamics in capital market development, the government of Indonesia issued a series of fundamental deregulation measures concerning the securities exchange. Some of these, those issued on 23 December 1987, are known as the December Package. The main objective of the capital market deregulation is to promote further the role of the capital market as an alternative source of financing. As a result, issue requirements have been relaxed;[1] foreign investors are allowed to participate in the capital market; bearer shares have been introduced in addition to registered shares;[2] and a parallel market requiring a simpler issuance process and simpler issue requirements has been established.[3]

As a result of the December package, smaller and medium companies with good prospects (as well as newly established ones) are given equal opportunity to raise funds through the capital market. The activity of the capital market for the first 10 months of 1988 has increased dramatically. During this period, eight issues of bonds for seven companies were brought to the market and Rp320 billion was raised in the primary market. Four of the seven companies were newcomers to the capital market. The government measures aimed at generating a favourable climate for capital market development include equal tax treatment of time deposits/certificates of deposits and investment in shares and bonds. Banks and non-bank financial institutions can increase their paid-in capital through the capital market by issuing new shares. In order to increase the capital market instruments, especially shares, it is necessary to gain the support of the business community. Companies which plan to issue shares through the capital market have to present adequate disclosures which will, in turn, be used by investors in their decision-making.

With regard to control or ownership in general, most public companies issue their shares through the capital market for less than 50 per cent. The majority interest of the ownership is held by the founders or the existing shareholder(s). In addition, shares issued through the capital market are generally distributed among many minority interests. In these circumstances, final decisions are taken, more often than not, by the founders or the existing shareholders. Thus, diminishing control or ownership of the company does not constitute a major factor that prevents companies from offering their shares through the capital market.

A company qualifying for listing on the stock exchange must meet the following requirements:

1. be a limited liability company;
2. be domiciled in Indonesia;
3. have minimum fully paid-up capital of Rp200 million (US$117,000);
4. have recorded profits for the last two consecutive financial years;
5. for the last two financial years, the financial statements must have been audited by registered public accountants or state accountants (for state owned companies) with an unqualified opinion for the latest financial year;
6. in the case of a bank, it must have been classified as "sound" by Bank Indonesia for the latest year and at least classified as "sufficiently sound" during the two preceding years. The bank should also meet the capital adequacy requirements determined by Bank Indonesia.

A company which meets the requirements outlined above may apply to BAPEPAM to list its stocks on the stock exchange. Bearer shares can be issued for amounts up to a maximum of 49 per cent of the paid-up capital. However, the stock offered for registration must have a total minimum par value of Rp100 million, consisting of stocks with a par value of at least Rp1,000 per share. A company seeking an initial registration must submit a registration statement to the Chairman of BAPEPAM through the underwriter appointed by the issuer. The Registration Statement must be duty stamped and signed by an authorized person representing the company. The registration statement must be accompanied by a copy of the Articles of Association, draft of the prospectus, and financial statements.

Based on the decree of the Minister of Finance of the Republic of Indonesia No. 859/KMK.01/1987 on 23 December 1987 and on the implementation regulations, the public offering of bonds can be carried out only after the issuer has obtained the necessary licence from BAPEPAM. An issuer shall submit a registration statement to BAPEPAM through its underwriters. The issuer must meet the following requirements:

1. be a state or local government-owned company or a private enterprise which holds legal entity status;
2. be domiciled in Indonesia;
3. have a minimum paid-up capital of Rp200 million;
4. have net profits, at least for the last two consecutive financial years;
5. have financial statements which have been audited by a public accountant or a state accountant for the last two consecutive financial years, with an unqualified opinion for the latest year;
6. bonds to be issued must be secured by the assets of the issuer;
7. bonds to be issued should be limited to total liabilities (including bonds to be issued) not exceeding 80 per cent of total assets. A guarantor shall be appointed if this percentage is exceeded;
8. for banks or non-bank financial institutions, the Minister of Finance will decide the total amount of bonds which may be issued, based on the ratio of total liabilities to equity (gearing ratio) of the issuer. Specifically for banks, a recommendation from Bank Indonesia regarding the total amount of bonds which can be issued, is also required.

Bonds to be issued must also comply with the following requirements:

1. they must be expressed in Rupiah;
2. the value must not be less than Rp100 million;
3. the denomination must not be less than Rp10,000;
4. a trustee must be appointed for any bond issued;
5. the functions of trustee, guarantor and underwriter must be carried out by separate institutions;
6. a Sinking Fund must be established by the issuer.

Bonds which have obtained a license from BAPEPAM for offering may be traded on the stock exchange or over-the-counter (parallel market). A company qualifying for listing on the parallel market must meet the following requirements:

1. be a limited liability company;
2. be domiciled in Indonesia;
3. have a minimum fully paid-up capital of Rp100 million (US$59,000);
4. its statements must be audited by public or state accountants with an unqualified opinion.

For issue of shares, the other relevant stipulations are: (1) bearer shares can be issued up to a maximum of 49 per cent of the paid-up capital; and (2) foreign investors may buy shares up to a certain limit which is in accordance with prevailing regulations governing foreign participation.

For issue of bonds, the other relevant stipulations are:

1. Bonds to be issued should be limited to total liabilities (including bonds to be issued) not exceeding 80 per cent of total assets. A guarantor shall be appointed if the percentage is exceeded.
2. For banks and non bank financial institutions, the Minister of Finance will decide the total amount of bonds to be issued based on the ratio of total liabilities to equity (gearing ratio) of the issuer. Specifically for banks, a recommendation from Bank Indonesia regarding the total bonds which can be issued, is also required.
3. The bonds will be listed at the standard price list as stipulated by the Association for Money and Securities Trading (PPUE).

A company seeking to issue shares or bonds to be traded in the parallel market must submit a registration statement to the chairman of BAPEPAM through the underwriter appointed for the securities issue. The registration statements must be accompanied by a copy of the Articles of Association and its amendments, a draft of prospectus, and financial statements for the last two financial years (except for a newly established company which is required to submit only interim and/or annual financial statements on the basis of the company's establishment).

External Sources of Equity Funding and Technical Assistance

Besides shareholders' equity and liquidity loans from Bank Indonesia, there are two regional financial institutions that provide lines of equity financing to VCCs namely: Islamic Development Bank and the Asian Development Bank.

The basic condition for IDB membership is that a country should be a member of the Organization of Islamic Conference (OTC) and be willing to accept such terms and conditions as may be decided upon by the Board of Governors. Indonesia is a member country, and upon the request by Junior Minister of Finance, Bahana Venture Capital Company was approved by IDB to function as an executing agency.

The IDB evaluation team visited Bahana twice in 1988. Subsequently, the IDB approved a line of equity for Bahana's investee companies to the tune of Islamic Dinar (ID) one million or US$1.12 million. The smallest nominal equity participation is ID 100,000 which accounts for one-third of paid-in capital. Its equity will be matched by Bahana and the entrepreneur on equal footing. Besides, IDB will provide instalment sales (a minimum of ID 250,000 and a maximum of ID2 million to each investee company) in addition to technical assistance.

Since 1983, the ADB has placed increasing emphasis on its efforts to promote healthy private sectors in its developing member countries and they have since identified venture capital as a potentially important ingredient in that process. The ADB's regional study of venture capital financing, undertaken during 1986, has provided a strong basis for ADB's future involvement in this new area of enterprise financing. The ADB is currently evaluating the feasibility of establishing venture capital companies in several member countries including Indonesia. Recently, the ADB played a leading part in setting up a regional mutual fund called the Asian Development Equity Fund to facilitate transfer of surplus resources in developed countries into equities in developing countries in the region. Similarly, the ADB is also exploring the possibility of setting up another regional mutual fund that would encourage and invest exclusively or largely in venture capital financing operations in the member countries.

PT Bahana Pembinaan Usaha Indonesia

Bahana was incorporated in April 1973 as a state-owned development finance corporation. The company is based in Jakarta without branches or representative offices in other parts of the country or abroad.

Bahana was established to help develop the small- and medium-sized private indigenous firms to be larger in size and scope of operation, better managed and more bankable. The major instruments to implement this task comprise equity financing, bridge financing, and technical and management assistance. In addition, the company operates in the money market to generate supplementary income. Until recently Bahana had relied on their own internal funds and liquidity loans from Bank Indonesia as sources of funding in money market operation.

Background

With the decrees of Minister of Finance (SK Men Keu 792/MK/IV/12/1970 and SK Men Keu 38/MK/IV/1/1972) the government of Indonesia paved the way for the establishment of non-bank financial corporations. These corporations are allowed to collect funds from the public through capital and money markets in the form of marketable securities. The decrees, issued in 1970 and 1972, were followed by the establishment of two joint venture development finance corporations between Indonesian banks and foreign institutions (PT. Private Development Finance Company of Indonesia and PT. Indonesian Development Finance Company), one state financial development corporation, Bahana, and nine investment finance corporations. In addition to their main function of providing medium- and long-term loans and making equity investments, the development finance corporations are eligible by law to operate in the Indonesian money and capital markets. The money and capital market activities in which the development finance corporations are permitted to operate include collection of funds from the public by issuing and dealing in commercial papers and long-term securities, and playing roles as brokers and traders/dealers in these markets.

The investment finance corporations have similar functions to those of the development finance corporations. However, they are not allowed to make direct loans. Nor can they extend credit, though they are eligible to lease capital goods, finance hire purchases, issue guarantees and discount promissory notes, bills of exchange, and trade bills.

By the Finance Minister's decree on 30 November 1973, Bahana was categorized as a development finance corporation and therefore, by law, the company is entitled to conduct a full range of money and capital market activities. In Clause 3 of the Company's Articles of Association, it is stipulated that the money and capital market activities include issuing marketable securities as one of their activities. Thus, Bahana is licenced to operate in the money and capital markets as a non-bank financial institution and in a developmental capacity as development finance institution (DFI) in Indonesia.

The company participates in the implementation and in support of the government policies and programmes by means of generating and fostering the entrepreneurial spirit and business capability of small indigenous businessmen within the framework of ethnic business principles and ethics.

To achieve the company's objectives, Bahana is carrying out the following activities:

- participation in capital investment and credit extension to small- and medium-sized companies through the establishment of new companies and through the expansion, modernization and rehabilitation of existing ones;
- expansion of equity capital through the issuance of securities in the market place; and
- provision of services to small- and medium-sized private companies in the form of:

  1. management consultancy to enhance the capability of corporate planning, technology, production, marketing, finance, personnel, administration, and legal and general management practices,

2. provision of expert staff to handle problems confronted by such companies in the fields of production technology, marketing, administration, and finance,
3. assistance to obtain local and international capital in the form of equity investment and loans, and
4. assistance in providing local partners for joint ventures.

Funding

Bahana relies on two principal sources of funding, namely shareholder funds and a liquidity loan from Bank Indonesia. Total paid-up capital as of December 1987 is Rp6 billion and the outstanding balance of the Liquidity Loans is Rp8.5 billion. The Liquidity Loan was originally for a term of 10 years including four years grace, and carries interest ranging from three per cent to 12 per cent per annum depending on the use to which the loan is applied.[4] The first instalment of repayment of the Liquidity Loan was originally due in June 1986. However, since divestment of the equity investments has been relatively slow, while returns on existing equity portfolios are low, Bank Indonesia has extended the grace period for an additional four year period to June 1990.

As of 31 December 1987, the authorized capital is Rp10 billion with a total paid-up capital of Rp6 billion. The number of shareholders of the company as of 31 December 1987 is shown in Table 7.4.

Financial Performance

A comparative statement for composition of revenues from investment-related activities for the past seven years (1982–88) is presented in Table 7.5.

Loan interest is based on 12 per cent per annum for credit not exceeding Rp75 million, and 18 per cent per annum for Rp75 million and over, while the front-end fee is 1 per cent of total loan required. Commitment fee is 25 per cent per annum of an undrawn sum of the total loan. Maximum fee for preparation of

TABLE 7.4
Shareholders of Bahana, 31 December 1987
(In million rupiahs)

	Preferential Shares	Common Shares
Ministry of Finance	1,600	400
Bank Indonesia	2,400	1,600
Total	4,000	2,000

TABLE 7.5
Bahana's Revenues from Investment-Related Activities, 1982–88
(In million rupiahs)

	1982	1983	1984	1985	1986	1987	1988*
Interest and front-end fee	93	98	116	123	169	150	126
Commitment fee	7	3	3	12	15	6	8
Feasibility study	11	1	1	1	14	5	7
Consultancy fee	7	11	15	18	21	27	30
Dividend	0	5	1	16	37	26	15
Total	118	118	136	170	256	214	186

* Unaudited

project feasibility study is Rp2 million. Technical and management advisory services are based on a monthly retainer fee of Rp50,000 to Rp100,000. As in other developing countries, the small- and medium-sized companies, especially the smaller ones, are weak in many aspects of business. Compared to the total equity financing Bahana has made, the dividends received in 1987 (in terms of return on investment) were only 1.3 per cent which was less than the interest paid to Bank Indonesia for the latter's liquidity credit.

Total revenues from the investment portfolio have not covered the company's operating expenses. For comparison, listed in Table 7.6 are total revenues from investment portfolio against the company's operating expenses for seven years (1982–88). From Table 7.6 it can be seen that the deficit has been significant in recent years. The deficit in 1988 is equivalent to approximately

TABLE 7.6
Bahana's Total Revenues and Operating Expenses, 1982–88
(In million rupiahs)

	1982	1983	1984	1985	1986	1987	1988
Income from investment	118	118	136	170	256	214	186
Operating expenses	804	1,033	2,467	2,011	1,706	1,640	1,689
Deficit	686	915	2,331	1,841	1,450	1,426	1,503

TABLE 7.7
Contribution to Bahana's Profits, 1982–88
(In million rupiahs)

	1982	1983	1984	1985	1986	1987	1988
Interest income	616	1,253	2,053	2,016	1,615	1,698	1,623
Direct expense*	357	592	975	972	888	838	744
Profit contribution	259	661	1,078	1,044	727	860	879

* Represent interest on the liquidity loan from Bank Indonesia.

25 per cent of the company's total paid-up capital. To cope with the problem of annual deficit, Bahana has set aside and invested part of its capital in the money market operation.

Total annual contribution to the company's earnings, which is calculated by interest income derived from the purchases and holdings of promissory notes (through money market dealings), and the interest Bahana has to pay for the Liquidity Loan from Bank Indonesia during 1982–88, are shown in Table 7.7.

Organizational Structure

Project application and evaluation for financing (equity participation) rests with the Board of Directors. The Board of Directors consists of a President and two Managing Directors who are appointed for a term of five years, which may be extended. They report to the Board of Commissioners, which consists of two members, one of whom acts as the Chairman.

The Head of the Project Equity Financing Department is responsible to the Board of Directors and is supported by two Regional Divisions which conduct the same function in each of two respective regions and have several professional staff from a variety of educational backgrounds and work experience. The Project Equity Financing Department has three main tasks, that is sourcing new clientele, project proposal evaluation, and management consultancy services.

The Finance and Fund Management Department is responsible for the operation of the money and capital market activities and functions as the Company's Treasury. The Corporate Secretariat is responsible for general affairs, human resource development and secretarial activities of the Board of Directors. Other organizational units supporting and facilitating Bahana are the Legal Department and Research and Development Department with responsibility to the Board of Directors, while the Internal Audit is solely responsible to the President as stipulated by Government Regulation No. 3 of 1983. Bahana workforce numbers

TABLE 7.8
Breakdown of Bahana Employees' Job Responsibilities

Job Responsibility	No. of Personnel
Operational staff	16
Auditors	4
Lawyers	2
Research and Development	2
Accounting and Money Market	9
General Affairs and Secretariat	29
Total	62

62 personnel and the breakdowns according to job responsibilities and qualifications are given in Tables 7.8 and 7.9.

An Evaluation
During its first 11 years (1973 through 1984), Bahana's shareholders mistakenly thought that Bahana's success was indicated by the sheer number of companies in which it had invested. In reality, the profits accruing from these investments, on average, were negligible, and by the end of 1984, Bahana was running at a loss totalling Rp447 million. The reasons for this loss were two-fold. First, the cost of operations dramatically increased as additional staff were hired to provide management services for the increasing number of companies in the portfolio (a total of 42 companies). These costs could not be offset by dividend earnings. Second, most investee companies did not perform well. Total cumulative dividends received over the 11-year span were Rp79.3 million against cumulative equity portfolio of Rp602 million.

TABLE 7.9
Breakdown of Bahana Employees' Qualifications

Qualifications	No. of Personnel
University graduates	20
Diploma holders	17
High school graduates and under	25
Total	62

Most companies did not perform well for a number of reasons. First, the average equity portfolio was very small, only Rp14.34 million. Second, project locations were spread almost randomly and were distant from Bahana's Jakarta headquarters, making monitoring and management services very costly. Third, management policy aimed at small projects. Fourth, Bahana's funding was inefficiently organized. Its exposure of Rp3.7 billion (Rp602 million equity and Rp3.15 billion loan) represented fully 50.2 per cent of project costs of the entire portfolio of Rp7.5 billion. Last but not least, the decision-making process for Bahana's equity participation was very slow, since the Board of Directors was required to submit each application first to the Board of Commissioners for its approval. It was obvious that Bahana had neither generated new entrepreneurs, investors or companies needed to accelerate national development, nor had it operated profitably by itself. All this call for a new approach.

Recent government regulations stipulate that all government undertakings, particularly the PESERO (Government undertakings established as limited liability companies under Indonesian commercial law) must be managed as efficiently and effectively as possible. PESERO companies are mandated to produce profits while playing a specific role as government agent in the national economic development process.

An important part of national development involves strengthening the private sector. Particular focus must be placed on promoting small- and medium-scale industries and businesses. To do this, entrepreneurs must be identified and encouraged, and business culture concepts and values must be taught and reinforced. Bahana understands itself to be a catalyst in this process of "engineering" a business environment, that is, an environment where business methods are understood and pursued, and entrepreneurs are encouraged to develop their new products and services, thereby adding to increased employment and profit.

Bahana accomplishes its mission by forming business partnerships with entrepreneurs. PT. Bahana provides equity financing, assists with management development, and offers advice based on its business experience. As each new business venture establishes its ability to develop independently, Bahana divests its financial interest and looks for other entrepreneurs with whom it can form new partnerships. Through this process, Bahana contributes to the growth of the private sector. Bahana can help accelerate national development by encouraging new business ideas, building a larger equity market, generating employment and adding to the country's foreign exchange earnings.

Venture capital financing is the most appropriate method to breed astute entrepreneurs and professional managers, because it provides financial and management assistance, and then through divestiture allows businesses to grow on their own.

As these new companies develop, the success inspires other entrepreneurs to develop their new ideas, and other investors/shareholders to mobilize new sources of funding to take advantage of new business opportunities.

Additional equity investment, leading to more competitive products and services, also helps generate increased consumer spending. This mechanism is the key to the emergence of a middle class and accelerated development.

In carrying out the dual missions (profit making and developmental roles), Bahana operates in two fields of activities, namely "Venture Capital Business Operation" and "The Capital Market Operation". Accordingly, Bahana was declared as a Venture Capital Company effective from early 1985.

Bahana's indicator of success as a business entity will be profit and growth of assets, while its mission in business engineering will be measured by the number of successful investee companies in which Bahana has divested its holdings. Consistent with Bahana's developmental mission, the targetted ratio of small to medium-sized companies is three to one. Every medium-sized company must be matched by three small-sized companies.

However, Bahana aims at the young, energetic, talented, skilled and well-educated entrepreneurs as its main target group. There is no set industry criteria for investments. Nonetheless, industrial sectors receiving high priority are: manufacturing industries and workshop services; agriculture and aquaculture businesses oriented toward commercialization and biotechnology applications; tourism, especially hotel and restaurant support; any other business activity with good potential of exporting goods and services.

In the context of the National Economic Development Programme, Bahana is appointed to assist in the promotion and development of small and medium scale entrepreneurial activities in the private sector. Bahana is looked upon as a business entity for business engineering, implementation and production. In this respect, Bahana provides venture capital financing to entrepreneurs in need of establishing viable projects. Bahana's commitment takes the form not only of venture capital but also of project management consultancy. As the entrepreneurial company achieves a strong and mature business foundation of positive growth and development, Bahana divests its holdings in the enterprise, with reasonable capital gains at the time of divestiture.

Investee companies with total project cost (fixed investment and working capital) of up to Rp750 million are categorized, in Bahana's context, as "small", while those with project costs ranging from Rp750 million to Rp2,000 million are classified as "medium". The equity financing requirement by either one of those two groups of companies should be a maximum 20 per cent of the project cost; otherwise, the Board of Commissioners' approval is needed for Bahana to join such an investee company as a shareholder. The nominal maximum share capital Bahana can invest in a company without the prior approval of the Board of Commissioners is presently Rp150 million for a small-scale company and Rp200 million for the medium-sized company. The bridge (interim) financing facility is granted in the form of a temporary loan financing to bridge the gap between the date of funds as required for investment purposes and loans from other banks or non-bank financial institutions extended to the companies receiving equity participation form Bahana. This facility is intended to replace the medium-term loan financing which had been given by Bahana until 1985. Project proposals submitted to Bahana need a fixed asset foundation in the overall investment programme. Bahana does not finance working capital needs as a single entity.

Equity financing from Bahana is not intended to exceed the total equity of the entrepreneur. However, Bahana's equity investment may exceed the entrepreneur's contribution on a case-by-case basis, subject to approval by the Board of Commissioners. The normal debt/equity ratio is 2:1, although a ratio in excess of 2:1 but less than 3:1 may be considered in special projects.

In cases where the total amount of share capital from both parties is insufficient, a temporary loan or bridge financing may be considered to meet the balance, but it must be supported by a guarantee from a financing institution for Bahana no longer provides loans and restricts itself to venture capital financing. Supplemental income hitherto derived from money market operations will be gradually phased out.

Soon after Bahana started to function as a Venture Capital Company in early 1985, it divested the first of a series of holdings acquired since its inception in 1973. Holdings in four investee companies over a four-year span (1985–88) were divested (Table 7.10).

Investments under the Venture Capital Business Operation have not generally been self-liquidating at least in the short term. Minority investments of Bahana, particularly in private companies, have had unusually long gestation periods not normally required for investments to mature. For such tasks, Bahana has assumed the role of a development agent and has therefore not expected good profits. Experience has shown that, on average, a period of eight years is needed before Bahana is able to divest their venture capital investment. Meanwhile, a certain period of deficit appears between the time when Bahana invests its funds into a private enterprise and the first dividend payments are received from the private enterprise. The income from dividends, as mentioned earlier, has been too small to cover the Company's operating expenses.

Referring to Table 7.11, of all funds invested, Rp7,312 million, or 43.18 per cent is still on the move. The specifics of venture capital investing are such that a relatively small proportion of on-going invested funds is likely to make up for a capital loss through substantial capital gain. Comparative achievements between the holding company era and venture capital era may be described as follows (Table 7.12):

1. Foremost of all is the cumulative equity portfolio (Table 7.6) as a strategic key toward self-sustained growth. It has dramatically increased over a four-year span to a total of Rp 1,675.500 million (position as of

TABLE 7.10
PT. Bahana Pembinaan Usaha Indonesia
Divestment Cases

	Remarks	Units	Investee Companies			
			PT Amal Wahana	PT Bali Post	PT Fajar Mulia Pradipta	PT Dunia Rotan Sentosa
1	Line of Business		Shrimp Cold Storage (Export)	Printing and Publishing	Ornamental Cast Iron	Rattan Furniture
2	Equity Participation					
	No. of shares	Pieces	350	351	5	100
	Percentage of shares	%	50	16	4	18
	Nominal Value	Rupiah	200,000	100,000	500,000	100,000
	Equity Value	Rupiah	70,000,000	31,500,000	2,500,000	10,000,000
3	Dividend on Equity Disbursed	Rupiah	56,500,000	55,750,000	2,319,665	6,183,522.50
4	Divestment					
	No. of shares	Pieces	350	315	5	100
	Percentage of shares	%	50	16	4	18
	Value per shares	Rupiah	450,000	350,000	2,000,000	287,500
	Value of shares	Rupiah	157,500,000	110,250,000	10,000,000	28,750,000
	Year	–	1985	1986	1987	1988
5	Capital Gain					
	Value	Rupiah	87,500,000	78,750,000	7,500,000	18,750,000
	Percentage of Equity	%	125	250	300	187.5
6	Income from Equity Participation					
	Value (3+5)	Rupiah	144,000,000	134,500,000	9,819,665	24,933,522.50
	Percentage to Equity	%	206	427	393	250
7	Evaluation					
	Period of Participation	Years	8.00	7.00	6.00	7.50
	Capital Gain Per Year	%	15.63	35.71	50.00	25.00
	Capital Gain Per Year (Compounded)	%	10.50	23.00	26.00	18.00
8	Follow Up Financing					
	Institutions	–	BDN	BRI	BBD	BBD
	Loan	Rupiah	160,000,000	110,000,000	2,300,000	75,000,000

TABLE 7.11
Present Status of Investee Companies

	Investee Companies		Fund Invested (Rp millions)					
Condition	Total	%	Equity	Loan	PH	Others	Total	%
Divested	4	6	114.0	–	–	–	114.0	1
Sound	15	25	1,335.8	718.1	–	2.8	2,056.7	27
Unsound	6	10	335.0	987.4	251.0	0.3	1,573.7	21
Distressed	15	25	1,282.0	1,315.3	43.0	52.8	2,693.4	35
Stranded	12	20	85.6	761.3	209.3	3.7	1,160.2	15
Liquidated	7	14	22.5	162.5	–	2.0	187.0	1
Total	59	100	3,194.9	3,944.6	503.3	61.6	7,785.0	100

December 1988 is Rp2,277.850 million versus Rp602,000 million at year end of 1984).

2. The average equity portfolio during the venture capital era is Rp133,991 million versus Rp14.34 million during the holding company era.
3. Ratios of equity versus loan, equity versus total cost of project, loan versus total cost of project, and Bahana total exposure (equity loan) versus total cost of project are in favour of the venture capital era.

Future Investment Plan

For the next five years (1989–93), Bahana plans to make new investments in a total of 57 small- and medium-scale private enterprises. Total new private firms in which Bahana plans to enter as a venture capitalist in 1989–93 are shown in Table 7.13. Subsequently total maximum new share capital to be invested in 1989–93 is shown in Table 7.14.

In order that the company can attain the stage of self sustained growth, its cumulative equity portfolio at the end of 1993 must reach Rp16 billion. Provided that a return on investment in excess of 25 per cent compounded per annum can be realized in the four-year span, the company will be sound and profitable in all aspects.

On the other hand, Bahana plans to divest its equity investments in private firms from 1989–93 as follows. The joint venture partner(s) of Bahana will have the first right of refusal to purchase or buy back the shares to be divested by Bahana. In case they do not exercise their option to buy back, Bahana will be free to offer the shares through the capital market or directly to other prospective buyers.

TABLE 7.12
Comparative Performance Between Two Eras
(Rp thousands)

Remarks	Holding Company Era 1973–84					Venture Company Era 1985–88				
		Investment					Investment			
	No. of Companies	Equity	Loan	Total	Total Cost of Project	No. of Companies	Equity	Loan	Total	Total Cost of Project
Manufacturing	20	262,305	1,836,209	2,098,514	4,014,483	13	1,525,991	1,242,863	2,768,854	12,096,547
Tourism	2	38,250	66,875	99,125	355,317	1	116,000	161,000	277,000	467,542
Agribusiness & Poultry	15	260,595	1,013,817	1,274,412	2,375,670	3	635,859	618,807	1,254,666	2,949,000
Others	5	41,200	250,099	291,299	745,501	–	–	–	–	–
Total	42	602,350	3,161,000	3,763,350	7,490,771	17	2,277,850	2,022,670	4,300,520	15,513,116
Modes of Financing										
Equity vs Loan			16.0% : 84.0%					52.96% : 47.04%		
Equity vs Total Cost of Project			8.0% : 92.0%					12.80% : 77.20%		
Average Equity			14,340					133,991		
Loan vs Total Cost of Project			42.2% : 57.8%					11.36% : 88.64%		
Total Exposure vs Total Cost of Project			50.2% : 49.8%					27.72% : 72.28%		

TABLE 7.13
Firms for Venture Capital Investments, 1989–93

	1989	1990	1991	1992	1993
Small-scale	8	8	8	9	9
Medium-scale	2	3	4	3	3
Total	10	11	12	12	12

TABLE 7.14
New Share Capital for Investment in 1989–93
(In million rupiahs)

	1989	1990	1991	1992	1993
Small-scale	1,600	1,800	1,600	2,300	2,000
Medium-scale	400	200	400	200	500
Total	2,000	2,000	2,000	2,500	2,500
Scheduled cumulative equity portfolio	7,000	9,000	11,000	13,500	16,000

Summary and Conclusions

The major thrust of venture capital financing is investment in small and medium-sized businesses with high growth potential. The three main characteristics of venture capital financing are identified as follows. First, venture capital financing involves equity or equity-related participation in the form of a direct purchase of shares, or through warrants, options, or convertible securities. Second, venture capitalists add value to investments by developing an active ongoing involvement in the strategic operational management of the investee companies, often through working representation on the Board of Directors. In addition to adding value to the investment by providing advice and assistance, the venture capitalist's involvement in management is also an effective way of monitoring the investee company. Third, venture capital financing is a long-term investment discipline that often requires a period of seven to 10 years before receiving any significant return on investment. The returns are derived from substantial capital appreciation. Investments are liquidated via an initial public offering or sale to another company or through buy-back agreements with the entrepreneur and the major shareholders.

An established Securities Market with a Stock Exchange is essential for the smooth functioning of a VCC. The venture capitalist views the Stock Exchange as an "exit vehicle" where he divests his stake in the VCC project after its initial gestation/establishment period, when the VCC project is no longer considered a "venture" in its true sense. Since the government's decision to reopen the Stock Exchange in 1977 as part of its new financial policy, the Securities Market has developed very slowly. By the end of 1987, only 24 companies had been listed on the Stock Exchange; and the 27 registered members of the Exchange comprised six private banks, six state banks, nine non-bank financial institutions (NBFIs), one investment company and five broker firms. The fact that the Securities Market is relatively undeveloped is itself an impediment to its development and that of the VCCs. The lack of favourable opportunities for investment results in a deterioration in the activities of the Securities Exchange and an environment not conductive to the promotion of public issues. Quite apart from that, Indonesian owners and managers of companies are not, as a rule, keen to issue a portion of their shares to members of the public. Fear of losing control over the company, exposing themselves to public or second-party scrutiny and reluctance to share profits are the major factors contributing to this aversion. The Indonesian investor is also new to the concept of "risk". The fear of not receiving the return that is expected or not being able to recover the initial investment prevails over other considerations. Investing in assets providing a fixed return is considered more prudent, such as time deposits. The introduction of bonds has also reduced interest in the share market in this respect. Since the Capital Market was reactivated in 1977, the composite price index reached its highest record in 1988, primarily because of the December package 1987 and the performance of the listed companies. After years of slumber, Indonesian's tiny stock exchange has awakened with a bang in early December 1988.

The boom is something of a mystery. Brokers and exchange officials have observed a torrent of money suddenly coming in to buy shares, which have long been undervalued and ignored. Much of the money is from overseas, although some orders are believed to be from large Indonesian business groups. Its index more than doubled within a week. A total of 153,137 shares valued at Rp1.66 billion (US$965,000) changed hands; and on 23 December 1988 a value of 4.2 billion also changed hands; the volume and value figures were by far the highest recorded. Until early 1988, daily trading for years often amounted to only several hundred shares whose total value failed to top US$5,000.

Indonesia has the largest concentration of Muslims in Southeast Asia, and therefore Muslims are economically and politically a dominant force in Indonesia. It is well known that Islam prohibits interest and encourages equity participation. Although many Indonesian Muslims do not heed these Islamic injunctions, there have been attempts to bypass interest payments through equity financing.

Some interesting experiments have been made by several financial institutions in promoting venture capital as a means of mobilizing funds for investment and spawning new astute entrepreneurs and new companies through divestiture. Bahana represents one such experiment.

Over a fifteen-year span (1973 through 1988), the progress achieved by Bahana as a business entity by all accounts has been desperately disheartening. Its survival has been made possible by the shareholders through money market operations. Yet its developmental mission was convincing that the Islamic Development Bank in November 1988 confirmed provision of an equity line to be extended to Bahana's new investee companies of a total of ID one million, equivalent to US$1.2 million. The smallest nominal value of IDB's equity is ID100,000 which accounts for one-third of paid up capital. IDB's equity will be proportionately matched by Bahana and the business partner on equal footing. The ID300,000 paid-in capital will be strengthened by instalment sales. It implies that the investee company does not necessarily resort to conventional interest-bearing loans. Of the total investment consisting of fixed assets and working capital, the entrepreneur is obligated to provide only 22 per cent equity. IDB also provides facilities for education, on-the-job training, and apprenticeship in other companies in the member countries. Besides IDB, Asian Development Bank stands ready to provide an equity line, and in October 1988, ADB confirmed its technical assistance of US$75,000.

In the context of Islam and the economic development of Southeast Asia, given the importance attached to private initiatives in Islam and the fact that private enterprises form the backbone of the Southeast Asian economies, venture capital investing is seen as an appropriate mode of financing for Muslim business communities. It is the best vehicle for entrepreneur creating operations particularly along the line of *musharakah* (joint-venture profit sharing). Venture capital financing is far advanced and dynamic relative to common equity-based participation in that it spawns new astute entrepreneurs and companies through divestiture.

NOTES

* The author wishes to acknowledge help provided by the various government agencies, the Islamic Development Bank and the Asian Development Bank in the compilation of data used in this study which also draws heavily from an ADB study on venture capital financing in Indonesia conducted by Ernst and Whinney.

1 Before the "December package" was undertaken by the government, issue requirements were tighter than they are at present. For example, a minimum profit requirement—10 per cent of the owners' equity in the latest year—is no longer mandatory for a company to be listed in the Capital Market; the 4 per cent daily limit for price fluctuations of shares traded in the stock exchange has also been removed.

2 This policy is designed to increase the numbers of transactions and instruments of the capital market.

3 The Parallel Market differs from the regular market in various ways. One of the major differences is that the parallel market allows a newly established company or even an unprofitable company to enter the market. It should be noted that the management and operation of this market are assigned to a private institution, the Association for Money and Securities Trading (PPUE).

4 For example, an interest rate of three per cent per annum is charged on funds extended to finance equity investment/participation; three per cent interest is also charged on funds extended to finance provision of a loan not exceeding Rp75 million; eight per cent interest is charged on funds extended to finance provision of a loan of 75 million or over; and a 12 per cent interest is charged on funds mobilized under the Money and Capital Market Operation.

References

Ariff, Mohamed. *Islamic Financial Instruments*. Kuala Lumpur: Al-Nahdah, 1985.

Asian Development Bank. "A Study of Venture Capital Financing in Indonesia". Final Country Report June 1986 by Consultants Ernst & Whinney.

Sadli, Mohammad. "The Indonesian Economy and Impact of Financial Developments". Paper presented at Seminar on the Development of Capital Markets and Investment Opportunities in Indonesia, Jakarta, 6 July 1988.

———. "The Private and State Enterprises Sectors in Indonesia". Paper presented at Indonesia–Turkey Bilateral Seminar, Grand Tarabya Hotel, Istanbul, 12–17 October 1987.

Tanaka, Toshiaki. "Venture Businesses and Venture Capital in Japan, the Present State and out-look". *LTCB Research Monthly Economic Review*, no. 76 (October/November 1984).

Tsusaka, Akira. "Welcoming Remarks", Venture Capital symposium in the Asian and Pacific Region, Bangkok, 7–9 April 1988.

Usman, Marzuki. "Capital Market Development in Indonesia". A paper presented at Seminar on "Emerging Power in the World Economy". Singapore, 21 November 1988.

Zakaria Man. "Islamic Banking: The Prospects for Mudharabah and Musyarakah Financing". Paper presented at the International Seminar on Islamic Economics organized by International Islamic University, Malaysia, 6–9 July 1987.

Zimonyi, Ivan L. "ADB Overview of the Status of, Prospects for and Impediments to Venture Capital Financing in Selected Developing Member Countries". Introduction presentation, Bangkok, 7–9 April 1988 Symposium on Venture Capital Financing in the Asian and Pacific Region.

8 ISLAMIC INSURANCE IN MALAYSIA

Syed Waseem Ahmad

Islamic insurance is a relatively new enterprise. The first Islamic insurance company was established in Sudan in 1979. The theoretical work was done by many Muslim scholars and has been published in Arabic, Urdu and English.[1] Other Islamic insurance companies were established soon after not only in Muslim countries but also in Western countries. Syarikat Takaful Malaysia came into being on 29 November 1984 and started its business operations from mid-July 1985.

A period of two to three years is not sufficient to make any judgement about the success or failure of any insurance company. Nonetheless, it is important to watch and monitor the progress and performance of the company and to evaluate its performance so as to ensure that the Islamic alternative to conventional insurance is viable.

Conceptual Framework

Nature and Importance of Insurance

Insurance has been described as a device to cover losses when they occur by distributing them over a community or group.[2] "It is the community (or groups) pooling and the spirit of cooperation which has been described as the essence of insurance".[3] The aim of insurance is to make provision against the dangers to which a group of persons are all equally subject. Insurance is thus a mutual coverage of accidental loss, by a group of persons subject to a common danger.[4] In the present forms of insurance, losses are not distributed but funds are created to cover the losses calculated in advance with the aid of past experience.[5] Thus, we see that insurance involves the spirit of mutuality and co-operation.

The modern contract of conventional insurance seems to have its origin in the marine loans of ancient Greeks as described by Demosthenes.[6]

> Money was advanced on a ship or cargo, to be repaid with large interest if the voyage prospered but not repaid at all if the ship be lost, the rate of interest being made high enough to pay not only for the use of capital, but for the risk of losing it.[7]

According to Baron (1936),"The rate of interest includes together with other elements a premium for insurance in order to provide compensation for the loan to the lender, in case of a loss incurred through the bankruptcy of the borrower".[8] Thus it can be said that the modern contract of insurance is basically the same (usurious in nature) as the old marine loan of ancient Greeks.[9]

As against the usurious nature of the ancient Greek marine loan, the idea of mutual insurance finds its expression in the payment of blood money (blood-wite)[10] which was prevalent in Arab tribes during the Jahiliyya (pre-Islamic) period. This virtue of the Jahiliyya was approved and incorporated into Islam by the Prophet[11] and later acted upon by Caliph Omar.[12] The nature of blood-wite was neither usurious, nor exploitative. It ingrained the spirit of mutuality and co-operation, and eliminated the danger of wars of revenge which continued in pre-Islamic Arabia for decades and completely wiped out tribes involved in blood revenge wars. "Payment of blood-wite stands out as an example of mutual insurance—a community enterprise, social in character but economic in consequence".[13]

Leaving aside public insurance, Wagner divides all insurance into two groups, "pure mutual insurance organized in accordance with co-operative principles, and insurance with third persons as insurers".[14] In the former the aim is mutual service, in the later the aim is profit making. Being of a proprietory nature "the latter carries on its business for the purpose of providing profit to its shareholders by the insurance of others",[15] while the mutual insurance caters for social needs and is based upon the golden principle of "bear ye one anothers' burdens".[16] In a pure mutual insurance the insured themselves are the insurers. It has neither capital stock, nor any proprietory interest. Non profit-making and mutualization, that is, retirement of capital stock "are the two characteristics of real mutual insurance".[17] One can therefore conclude that the pure mutual insurance is acceptable and approved by Islam.[18] The Islamic idea of *takaful* thus embodies the principle of co-operation, mutual help and shared responsibility.

The importance of insurance in modern life can only be gauged by the fact that each and every facet of the normal activity of human life contains all types of risks and uncertainties. Life in the present modern world has become very complicated and is full of risks and uncertainties and the financial loss resulting from them is not dependent on one's voluntary actions. The economic and social progress of the human society will be hampered if no system is devised to offset, to compensate and to reduce, at least partly if not wholly, the financial loss resulting from these risks and uncertainties. The ever growing complexity of the economic system in this industrial age has (further) increased the importance of risk management, that is, reduction and removal of risks, in the productive process and commercial transactions.[19] The economic importance of risk reduction/elimination has become so overwhelming that without it the spirit of enterprise and the wheels of progress would be kept in jeopardy. The existence of pure risk obstructs the smooth conduct of business with which such a risk is associated.[20] If some measures are taken to decrease the financial losses and partly relieve the burden of losses associated with risks, it would facilitate the conduct of business and more people would be willing to do it.[21] Human ingenuity has improvised such a system through insurance. By meeting pure risks through insurance, the investor will be facing only normal business risk and uncertainty, which are inevitable in all investment—one earns profit only by taking such risks. By eliminating pure risk for a relatively small outlay, it becomes possible to run large-scale business smoothly. The reality of life requires that insurance be treated as a basic human need[22] which has acquired greater importance in the increasingly scientific, technical and fast growing complex world.

> Insurance is a basic human need. It is concerned with the financial implications of measurable pure risks. Insurance is concerned only with devising means of compensation for a person who has incurred financial loss in any actual accident. Insurance does not concern itself with other non-financial implica-tions involved in every peril. It is a different matter if financial compensation to some extent relieves one or some of the burden of other losses (such as psychological, moral, social and political) as well. All that can be hoped for from insurance is that it should remove, as far as possible, the defect of indeterminancy in the measurement of losses and to have objective bases for the calculation instead of having just subjective estimates.[23]

Objections of Islamic Jurists to Conventional Insurance

Up to the middle of the twentieth century, the generally agreed view of the Muslim Jurists was that, besides other elements not allowed by the rules of Shariah, the practice of insurance contained an element of gambling (*al-maisir*) which is prohibited by Islam.

The operation of conventional insurance does not in its present form conform to the rules and requirements of the Shariah since it embodies the following three elements, namely: *al-maisir*, *al-harar* (ambiguity or indeterminancy) and *al-riba* (usury/interest). Besides gambling and usury (interest), other evils which the Shariah wishes to eliminate from human affairs, especially in business activities are: (1) Coercion *(ikrah);* (2) Exploitation of distress; (3) Fraud and cheating;

(4) Obvious indeterminancy and hazard (*al-gharar*) and ignorance (*jalh*) likely to cause disputes; (5) Detriment (*darar*).[24]

An overview of recent literature published in English reveals that one prominent and distinguished Muslim jurist has concluded that, of the five evils mentioned above, the first three are not inherent nor are they present in the concept of insurance. He writes "On thoroughly examining insurance one finds it is free from the first three evils. Insurance is also free of the fifth evil—(*darar*) detriment. No third party is harmed by an insurance contract, nor is any collective interest harmed by it. Rather the contrary is true".[25]

For the benefit of readers, we reproduce and quote below the arguments and reasoning of Siddiqi at length. Siddiqi[26] has divided risks into three categories namely: (1) business risk and uncertainty; (2) pure risk, and (3) the risks on which one has an optional control.

The third category of risk is the one which is involved in gambling and in games of pure chance which is not allowed by Shariah. The first two categories of risks are of the kind in which a person has no optional control as they are necessarily entailed in the normal activities of everyday living and working.

Experience shows that by and large the profit outweighs loss in these categories of risks. The insurance system has been devised to face these risks, that is, business risk and uncertainty and pure risk on which a person has no optional control. Pure risk is the risk which has only fear of loss without any hope of gain. Thus, there is a clear distinction between the type of risk involved in gambling and the risks for which the insurance is designed to provide the coverage.[27]

Let us now proceed to the arguments which Siddiqi puts forward to show that the nature of insurance in itself does not inherently contain any element of gambling. In what manner the nature of gambling is different from that of insurance can be seen from the following lengthy quotation:

> The evil of gambling lies in the fact that the gambler wilfully seeks out, through betting and wagering, risk which was not there earlier or which, even if did exist, did not personally concern him. ... All possible forms of gambling and its current practices have one thing in common—the risk of financial loss that the gambler courts by betting or wagering could have been avoided if he wanted to do so—in other words the risk is optional and is willingly being sought for.
>
> The case of insurance is fundamentally different. The occurrence of peril against which and the effect of which the insured seeks protection does not depend on whether he is insured or not. The insured is not optionally seeking peril. All such perils entail financial loss either to the insured or to his dependents. Unlike the gambler, the passenger or the owner of a vehicle or house does not wilfully imperil himself by seeking out an accident involving financial loss. In all cases such as that of fire and accident, the chances

> of peril and its consequent financial loss are present irrespective of whether they have been insured or not.
>
> The second fundamental difference between gambling and insurance relates to the hope of gain.
>
> The financial motivation of gambling is provided by the gain in the event of winning, while in the case of insurance it consists in the desire to have protection against loss that one is to suffer in the event of the occurrence of the apprehended peril. The amount received by the insured cannot be considered as profit since it only provides him relief from the burden of loss that he has already incurred. The money won by the gambler is in the nature of profit for it increases his wealth. The motivation of the gambler and of the insured are altogether different. The gambler seeks clear profit while the insured seeks protection against probable loss.[28]

The above discussion removes any misunderstanding that insurance and gambling share any common characteristics or that gambling is in any way inherent in insurance. Rather, in their social and economic roles, they are diametrically opposed to each other. Thus it has been shown that insurance does not contain the element of gambling and that evils such as coercion, exploitation, fraud and cheating are not inherently present in insurance and can be eliminated through legal means. We can therefore conclude that the conventional insurance industry is plagued by the existence of *al-gharar* and by the practice of *al-riba*.

Al-gharar is an Arabic word which means obvious indeterminancy, hazard and ignorance that is likely to cause disputes which, when applied to insurance, means the presence of unknown and uncertain factors in the operation of a contract. This factor is present in the contract and operation of conventional insurance. The uncertainty relates to the fact that the insured or the policy holder is not informed of how the amount of compensation that the company will pay him is to be derived.

The conclusion is that, there is nothing unIslamic about insurance *per se*, provided an insurance system is devised and operationalized in a manner which not only eliminates *al-gharar* and *al-riba*, but also ensures that the elements which are not in accordance with Shariah do not creep in.

Principles of Islamic Insurance

The Concept of Takaful

The word *takaful* in Arabic means "joint guarantee". This concept embodies the principles of co-operation, mutual help and shared responsibility. It can be seen as a method of joint guarantee among a group of members—that is, participants in any scheme against loss or damage that may fall upon any of them. It does mean that participants pledge mutual help amongst the group. Each member of the group pools efforts to support the needy.

The concept of *takaful* has been developed as a form of business and the principle of *al-mudarabah* (profit sharing) has been applied in the contract between the *takaful* operator and the participants. Syarikat Takaful Malaysia acts as an entrepreneur (*al-mudarib*) and accepts *takaful* contributions (instalments/*rasul-mal*) from participants who are treated as investors or providers of capital (*sahibul-mal*).

The *takaful* contract specifies how the profit (surplus) from the operations of *takaful* is to be shared between the participants and the *takaful* operator.

The contract states clearly the rights and obligations of both the participants and the *takaful* operator. In the case of Family Takaful business, the profit sharing ratio is 7:3 between the participants and the Syarikat Takaful Malaysia. In the case of General Takaful, the ratio is 6:4 between the participants and the *takaful* operator.

The Concept of Tabaruk

Another special feature of *takaful* contract is the concept of *tabaruk* which means to donate, to contribute. Under the *takaful* contract the participants agree to relinquish as donations, in accordance with the concept of *tabaruk*, a certain proportion of their *takaful* contributions in order to fulfil the obligations of mutual help as embodied in the concept of *takaful*. In this manner the participants help in fulfilling their obligations in assisting and helping fellow participants who might suffer a loss or damage due to death, or disasters. The sharing of the profit (surplus) from the operations of *takaful*, according to the principle of *al-mudarabah*, is made only after the obligations of assisting fellow-participants have been met. The *takaful* operator has to meet these obligations as well as generate a reasonable level of profits by maintaining adequate assets in its *takaful* funds whilst at the same time striving prudently to protect the funds against undue exposure.

The objectives of the Family Takaful Plans have been described to enable a person:

1. to save regularly;
2. to invest this saving with a view of earning profits in accordance with the rules and requirements of the Shariah;
3. to avail the cover in the form of payment of *takaful* benefits to heir(s) should a participant die before the maturity date of his Takaful Plan.

Operation of Family Takaful Plans

A person who wishes to insure himself becomes a participant in the family *takaful* scheme by choosing one of the types of plan (10, 15 or 20 year term) offered by the company and by agreeing to pay regularly to the *takaful* operator (company) the *takaful* contribution/instalment (premium), monthly, quarterly or annually, signs a *takaful* contract with the *takaful* operator (company) based on the principle of *al-mudarabah*. This *takaful* contract, prepared by the *takaful* operator with its terms and conditions, clearly spells out the rights and obligations of the parties to the contract.

The participant decides on the amount of *takaful* contribution/instalment that he wishes to pay during the term of his *takaful* plan subject to a minimum fixed by the *takaful* operator (which at present is M$15 per month) payable on a monthly, quarterly or yearly basis. The amount of contribution/instalment should of course be within the financial means of the participant.

Each *takaful* contribution paid by the participant is credited into the account of Family Takaful business and shall be divided and credited by the operator into two separate accounts namely:

1. The Participant's Account (PA)
2. The Participants' Special Accounts (PSA)

What proportion of the instalment goes into each account depends on the *tabaruk* (donation) proportion which in turn depends on the age group and maturity period (Table 8.1). The *tabaruk* proportion is worked out by the actuaries taking mortality by age into account, and the method and techniques of determination are the same as in conventional insurance. In the determination of *tabaruk* proportion there is nothing objectionable from the Shariah viewpoint.

The *tabaruk* proportion (which varies from two per cent to nine per cent as shown in Table 8.1) is credited into the PSA. The remaining proportion of the instalment is credited into the Participant's Account. It is out of the PSA that the operator is to pay the *takaful* benefits to the heir(s) of a participant who may die before the maturity of his family *takaful* plan. The purpose of the *tabaruk* proportion that goes into the PSA account is to create a form of mutual fund.

TABLE 8.1
Tabaruk Proportion in Family Takaful Plan
(Percentages)

Age Group (years)	Maturity Period (years)		
	10	15	20
18–30	2.0	3.5	5.0
31–35	2.5	4.5	6.5
36–40	3.5	6.0	9.0
40–45	5.0	8.5	
45–50	7.0		

The *tabaruk* proportion increases with the length of maturity of the Family Takaful plan as well as with the age of the participant at entry. The factors determining the *tabaruk* proportion in the family *takaful* plan are the age at entry and the time frame of the contract. These factors are the same as those determining the annual cost of a term assurance policy in conventional insurance. In conventional insurance, the premium rate rises both with age at entry and the length of the maturity period. In the case of Family Takaful the contribution/instalment remains the same but the *tabaruk* proportion rises.

The distribution of profit realized from investment by the company is first divided according to the profit sharing agreement (in this case 70 : 30), between the participant and the company. The proportion (30 per cent) allocated to the company goes into the profit and loss account of the company. The profit accruing to the participant (70 per cent) is then further divided into PA and PSA (Figure 8.1).

One of the functions of the *takaful* operator in managing family *takaful* scheme is the investment of *takaful* instalments. For this purpose the instalments credited into the two accounts (PA & PSA) are pooled as a single fund. The profits generated from the investment are shared between the participants and the operator in a ratio mutually agreed (in advance through the contract) between them (Table 8.1 and Figure 8.1).

A participant in the age group of 36–40 taking up a 20-year plan under Family Takaful will have nine per cent in PSA and 91 per cent in the PA. Similarly, out of the agreed-to proportion (70 per cent) of the share of the profits (derived from investments of the participant), the *tabaruk* proportion will be deducted and credited into PSA (nine per cent of the 70 per cent of the profit) and the remaining (91 per cent) will go into PA.

Under the Family Takaful scheme, the *takaful* benefits shall be paid to the participants or their heir(s), as the case may be, in the following manner:

Case I The participant dies before the maturity of his Takaful Plan.

Case II The participant survives the maturity of his Takaful Plan.

In the first case the *takaful* benefits shall be paid to the beneficiary [heir(s)] as follows:

1. From PA
   a. the total amount of *takaful* instalments paid by the deceased participant from the date of entry of his Takaful Plan to the due date of payment of the instalment prior to his death; and
   b. his share of the profits from the investment of the instalments which have been credited into his PA;

FIGURE 8.1
Family Takaful Business

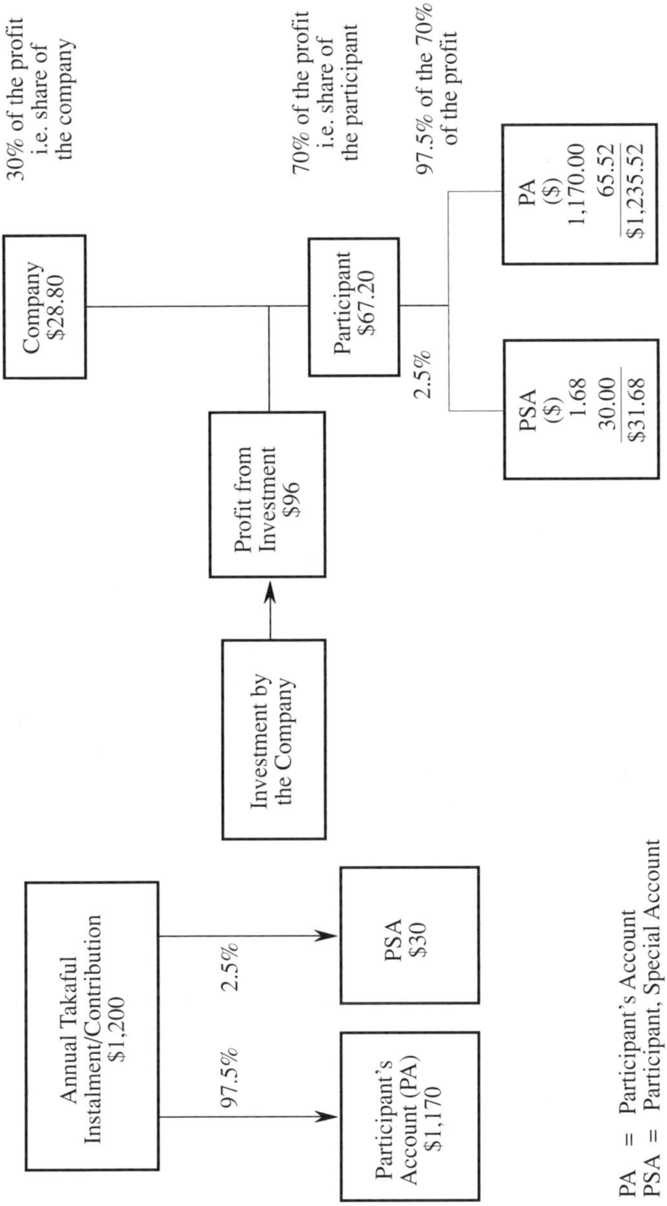

2. From PSA
   The outstanding *takaful* amounts which would have been paid by the deceased had he survived. This amount is calculated from the date of death to the date of maturity of his Takaful Plan.

In the second case (participant surviving the maturity period of his Takaful Plan) the *takaful* benefits that shall be paid to him will come:

1. From PA
   a. the total amount of *takaful* instalment paid by the participant during the tenure of his participation; and
   b. the share of profits from the investment of the *takaful* instalments credited into his PA.
2. From PSA
   The net surplus allocated to the participant as shown from the last valuation of the PSA.

In case of surrender or discontinuation the participant shall be entitled to surrender benefits. There is no minimum period of payment of *takaful* instalments after which the participant is entitled to surrender benefits, while in conventional insurance the insured becomes entitled to surrender benefits only if he has paid his premium instalments for a minimum period (usually three years). There is no forfeiture in the Family Takaful Plan. The surrender benefits shall be the proportion of his *takaful* instalments which has been credited into his PA plus his share of the profits from investment of the instalments as credited into the PA. The proportion of *takaful* instalments which had been credited into the PSA as *tabaruk* shall not be refunded to the participant. These terms are far better compared to the forfeiture and surrender benefits provided by the conventional insurance industry. Hence, the injustice of conventional insurance as seen from the Shariah viewpoint.

Principles and Operation of General Takaful

The General Takaful scheme provides cover for an individual or a body corporate against loss or damage consequent upon a catastrophe or disaster, usually inflicted upon properties or assets, including personal accidents. The scheme is not structured to function as a means of savings, although the participant is entitled to some form of profit sharing as expressed in the principle of *al-mudarabah*. However, under the General Takaful scheme the entire contributions are paid as *tabaruk* for the purpose of creating a defined asset or fund (General Takaful Fund) to pay against a defined loss.

The *takaful* operator invests the General Takaful Fund; and all returns on such investments shall be funnelled back into the Fund. It is out of this Fund that compensation or indemnity is paid to any participant who suffers a defined loss or damage consequent upon the occurrence of a catastrophe or disaster. All operational costs for managing the General Takaful business, including the costs of re-*takaful* (re-insurance) and setting up of a reserve, shall be borne by the Fund.

The amount of *takaful* contributions will depend on the value of the property or asset to be covered. In the determination of general *takaful* contributions, the same principle, methods and techniques apply as in the case of conventional insurance. The difference from conventional insurance lies in sharing the surplus (profits), if no claims are made. This surplus arises after deducting all operational costs. The sharing of the surplus will be made in a ratio agreed to in advance in accordance with the principle of *al-mudarabah* (in the case of Syarikat Takaful Malaysia the ratio at present is 6:4 between the participants and the *takaful* operator).

As agreed to under the *mudarabah* contract, 40 per cent of the net contributions go to the company which were M$397,447 in 1986 and this forms part of the operating revenue of the company. From the operating profit (composed of underwriting profit plus returns from investments) 40 per cent (the share of the company in the profits) accrues to the company and is transferred to the profit and loss account of the company. They amounted to M$129,825 in 1986. The remaining 60 per cent of the operating profit accruing to the participants is transferred to the General Takaful Fund. This component amounted to M$194,737 in 1986, M$0.97 million in 1987, and M$1.85 million in 1988.

Company Structure and Performance

Institutional Framework

Islamic insurance does not come under the conventional Insurance Act 1963. For establishing Islamic insurance a special act called the Takaful Act was passed in 1984. Under the Act only one licence has so far been issued. This was granted to Syarikat Takaful Malaysia Syndicate Berhad. The company is a subsidiary of Bank Islam Malaysia.

Syarikat Takaful Malaysia Sendirian Berhad was incorporated as private limited company under the Companies Act 1965 on 29 November 1984. The Islamic character of the company is clearly stated in its Memorandum of Association: "All businesses of the company will be transacted in accordance with Islamic principles, rules and practices". Accordingly, the company has set up a Religious Supervisory Council to ensure that all its operations comply with the rules of Shariah.

The authorized capital of the company is M$100 million divided into 100 million ordinary shares of M$1 each. At present its paid-up capital is $10 million held by the following institutions as shown in Table 8.2.

Syarikat Takaful Malaysia Sdn Bhd was given two separate licences to operate the two kinds of insurance, namely Family Takaful Business and General Takaful Business. Section 16 of the Takaful Act 1984 requires that separate accounts be maintained for each category.

TABLE 8.2
Paid-up Capital of Syarikat Takaful Malaysia

	M$ million
Bank Islam Malaysia Berhad	5.1
State Religious Councils and State Religious Agencies	4.9
	10.0

The company does not have an agency system. Instead, it operates "Takaful Desks" in the branches of Bank Islam Malaysian Berhad (BIMB) that are manned by full-time paid officers of the company. A Takaful Desk is a one-man operation by the company's employee under the supervision of the Head Office or nearby Branch. It works as a secondary outlet for the expansion of the company's sales and services. The company was also granted permission by Majlis Agama and Religious Departments of States to open Takaful Desks in the offices of Kadi Daera (District Kadis). At the end of two years of operation, Syarikat Takaful had established seven branches and 19 Takaful Desks. Some of Takaful Desks located in the offices of Daera Kadi were temporary and their officers worked part-time only. In the third year of its operations (1987–88) the company did not open any new branch but concentrated on the expansion of permanent Takaful Desks. It opened 13 new Desks, nine of which are located at the branch offices of BIMB and four at district offices of the Haj Pilgrimage and Management Board.

At the end of the third financial year ending 30 June 1988, the company had a total staff strength of 86 (as against 64 in the previous year and 49 in the first year of operation), consisting of 26 executives (25 in the preceeding year), 57 in clerical (against 36 previously) and three in non-clerical positions.

Nature of Business

As mentioned earlier, the company operates Family Takaful and General Takaful on the basis of the Islamic principle of *al-mudarabah*.

Two groups of Family Takaful are offered by the company: (1) Takaful plans with a maturity of (a) 10 years, (b) 15 years and 20 years which must mature before the participant reaches the age of 60 years, and (2) Takaful Mortgage Plans which consist of (a) Takaful Plans for Education and (b) Group Takaful Plans.

The age groups covered under the Family Takaful plans with various maturity periods range from 18 to 50 years.

The main types of General Takaful scheme comprise the following:

1. Fire Takaful Scheme subdivided into: (a) basic fire; (b) house owner; and (c) householders.
2. Motor Takaful Scheme for motor cars and motor cycles.
3. Accident/Miscellaneous Takaful Scheme which covers: (a) personal accident; (b) all risks; (c) workmen's compensation; (d) public liability and (e) money.

During the third year, the company introduced three new schemes under the Miscellaneous Takaful Scheme namely: (a) equipment all risks; (b) burglary and (c) employers' liability.

General Takaful

The gross *takaful* contributions booked in the General Takaful schemes registered M$1.4 million in the first year and increased by 233 per cent to M$4.7 million at the end of the second financial year. During the third year, it further jumped to M$9.7 million, recording an increase of 107 per cent over the previous year.

After deducting the refunds[29] (during the year) from the contributions booked in a given year gross contributions are arrived at. The gross *takaful* contributions received during the second year from participants in the various *takaful* schemes amounted to M$4.6 million, an increase of 232 per cent over the previous year's figure of $1.4 million. In the third financial year, the figure shot up to M$9.5 million by 106 per cent.

Net contributions are derived after deducting re-*takaful* (reinsurance) from gross *takaful* contributions received. In the first financial year, net contributions came to M$993,617 (after allowing for re-*takaful* of M$402,353). Claims paid amounted to M$25,675, giving an overall loss ratio of 2.6 per cent. There were no claims in the fire, personal accidents and miscellaneous categories in the first year of operation. The total claims of M$25,675 on motor cars and motor cycles against net contributions of M$490,991 yielded a loss ratio of 5.2 per cent.

In the second financial year, after deducting reinsurance of $936,202, net contributions stood at M$3.7 million. Total claims during the second year were M$537,181 giving an overall loss ratio of 14.5 per cent as compared with 5.2 per cent of the previous year. The loss ratio was 7.9 per cent for fire, two per cent for motor car and 21 per cent for motor cycles and 12.6 per cent for the miscellaneous category. The details are provided in Table 8.3. Total claims for 1988 amounted to M$3.2 million as against M$0.9 million for 1987 and M$0.1 million for 1986.

The distribution of *takaful* contributions (gross and net), reserves for unearned *takaful* contributions and income from contributions after reserves, together with expense and net income from general *takaful*, by categories of general *takaful* are presented in Table 8.4.

TABLE 8.3
Distribution of Net Contributions and Claims by Category of Insurance
(In Malaysian dollars)

Year	Items	Fire	Motor		Miscellaneous Accident	Total
			Act	Others		
1986	Net Contributions	271,326	490,991		231,299	993,617
	Percentage	27.3	49.4		23.3	100
	Claims	–	25,675		–	25,675
	Loss ratio	–	5.2		–	2.6
1987	Net Contributions	629,733	560,256	1,901,775	609,958	3,698,722
	Percentage	17.6	15.2	51.4	15.8	100
	Claims	49,622	11,286	399,861	76,412	537,181
	Loss ratio	7.9	2.0	21.0	12.6	14.5

SOURCE: Laporan Tahunan Ketiga Ketua Pengarah Takaful bagi Tahun berakhir 31hb Disember, 1987, p. 5.

At the end of second financial year, total assets under General Takaful were M$4.1 million, compared with M$1.3 million in the previous year. Of the total assets, 15.4 per cent were in the form of Malaysian Government Investment Certificates, exceeding the 15 per cent minimum required by Section 17(2)(b) of the Takaful Act 1984. Over M$3 million was in the form of cash and investment account with the holding company (that is, Bank Islam Malaysia), constituting 75.2 per cent of the total assets.

Income from *takaful* contributions is derived after deducting re-*takaful* payments and allowing for reserves for unearned *takaful* contributions from the gross *takaful* contribution received.

The amount of re-*takaful* registered an increase of 132.6 per cent in 1987 over the previous year, but when expressed as percentage of gross *takaful* contributions (received, not booked) the percentage went down to 20.2 per cent in 1987 compared with 28.2 per cent the year before. During the third year (1988), re-*takaful* as a proportion of gross *takaful* contributions further declined to 15.3 per cent, although the amount of re-*takaful* increased in absolute terms by 55.5 per cent.

Reserves for unearned *takaful* contributions increased in absolute terms by 137 per cent in the second year and by 64 per cent in the third year; but as a percentage of gross *takaful* contribution received, they declined to 22 per cent in 1988 from 28 per cent in 1987 and 39 per cent in 1986. The percentage declines in re-*takaful* and

TABLE 8.4
Percentage Distribution by Category of General Takaful

Item	Year	Category of General Takaful			Total
		Fire (%)	Motor (%)	Miscellaneous/ Accident (%)	$
(a) Gross Takaful	1986	42.8	38.0	19.2	1,395,970
	1987	30.0	54.3	15.7	4,634,924
	1988	n.a.	n.a.	n.a.	9,536,218
Less:					
(b) Re-*takaful*	1986	81.2	9.2	9.1	402,335
	1987	78.9	5.6	15.5	936,202
	1988	n.a.	n.a.	n.a.	1,456,125
(c) Net Contributions	1986	27.3	49.4	23.3	993,617
	1987	17.6	66.6	15.8	3,698,772
	1988	12.7	77.4	9.9	8,080,093
(d) Reserves for unearned Takaful contributions	1986	20.5	61.1	18.3	549,642
	1987	8.1	77.3	14.6	1,301,089
	1988	5.0	94.0	1.0	2,132,309
(e) Income from contributions after reserves	1986	35.7	34.9	29.4	443,975
	1987	22.9	60.7	16.4	2,397,633
	1988	15.5	71.4	13.1	5,947,784
(f) General Takaful expenses	1986	8.9	85.0	6.1	127,989
	1987	12.7	74.9	12.4	902,261
	1988	5.3	86.7	8.0	3,263,362
(g) Net income from general Takaful or underwriting profit	1986	35.7	34.9	29.4	315,986
	1987	22.9	60.7	16.4	1,495,372
	1988	27.9	52.7	19.4	2,684,422

n.a. = not available.

SOURCE: Compiled from Annual Reports of Sharikat Takaful Malaysia Sdn. Bhd., 1986, 1987 and 1988.

reserves for unearned *takaful* contributions led to an increase in the ratio of income from *takaful* contributions to gross *takaful* contributions received. This proportion went up to 62 per cent in 1988 from 52 per cent in 1987 and 32 per cent earlier, reflecting an improvement in the functioning of the company.

Expenses consist of claims (paid and outstanding), levy and survey fees. The last item was found only in the initial year. Claims ratio as well as the expense ratio both worsened in the second financial year. In the third financial year, claims ratio further went up to 54.0 per cent from 36.6 per cent the year before and 26.9 per cent in 1986. The expense ratio also shot up from 28.8 per cent in 1986 to 37.6 per cent in 1987 and to 54.9 per cent in 1988. The composition of these claims and their distribution by category of General Takaful can be seen in Table 8.3. About 76.5 per cent of net claims in 1987 was for vehicles, 14.2 per cent for miscellaneous accidents and 9.2 per cent for fire.

After taking into account the operational costs comprising of payments for re-*takaful*, increase in reserves for unearned *takaful* contributions and claims incurred, underwriting profit is arrived at. The underwriting profit for the second financial year was M$1.5 million as against M0.3 million previously. In the third financial year, the underwriting profit recorded a growth of 79.5 per cent, reaching M$2.7 million.

There are also incomes from (1) returns on investments and profits from the disposal of quoted shares, (2) dividends from shares quoted in Malaysia and (3) profit on disposal of Malaysian Government Investment Certificates (MGIC). Returns on investment of the fund during 1987 financial year amounted to M$122,688 as against M$8,576 in the previous year. In 1988, the return on investments reached M$421,976, an increase of 244 per cent over 1987.

Underwriting profit and income realized from investments of the Fund add up to the total profit accruing to the company and the participants in accordance with the terms of *al-mudarabah* (profit/loss sharing) contract. As was noted earlier 60 per cent of the total profit goes to participants and 40 per cent to the company. The total profit amounted to M$1.6 million in 1987 as against M$0.32 million in the previous year. In 1988, the total profit jumped by 92 per cent to M$3.1 million.

In 1987, the company transferred M$0.97 million to the General Takaful Fund as profit attributable to participants as against M$0.19 million in the preceding year. It is from this account that actual profits are paid to the participants at the current rates of profits upon the expiry of their *takaful* contracts. The current rates of profits are calculated monthly. The rates had varied from month to month ranging from 29.03 per cent to 36.14 per cent per annum during the second financial year. In the third financial year, the company transferred M$1.9 million (90 per cent higher than a year before). During the third financial year, over M$1.2 million was paid to 22,005 participants, compared with M$0.42 million paid to some 5,548 participants in the second financial year.

The General Takaful Fund consists of (1) reserves for unearned *takaful* contributions and (2) profits attributable to participants. The General Takaful Fund amounted to M$2.6 million on 30 June 1987 as against M$0.7 million a year ago. At the end of 30 June 1988, the Fund rose to M$5.4 million.

Family Takaful

Tables 8.5 and 8.6 provide statistics relating to family *takaful* on total participation and annual contributions for the years 1986 and 1987. During the second year of business, Family Takaful issued 942 new certificates (policies) as against 834 in the first year. The total participation (sum insured) in the second year from the issue of new certificates amounted to M$13.9 million as against M$17.4 million in 1986, showing a decline of 20.4 per cent. There were 116 terminations

TABLE 8.5
Total Participation

Year	No. of Certificates	Total Participation		
		New (sum insured)	Terminations (sum insured)	Business in Force (in Malaysian dollars)
1986	834	17,410,760	705,000	16,705,760
1987	942	13,867,459	3,363,301	10,504,158
Cumulative				27,209,918

SOURCE: Laporan Tahunan Ketiga, Ketua Pengarah Takaful, 1987.

TABLE 8.6
Annual Contributions Instalments
(In Malaysian dollars)

Year	New	Terminations	Business in Force
1986	943,835	40,560	903,275
1987	788,688	111,431	675,257
Cumulative			1,578,532

SOURCE: Laporan Tahunan Ketiga, Ketua Pengarah Takaful, 1987 out of 942 new certificates issued in 1987 (as against 42 in 1986). After allowing for the amount surrendered due to terminations during the year, the total participation in the "active" sense registered a decline of 37 per cent from M$16.7 million in 1986 to M$10.5 million in 1987. However, the cumulative sum for business in force reached M$27.2 million registering an increase of 75 per cent.

The amount surrendered in the second year reached M$3.4 million from M$705,000 in the previous year. The surrender rate (5 per cent in 1986 and 7 per cent in 1987) is apparently higher than that experienced in conventional insurance (2.3 per cent in 1986). However, there are no forfeitures in *takaful*, unlike conventional insurance where the forfeiture rate has been rising from 17 per cent in 1982 to 39 per cent in 1986 in Malaysia.

The annual contributions due for the new business in force (Table 8.6) also registered a decline of about 25 per cent in 1987 over the previous year. The cumulative annual contributions at the end of the second financial year reached M$1.58 million from the initial figure of M$0.9 million as at 30 June 1986. However, contributions actually received from the participants were only M$584,999 in 1986, and they increased to M$1.1 million at the end of the second financial year.

The distribution of gross *takaful* contributions among the Family Takaful plans (of varous maturities) and mortgages during the first two years is presented in Table 8.7. It is clear from the table that the proportion of contribution received from mortgages declined from 38.5 per cent in 1986 to 11.0 per cent in 1987. There was also a decline of 47.0 per cent in the amount of contributions received from mortgages in 1987. The gross contribution received from the various plans of Family Takaful increased sharply by 170 per cent in the second year reaching M$972,181, increasing the proportion of Family Takaful in the total to 89 per cent in 1987 from 61.5 per cent in the previous year.

TABLE 8.7
Distribution of Gross Takaful Contributions for 1986 and 1987
(In Malaysian dollars and percentages)

Year	Family Takaful Plans	Mortgages	Total
1986	359,812 (61.5)	225,187 (38.5)	584,999 (100)
1987	972,181 [+ 170%] (89.0)	120,385 [- 47%] (11.0)	1,092,566 (100)

Note: Figures in brackets show percentage change over the previous year.

SOURCE: Same as for Table 4.

TABLE 8.8
Average Size of Sums Insured in Force by Type of Plan

Type of Plan	Average Size 1986 $	1987 $	% Change
10 years	8,746	6,807	–22.2
15 years	18,666	16,275	–12.8
20 years	16,531	14,432	–12.7
Mortgages	104,169	78,307	–24.8

SOURCE: Laporan Tahun Ketiga, Ketua Pengarah Takaful, 1987.

A comparison of the two financial years shows that the average size of the sums insured in force by various types of plans has declined during the second financial year. This is depicted in Table 8.8. The decline in business volume and consequently also in the average size of the sum insured in force may be attributed at least partly to the lagged effect of the economic recession during 1985–86.

Assets of the Family Takaful Fund showed an increase of 187 per cent at the end of the second financial year when they stood at M$1.7 million compared with M$0.6 million in the previous year. About 17.9 per cent of the total assets were in the form of Malaysian Government Investment Certificates and the remaining are in the form of cash and deposits in the first financial year. In the second financial year, the proportion of Government Investment Certificates in the total assets was 15.7 per cent while the share of cash and deposits also declined to 72.3 per cent, with the slack being taken up by other investments (12 per cent).

The gross *takaful* contributions from the participants in the various *takaful* plans and mortgage received during the second financial year amounted to M$1.09 million compared with M$0.58 million in the initial year. The sum received from new business was M$0.74 million, an increase of 26.8 per cent. In the third financial year, the gross *takaful* contribution recorded a rise of 94 per cent reaching a total of M$2.1 million. *Takaful* contributions received from new business during the year amounted to M$1.2 million, an increase of 58 per cent over the previous year.

Re-*takaful* payments increased from M$4,980 in the first year to M$9,936 in the second year but declined to M$8,352 in the third year. As a proportion of gross *takaful* contribution, re-*takaful* payments have shown a decline from 0.91 per cent in 1987 (and 0.85 per cent in 1986) to 0.39 per cent in 1988.

Operational costs consist of claims (paid and outstanding), surrenders and levies. In the first year, there were no claims. Consequently, the operational costs

(M$8,943) formed only 1.5 per cent of the gross *takaful* contributions. In the following year (1987), operational costs rose to M$99,285, constituting 9.1 per cent of the gross *takaful* contributions. In 1988, these costs rose further to M$237,545 and represented 11.2 per cent of gross *takaful* contributions. The significant rise in these costs is obviously due to increase in surrenders that accounted for 89 and 85 per cent of the operational costs in 1987 and 1988, respectively. After deducting payments for re-*takaful* and operational costs, the net retained contributions at the end of the year rose to M$0.9 million in 1987 from M$0.57 million in the previous year. In 1988, the net retained contributions reached M$1.9 million. The cumulative figure of net *takaful* contributions at the end of the third financial year amounted to M$3.4 million.

Profit from the investment of the fund increased from M$6,011 in 1986 to M$73,373 in 1987 and M$131,126 in 1988. Following the profit sharing ratio (70:30) agreed to in the *al-mudarabah* contract between the participants and the company, 30 per cent of the profit (M$1,803 in 1986, M$22,012 in 1987 and M$39,338 in 1988) was transferred to the profit and loss account of the company, and the remaining 70 per cent (M$4,208 in 1986, M$51,361 in 1987 and M$91,788 in 1988) to the Family Takaful Fund.

During the second financial year, the company credited a sum of M$37,439 (M$4,208 in the previous year) into the account of profits attributable to participants. The rate of profit as at the end of June 1987 was 3.21 per cent per annum, compared with 1.67 per cent a year before. The rate of profit as at 30 June 1988 was 2.67 per cent. It is not clear how the company decides what rate of profit is to be given each year. According to the company's 1988 Annual Report, profits attributable to the participants for the year were M$91,788 (78.7 per cent higher than the preceding year), but the rate of profit distributed in 1988 was 0.54 percentage points lower than in 1987.

Net retained contributions and the profit attributable to participants minus the amount paid during the year, which make up the Family Takaful Fund, amounted to over M$1.0 million in 1987 (M$0.6 million in 1986). Cumulatively, the Fund stood at M$1.6 million at the end of second financial year, and reached M$3.6 million as at 30 June 1988.

Performance of Syarikat Takaful Malaysia

Syarikat Takaful Malaysia has done well in the third financial year of its operations. Some idea of the performance of a company can be obtained by examining its balance sheet. A brief look at the balance sheet shows that, over the three years, the current assets have increased by 59 per cent. Although its current liabilities have grown, as would be normal with any growing company, its net current assets improved by 24 per cent and investments more than tripled. Fixed assets have remained the same and intangible assets have been eliminated. Term financing and loans have slightly increased in absolute but not in relative terms.

At the end of the third financial year, the investment account with the holding company increased by M$1.8 million or 15 per cent, compared with an increase of 23.9 per cent in the previous year. The proportion of investment account with the amount due from the holding company has been declining from 99.2 per cent in 1986 to 92 per cent in 1988, due to diversification of investment activities.

The operating revenue of the company increased by 119 per cent in the second year and by 74 per cent in the third year. As shown in Table 8.9, income from the investment account with the holding company forms a decreasing proportion of the total operating revenue, its share shrinking from 61 per cent in 1986 to 13 per cent in 1988, while the share of income derived from General Takaful has risen from 38 per cent to about 86 per cent. In absolute terms, it has grown from M$0.4 million in 1986 to about M$3.4 million in 1988.

The activities of the company have been financed by the Shareholders' Fund, Family Takaful Fund and General Takaful Fund. After taking account of accumulated losses in the initial years, the Shareholders' Fund stood at M$9.8 million at 30 June 1988 compared with M$9.4 million a year earlier. With the increase in Family Takaful Fund and General Takaful Fund, the proportion of Shareholders' Fund in the total decreased as shown in Table 8.10.

TABLE 8.9
Composition of Operating Revenue of Syarikat Takaful Malaysia

Operating Revenue	1986 $	1987 $	% Growth	1988 $	% Growth
Operating revenue consists of the following:					
Takaful contributions less re-*takaful* attributable to the company: i.e. 40% of net contribution					
General Takaful	397,447 (38.2%)	1,479,489 (64.9%)	272	3,394,241 (85.6%)	129
Dividend received	6,235 (0.6%)	36,076 (1.6%)	478	56,526 (1.4%)	57
Income from investment account with holding company	637,302 (61.2%)	762,618 (33.5%)	20	514,538 (13.0%)	–33
Operating Revenue	1,040,984 (100%)	2,278,183 (100%)	119	3,965,305 (100%)	74

SOURCE: 1987 and 1988 Annual Reports of Syarikat Takaful Malaysia Sdn. Bhd.

TABLE 8.10
Proportion of Shareholders, Family Takaful and General Takaful Funds in Financing

	At 30 June 1988		
Item	1986 %	1987 %	1988 %
Shareholders Fund	87.7	69.0	52.1
Family Takaful Fund	5.4	11.8	19.1
General Takaful Fund	6.9	19.2	28.8
	100	100	100
Total (in Malaysian dollar)	10,743,215	13,654,027	18,738,782
Annual Growth Rate		27.1	37.2

SOURCE: Balance Sheet shown in Appendix of the 1988 Annual Report, Syarikat Takaful Malaysia Sdn. Bhd.

The company derives its income from the investment of its Shareholders' Fund as well as from its share of the profits from General Takaful Fund and the Family Takaful Fund.

The company incurred a loss of M$569,719 in the first year of its operation before *zakat* and taxation, while in the second year it managed to break even, showing a small operating profit of M$434. In the third financial year the company recorded a profit of M$603,957 before *zakat* and taxation. Accumulated losses after the payment of *zakat* stood at M$0.58 million at the end of the second year. In the third year, accumulated losses were reduced to M$0.23 million, thanks to a profit of M$347,357 (net of *zakat* and tax) in 1988.

Some Observations

Comparison with Conventional Insurance

Conventional insurance provides the following categories of policies under life cover: Whole-Life Policy (par and non-par), Endowment Policy (par and non-par) and Term Assurance Policy.

A non-par (non-profit) whole-life policy does not entitle the policy-holder to a share in the profits of the company, but pays compensation on the death of the insured. "This type of policy is really a combination of a decreasing term assurance and a fixed interest saving plan", writes an insurance consultant.[30] He further adds that "the non-profit whole life policy has traditionally been regarded as a useful method of obtaining permanent cover for a younger man but the events of the last two decades have undermined its value for this purpose"[31] as the effect of the inflation has eroded the value of the sum insured.

A whole-life policy at par (that is, with profit) means that the policy-holder is entitled to share in the surplus. The surplus can be allocated to the policy by means of reversionary bonuses, every one, two or three years. The bonus is decided by the company. The insured is not told how much or when or on what basis bonus payments are to be made. A reversionary bonus is a sum added to the sum insured, but this becomes payable in full only when the policy matures or is terminated by death.

In both par and non-par whole-life policies, if the insured stops payment of premium before the completion of the first three years, the policy is forfeited, and the insured gets nothing. This is unjust, given the high rate of forfeitures in the Malaysian insurance industry. The premium of policies with a profit share is higher than that of non-profit policies, which means that the insured is already paying through higher premium rates for an uncertain share in the profits.

Whole-life policies can be used as collateral to raise a loan. Life insurance companies themselves will usually loan up to a maximum of 90 per cent of the surrender value to the holder at an interest rate. This again is unjust because the loan is being given out of the funds generated by the insured himself. It is the saving of the insured in the hands of the company. The insured is made to pay the interest on his own savings.

The whole-life policy may be made paid-up. This means that the policy holder stops paying premiums, after the period of forfeiture has passed, and the company keeps the policy in force with a reduced sum insured. The whole-life policy is not offered by Syarikat Takaful Malaysia for the simple reason that it is unjust by the standards set out by Shariah.

A term assurance is basically a pure life insurance cover for a stated period and it works on the same basis as fire or motor insurance. The factors determining the cost of a term assurance policy are the age at entry and the number of years it is to run. It provides cover only for a specified number of years. The policy-holder agrees to pay the set annual premium, and his heirs will get the stated benefits (the sum assured) only if he dies within the term; but if he survives the term neither he nor his dependents get anything whatsoever. This category of insurance is not provided by the Syarikat Takaful Malaysia. The term assurance is also used in covering personal debts, that is, to protect the family from debts due to business, mortgage and other creditors in the event of death of the breadwinner. The most widely used variant of the term assurance is a policy called the "decreasing term assurance" policy. This policy is used to ensure that a mortgage debt is repaid in the event of the borrower's death. Some banks require that such a policy be taken up in conjunction with the loan granted for the purchase of a house. This type of assurance is provided by the Takaful Malaysia with its mortgage plan under the Family Takaful Scheme.

Under a decreasing term assurance policy, the sum assured (of the policy) matches the amount of the loan outstanding and it also matches the period of mortgage. The premium is low for two reasons: firstly as the loan amount declines every year, the sum insured is reduced directly, and secondly the sum assured declines as age mortality increases. As the premium is low the policy holder is given the choice to pay his premium either yearly or in one single payment. If a single payment is made (which is preferred by the lender and generally adopted by the borrower) the payment will cover the entire loan period. Some financial institutions are even prepared to include this premium in the amount of the loan so that the cost becomes part of the normal mortgage repayment.

Now, let us look at the endowment policy. The distinctive feature of the endowment policy is that it has a specified maturity date on which the proceeds of the policy are payable to the policy holder. In case of death before maturity, the benefits are payable to the beneficiaries. Endowment policies in conventional insurance are available, like whole life policies in two forms—par and non-par (with profit and without profit). Annual premiums for endowment policies with profit are higher than those without profit, meaning that the policy holder has to pay more for sharing the uncertain profits of the insurance company that may be paid through reversionary bonus scheme to the insured.

The Family Takaful plan of the Islamic insurance system resembles in certain aspects the endowment policies provided by conventional insurance. There are also fundamental differences between the two. Some of the similarities and differences are listed below:

Common features

- Both have specified maturity periods.
- The sum insured is payable to the policy holder if he survives.
- The benefits are paid to the beneficiaries in case of premature death.
- Calculation of premium is done by the actuaries taking the same factors into account.
- In the case of Family Takaful, the *tabaruk* proportion is determined by the actuaries taking the same principles into account as in the case of conventional insurance.

Distinguishing Features of Family Takaful

1. No element of forfeiture
2. No non-profit policies
3. Same contribution/instalment (premium) since there is no policy which does not share profits.

4. Profit sharing ratio is clearly stated in the *al-Mudarabah* contract and the method of determining profit is known to both parties.
5. Profit is calculated on a monthly basis and accredited to the account of the participant at the annual rate of profit every month.
6. The insured are participants.

Distinguishing Features of Conventional Insurance
1. Forfeiture if premiums are stopped before three years usually.
2. Come under par (with profit) and non-par (without profit) forms.
3. Premiums are high for part policies.
4. Uncertain how profits are determined and what proportion of the profits are attributable to the policy holders.
5. Interval of determining the bonus is not known.
6. The insured are clients but they do not have participant status.

Mortgage Takaful Plan is basically the same as the Decreasing Term Assurance Policy which is used to ensure that a mortgage debt is repaid in the event of the borrower's death. The difference in the case of Mortgage Takaful is that the company does not engage in practices which are not disallowed by the Shariah such as *riba* or interest.

General Takaful in the case of fire, motor and accidents is technically a term assurance—that is, unless a claim is made no benefit can be paid. In this respect there is no difference between *takaful* and the conventional insurance. The tariff for basic fire is standardized—same for all companies. Hence the tariff rates for conventional insurance and for *takaful* are the same. However, underwriting guidance varies from company to company.

The coverage for house holders' policy depends on the choice of the house holder. For each category of coverage, additional premium at different rates are charged. Liabilities under these various covers are limited and vary from company to company. In general, this policy besides protecting one's household goods against damage or loss caused by factors such as fire, lightning, thunderbolts, explosions, aircraft or other aerial services, over flowing of water tanks, hurricanes, cyclones, typhoons, volcanic eruptions or floods caused by them, and theft, also compensates any loss of rent that ensues. For an additional premium, the policy can be extended to cover against damage caused by riots and strikes. Each company may have a different set or combination of coverage and rates vary only slightly.

The *takaful* structure is slightly different in the case of motor car insurance. Apparently, the rates (premiums) are higher but the coverage is also wider.

The Takaful motor assurance instalments include cover for breakage of windscreen and a personal accident cover of up to M$10,000. The conventional insurance companies charge separately for windscreen and personal accident cover. However, the cost for the latter is only about M$15. The windscreen cover charge may vary, depending upon the category of cars, starting from M$50 upwards. Radio cassette, air conditioners are inclusive in the *takaful* package, which also treats a married couple as one owner. There is an extra for the all drivers clause. The *takaful* does not provide any cover for vehicles covered under commercial use at present.

No-claim bonuses in conventional insurance companies increase in the absence of claims for each additional year up to a certain maximum and the percentages are fixed. The Takaful declares dividend at the end of each year depending on the profits made and based on the *mudarabah* concept. The difference in *takaful* from conventional insurance companies lies in the principles of its operations and the distribution of profits, if any, as has been explained earlier.

Concluding Remarks

The experience of three years of business operations of any insurance company is not sufficient to draw definitive conclusions about its success or failure. This is more so for a company founded on a new system of operation along Islamic principles. The acceptance of this system, not only in theory but also in practice, depends largely upon the extent of one's commitment to Islam as a way of life. Islam does provide principles that regulate one's entire life. The Takaful is an attempt to prove that these principles can be operationalized in the field of insurance.

In spite of this caution, an assessment of three years' experience does provide some insights into the problems and difficulties faced by the company. For an insurance company with only three years of business experience, the results are very encouraging. This is particularly so since the company is new in both conceptual and operational terms and given the extremely competitive environment. Its clientele wholly belongs to one faith, namely Islam, although the company's doors are open to all. An insight into the Islamicity of the operations of Syarikat Takaful Malaysia may be obtained by taking a closer look at its investments and the manner in which profits are shared with the participants.

The Takaful Act 1984 requires the company to deposit a minimum of 15 per cent of its assets in Malaysian Government Investment Certificates. The Government Investment Act 1982 specifies that the Finance Minister shall declare the rate of dividend to be paid on the Investment Certificates without stating how the rate of dividend is to be determined. Since the rate of return is neither fixed nor predetermined, and since the government is not obliged to pay any return, the rate of return on MGIC cannot be categorized as interest. But still one does not know how or from where the dividend is derived. Nor is there a separate account into which this money goes. It is this element of *al-gharar* which makes the return from MGIC doubtful from the Islamic point of view. Moreover, the government Treasury receives all kinds of receipts including interest and it is from this common fund that the government pays the "dividend".

Based on the *mudarabah* principle, a predetermined agreed share of profit is allocated to the participants (70 per cent in the case of Family *takaful* and 60 per cent in the case of General Takaful). Family Takaful Revenue Account for 1987 shows that profit attributable to participants and transferred to the Family Takaful Fund was M$51,361 but only M$37,439 was actually credited. It is not stated why the amount credited was less than the 70 per cent share (M$51,361) shown in the revenue account.

The Annual Reports of Syarikat Takaful Malaysia do not clearly state how the rate of profit as at 30 June of each year is determined, i.e. whether the whole 70 per cent share or only a certain portion is distributed. It is, therefore, suggested that the Annual Reports and the Financial Statements should provide more information on these aspects so that the element of *gharar* and *jahl* that appear to be present may be completely eliminated. The Company has to convince its prospective clientele that it is working completely and fully in accordance with the rules of Shariah, and ensure that its business principles and practices, taken from Islamic precepts, have been operationalized in a manner that befits the competitive, modern business world. Such considerations obviously place limits on the company in the employment of its funds to earn profits. It cannot resort to money market transactions or deal in futures markets. Even for investment in shares, it has to go through Syarikat Al-Wakala Nominees Syndicate Berhad, a subsidiary company of Bank of Islam Malaysia.

It is really not fair to compare the performance of Syarikat Takaful Malaysia with the conventional insurance (companies) at this stage for the simple reason that for any insurance company three years is not enough even to break even particularly in the post-recessionary period of the economy, when the entire conventional insurance industry is going through a very rough passage.

Needless to say, the *takaful* insurance company would be able to perform better if there are more Islamic investment outlets in the country. This observation calls for the establishment of other Islamic financial institutions such as Islamic Mortgage Bank, Islamic Development Bank, Islamic Finance companies and investment houses which would complement the existing Islamic financial and business institutions.

The conclusion that one arrives at after reviewing the literature on Islamic insurance is that it would be more appropriate to organize the business of Islamic insurance along the lines of mutual insurance societies. The idea of mutuality is closer to the custom of blood-wite that was incorporated by the Prophet into Islam than the concept of *kafala* from which the word *takaful* has been derived. Moreover, many large mutual insurance societies are being operated successfully in USA and Europe whose organizational models can be adapted after eliminating the practice of *riba* and other unislamic elements from them.

NOTES

I gratefully acknowledge the helpful comments and suggestions made during the workshop especially those by Monzer Kahf and Syed Othman Alhabshi. I also owe a particular token of gratitude to Mohammad Fadzli Yusof, Managing Director of Takaful Malaysia Sdn. Bhd. for his co-operation and assistance in the collection of data for this study. The responsibility for all errors is mine.

1 Mustafa Ahmad Al-Zarqa, Sheikh Mustaka Jabbar, and Sheikh Siddique Darir (among many others) have written in Arabic on the subject of insurance in Islam. Mustafa Ahmad Al-Zarqa in 'Aqd al-Tamin (pp. 23–24) quoted by M. Muslehuddin, op. cit., (p. 153) holds the view that insurance, in all its forms, is permissible in Islam. Another distinguished Muslim scholar in this area is Muhammad Nijatullah Siddiqi whose work on Islamic Insurance was first published in Urdu in 1973 and later translated into English 'Insurance in Islamic Economy' as recently as 1985.

2 Mohammad Muslehuddin, *Insurance and Islamic Law*. Fourth edition (Lahore: Islamic Publications Ltd., 1982), pp. 6–7.

3 Entry on Insurance in *Encyclopedia Chambers*. New Edition, vol. 7, p. 617.

4 Mohammad Muslehuddin, op. cit., p. 15.

5 H. Baron, *Cooperative Insurance* (London: Macmillan, 1936), p. 40.

6 Entry on Insurance in *Encyclopedia Britannica*. Eleventh edition, vol. 14, p. 657, quoted by Mohammad Muslehuddin, op. cit., p. 34.

7 Ibid., p. 34.

8 Baron, op. cit., p. 25.

9 Mohammad Muslehuddin, op. cit., p. 36.

10 T. W. Juynboll, "Akila" in *Encyclopedia of Islam* vol. 1, Leyden & London, 1913–34, 39–40, quoted by Mohammad Muslehuddin, op. cit., p. 14.

11 Mohammad Muslehuddin, op. cit., p. 30.

The custom of blood-wite became the most important virtue of the Jahiliyya. It was adopted by Islam in accordance with the saying of the Prophet that "Virtues of the Jahiliyya are acted upon in Islam".

See also Burhan al-Din al-Marghinani, al-Hidaya, Lucknow, 1896–1902, vol. 4, Kitab al Ma'aqil, p. 642 and Ibu Nujaim, Bahr al-Ra'ik, vol. 8, p. 400. The custom of blood-wite is found cited in the agreement between emigrants from amongst the Quraish (followers of the Prophet) and the tribes of Madina (including

Jewish tribes) and drawn by the Prophet himself. Clause 3 of this document states:

> *The emigrants from among the Quraish shall be responsible for their ward and shall pay their blood money in mutual collaboration as heretofore, and shall secure the release of their prisoners by paying their ransom themselves, so that the mutual dealings between the believers be in accordance with the principles of recognized goodness and justice.*

Clause 12.a states,

> *And verily believers shall not leave any hard pressed with debts without helping him in recognised goodness with regard to ransom or blood-money.*

Also see M. Hamidullah, *The First Written Constitution in the World*. Third Ashraf edition (Lahore: S.H. Muhammad Ashraf, 1981) pp. 41–42 and 44–45.

12 Mohammad Muslehuddin, op. cit., p. 30.

13 B.D. Mudgett, et al., *Modern Business* (New York: Macmillan, 1940) p. 1.

14 Mohammad Muslehuddin, op. cit., p. 183 and also see H. Baron, op. cit., p. 37.

15 E.J. MacGillivary, and Denis Browne, *Insurance Law*, (London. 1953), para 1.

16 Baron, op. cit., p. 38.

17 Ibid., pp. 100–01.

18 Mohammad Muslehuddin, op. cit., p. 182, and on p. 189 the same author writes,

> Pure mutual institutions accord with the spirit of Islamic law.

19 M.N. Siddiqi, *Insurance in an Islamic Economy* (Leicestor, U.K.: The Islamic Foundation, 1983), p. 23.

20 Ibid., p. 22.

21 Ibid.

22 Ibid., p. 23.

23 Ibid., pp. 20–21.

24 Ibid., pp. 39–40.

25 Ibid., p. 40.

26 Ibid., pp. 14–15.

27 Ibid.

28 Ibid., p. 27–34.

29 Gross *takaful* contributions booked minus refunds equal gross *takaful* contributions received. Refunds in 1986, 1987 and 1988 were M$10,796, M$55,634 and M$186,266 respectively. Consequently gross *takaful* contributions were M$1,395,970 for 1986, M$4,634,924 and M$9,536,218 for 1987 and 1988 financial years respectively.

30 Gerard Soong, "Benefits of the Whole Life Policy", *New Straits Times*, 28 August 1988, p. 7.

31 Ibid.

9 LANDOWNERSHIP AND LAND USE IN THE MALAY COMMUNITY

Salleh Ismail

Introduction

Land[1] is one of the most important assets of the Malays, especially for those living in the rural areas of Malaysia.[2] The majority of the Malays live in the rural areas and about 80 per cent of them are traditional farmers. They farm on small pieces of land and utilize redundant family labour. To them, land is the most important factor input in their traditional, agricultural production. The traditional Malay farmers in Malaysia are involved mainly in the plantation of rubber, palm oil and coconut, cultivation of padi, fishing industry and in other[3] agricultural production. In 1988, it was estimated that 423,000 farmers were involved in traditional agricultural production (Economic Report 1988/89). The landholdings of these farmers, on the average, were much below the optimum size. For example, the average land size of rubber smallholders, the largest group, is only 2.3 hectares.

The paddy planters, the second largest group of smallholders, operate on landholdings that average about 2.2 acres. As a result, the rural sector of Malaysia is distinctly characterized by the persistent prevalence of poverty. In 1984, of the total 1.6 million rural households, 0.4 million (25 per cent) were below the poverty line. Of these, 85 per cent were Malay households (Fifth Malaysia Plan 1986–1990).

It is, therefore, often argued that low income and high incidence of poverty among the rural Malays is due to the smallness of their farms. The land is said to be too small to generate income above the subsistence level (Aziz 1965; Chamhuni 1975; Shukor 1985, 1986; Salleh 1986, 1987). According to a World Bank study (1980), a Malaysian rural household involved in the cultivation of paddy requires at least five acres of land in order to generate income above the subsistence level.

As for the rubber smallholders, the World Bank study suggests that a minimum land size of five hectares of mature rubber is required to generate income above the subsistence level. The study, however, discovered that more than 50 per cent of the paddy planters owned land of less than five acres, and more than 50 per cent of the rubber smallholders owned less than five hectares of mature rubber.

In 1987, a study was conducted by Salleh et al. to identify factors that determine the level of income and well-being of the people in the rural district of Tumpat, Kelantan. The study discovered that land was one of the more important factors influencing the income and well-being of the Tumpat households. The study also revealed that the average landholding of the Malay farmers in the district was small, measuring only about 1.5 acres per family. This finding reinforces the earlier work done by Ungku Aziz (1964) and Shukor Kassim (1986).

It has been argued that small landholdings is an important factor influencing low income and poverty among the rural farmers, especially the Malays. It has also been argued by many that land fragmentation among the Malays has led to the smallness of their landholdings, thereby causing diseconomies of scale in their agricultural production, and resulting in low incomes and high incidence of poverty within the Malay community.

In this chapter, land "fragmentation" refers to the subdivision of Malay land as guided by the Islamic law of inheritance, while the "subdivision" means dividing the ownership of a piece or pieces of land that originally belonged to one person, usually the parent, to a number of other individuals, usually the children and close relatives who inherit the land. It has been argued that Islamic inheritance law tends to reduce the farm land owned by the Malays to sizes that eventually become too small to be of any use.

There are sound theoretical reasonings behind this thesis. Nevertheless, it is pertinent to point out that there are other salient points of view that are equally plausible in explaining the low income and poverty among the rural households involved in traditional agriculture. In fact, there are research findings suggesting that the Islamic law of inheritance did not necessarily contribute to the smallness of the farm landholdings. Evidence to the contrary shows instances where inheritance could complement the farm size that farmers already have.

While the pattern of landownership and use is an important factor of traditional agricultural production, it is also important to recognize the fact that land available for cultivation is finite and the country's population is growing at a fairly rapid rate. Contrary to Malthusian theory (Bondestam and Bergstrom 1980) that states that subsistence will grow only at arithmetic progression while population will grow at geometric progression, the Malaysian agricultural sector has been able to sustain its population, even though much of its agricultural husbandry is characterized by small-scale, traditional farming.

Another aspect of land size and land use in the rural areas of Malaysia is the separation ownership and enterprise. Like many other countries, there are individuals in Malaysia who own huge pieces of farm land. Very often, the big landowners do not work on their lands; instead they lease them to farmers or groups of agricultural producers. For the small farmers, the rent they have to pay for the land could be exorbitant, causing severe strains on their incomes. There are, however, cases of landowners not collecting the rental from the farmers.

The primary aim of this chapter is to try to understand the pattern of landownership and land use among the Malays in Peninsular Malaysia, and to address the relationship between land fragmentation, brought about by the Islamic law of inheritance, and the pattern of landownership and use.

This study uses two sets of data. The first set of data is derived from secondary sources in the form of published information from the Agriculture Census, the Malaysia Five Year Plans, the Treasury Economic Reports and other published and unpublished research reports. The second data set refers to primary data derived from a survey of farmers in the district of Bachok, Kelantan.

Landownership

In Malaysia, the laws and regulations pertaining to landownership and use are varied. This is because each state in the country has autonomous right over the land within its boundary. In simple terms, landownership refers to the right of an individual or individuals over a piece of land. In broader and more general terms, landownership also covers not only the right over the land but also its relationship with the relevant administration and controlling institutions, the land control system, land levies and tax on income generated by the land, etc. Landownership also refers to regulations on rights over the land, transfer and use of the land, and the duration of ownership and extension of that duration (Malaysia National Land Code 1987).

Types of Ownership

In Malaysia, land can be owned either individually or jointly. There are instances of land becoming public property without the public having legal ownership over the land. The following are the various ways in which land can be acquired.

1. Temporary occupational licence (TOL)
2. Appropriation
3. Inheritance
4. *Waqf* (endowment)
5. Purchase
6. Illegal occupation

Temporary Occupational Licence Land. TOL refers to land designated by the state governments to individuals for single or multiple purposes. The state authorities may permit the temporary occupation of land under licence of:

1. state land
2. mining land not for the time being used for the purposes of mining
3. reserved land not for the time being used for the purposes for which it was reserved (Malaysia National Land Code 1987)

A significant number of Malay farmers in the rural areas of Malaysia are provided with TOL land by the state governments for agricultural purposes. The sizes of these TOL lands usually range from two to five acres.

There are many instances of these TOL lands, after many years of temporary right and use, being converted or upgraded to grants. Through this process, the ownership acquires a new status. The owners of the land are given the land grants so that they have the legal right to dispose as well as to apply to change the status of the land through conversion procedures.

Appropriated Land. The state governments, from time to time, will decide to appropriate state lands to residents of the state, particularly the locals. Individuals can apply for such land through the district land office subject to approval by the State Executive Council.

Inherited Land. The law of inheritance is the dominant factor in the ownership and use of land among the Malays in Malaysia. Broadly, the law of inheritance can be categorized into: (1) the customary law of inheritance, and (2) the Islamic law of inheritance.

The customary law of inheritance, or commonly known as Adat Pepateh, is unique to the Naning community in the state of Malacca and the Minang community in the state of Negri Sembilan. The customary law of inheritance is also practised by the aborigines of the country.

Adat Pepateh is unique and complicated. In simple terms, Adat Pepateh states that property in general, and land in particular, if acquired by an individual or his family, is treated as a belonging of the community and that it should be kept within the community.

The custom classifies landownership into two categories, i.e. Tanah Pesaka (ancestral land) and Harta Carian (acquired land). Inherited land are derived along the matrilineal line. Under Adat Pepateh, the female heir becomes the sole owner of the inherited land except when there is a written will stating otherwise.

The customary law defines acquired land as land acquired by a person other than by way of inheritance, such as through purchases and land appropriation. The custom allows the acquired land to be disposed of by the holder without any restriction. However, the acquired land, once devolved to female heirs, will automatically become ancestral land. The acquired land can only be disposed of while the holder is still alive. On the death of the holder, the acquired land has to be appropriated according to the customary law (Ahmad Ibrahim 1975; Yong 1975).

The Islamic law of inheritance is clearly described in the Qur'an. For the purpose of this chapter only a brief discussion of the law will be presented. As written in the Qur'an, the property of the deceased can be appropriated among the heirs only after all costs of burial and the will of the deceased are fulfilled (An-Nisa, verse 11). According to the Qur'an, there are five members of the family who definitely cannot be omitted from being the heirs: (1) husband; (2) wife; (3) natural children; (4) father, and (5) mother.

It is also stated in the Qur'an that the son's portion of the inherited property is two times that of the daughter's (An-Nisa, verse 11). As stated in the Qur'an, there are two groups or categories of heirs, i.e. Dzu Fardlin and 'Ashabah. A brief explanation of these two categories of heirs is presented in Appendix A.

Waqf Land. *Waqf*, according to Imam Abu Yusuf, is the appropriation of a particular article or property in such a manner as to subject it to the rule of Divine property, whence the appropriator's right to it is extinguished and it becomes the property of God by the advantage of it accruing to His creatures (Ahmad Ibrahim 1975).

In order for a *waqf* to be valid, the founder (*waqif*) must be capable of declaring his wishes and must be able to dispose of his property of his own will and pleasure, and the subject of the *waqf* must be such that it can be used perpetually. To be sure, land can be a *waqf* property. In fact, there are Malay *waqf* lands in Malaysia. *Waqf* lands include plots on which mosques and *madrasah* are constructed, graveyards, and public resting areas found in the rural areas. Collectively these *waqf* lands are small relative to the total land area owned by the Malays.

Purchase Land. Agricultural land that is not caveated can be purchased and sold. A contract to sell land is made in the same way as any other contract. As soon as there is an agreement for valuable consideration between the parties, there is a contract; and such a contract, although not recognized by the Land Codeunder registration, is enforceable under the Contract (Malay States) Ordinance, 1950. Many of the agricultural landownerships are derived through purchases.

Illegally Occupied Land. Very often state lands are illegally occupied. In the rural areas of Malaysia, illegally occupied state lands are utilized for agricultural purposes. The acreage of illegally occupied lands relative to the total agricultural land is small.

Land Use

Peninsular Malaysia comprises an area of 13.2 million hectares. In 1987, it was estimated that 30 per cent of the total land was utilized for agricultural purposes. The agricultural lands were used for planting rubber, palm oil, cocoa, paddy, coconut, pepper, pineapple, tobacco and others, as can be seen in Table 9.1.

Rubber, palm oil and cocoa are the primary commodities of the country which are produced for export purposes. Rubber is the main agricultural commodity of the country, both in terms of production volume and the number of members of households involved in the production. In 1988, M$5.0 billion worth of trade was generated by the rubber industry which employed about 423,000 farmers. About 70 per cent of the country's rubber production is contributed by the smallholders who are mostly Malay farmers. However, in 1988, the smallholders were producing only 1,135 kilogrammes per hectare compared with 1,527 kilogrammes per hectare produced by the estate sector (Table 9.2). It is also pertinent to note that the average landholdings of the smallholders in 1988 were less than 2.3 hectares, and 52 per cent of the smallholdings were below two hectares.

Palm oil is Malaysia's second largest export commodity. In 1988, the palm oil industry produced about five million metric tonnes of crude palm oil and 610,000 metric tonnes of palm kernel oil (Table 9.3). The industry was able to generate export earnings of M$4.6 million. However, the smallholders account for only 8.0 per cent of the total output.

TABLE 9.1
Crops in Malaysia
(Hectares)

Item	1981	1983	1985	1987	1988
Rubber	2,006,070	1,971,260	1,959,000	188,300	187,000
Oil Palm	1,117,900	1,253,000	1,464,900	168,600	174,600
Cocoa	158,800	215,100	258,000	–	357,000
Paddy	767,640	764,200	775,220	609,600	596,100
Coconut	318,000	324,000	274,000	–	–
Pepper	13,405	11,360	10,000	–	862,200
Pineapple	11,600	11,050	10,250	–	–
Vegetable	12,250	7,620	8,090	–	–
Orchards[1]	87,800	90,000	94,000	–	–
Tobacco	14,290	9,440	9,190	12,300	9,700

[1] Includes fruit trees, bananas, and watermelon but excludes pineapple.

SOURCE: Various government agencies.

TABLE 9.2
Production of Rubber

	1986	1987	1988
Area of Production ('000 He)	1,702	1,883	1,870
Production kg (per hectare)			
Smallholders	1,072	1,107	1,135
Estate	1,497	1,531	1,527
Production ('000 metric tonnes)	1,539	1,581	1,612
Smallholders	1,042	1,083	1,145
Estate	497	498	467
World Production (%)	34.7	33.8	33.3

SOURCE: Economic Report 1989/90.

TABLE 9.3
Production of Palm Oil

	1986	1987	1988
Area of Production ('000 He)	1,543	1,686	1,746
Production ('000 metric tonnes)			
Crude Palm Oil (CPU)	4,544	4,532	5,000
Palm Kernel Oil	590	576	610
World Production (%)	60.7	59.0	59.2

SOURCE: Economic Report 1989/90.

Rice ranks third in terms of land use and employment in the agricultural sector. In 1988, 150,000 households were involved in the cultivation of rice on an area of about 596,000 hectares. The average paddy landholding is estimated at 1.25 hectares. It is also of interest to note that about 52 per cent of the paddy planters cultivate the crop on rented land.

Idle Land

"Idle land" is defined as agricultural land not put to good use for three consecutive years. The definition includes paddy land planted with a single crop where there

TABLE 9.4
Idle Padi Land Under the Ministry of Agriculture
(Hectares)

State	Continuous	Off-Season	Total
Perlis	–	1,880	1,880
Kedah	4,358	288	4,646
Pulau Pinang	5,633	840	6,473
Perak	9,027	2,744	11,771
Selangor	1,427	298	1,725
Negeri Sembilan	9,386	5,040	14,426
Melaka	3,250	3,334	6,584
Johor	1,682	881	2,563
Pahang	9,989	1,632	11,621
Terengganu	7,028	10,102	17,130
Kelantan	20,010	62,039	82,049
Total	71,790	89,078	160,868

Padi land	: 160,868 He
FELCRA	: 565,140 He
Various Agencies	: 163,997 He
Total	: 890,005 He

should be double cropping, and paddy land where there are untapped off-season facilities. In 1982, 890,000 hectares of land were left idle. Of the total idle land, 160,863 hectares were paddy land (Table 9.4).

There are various reasons why agricultural land is left idle. These include (1) topographical factors, such as types of soil, and inadequate infrastructure; (2) economic factors, which include the small size of farm holdings, and shortage of labour; (3) legal factors which dictate that only particular crops be grown; and (4) socio-demographic factors which include old age, migration of youthful population and inadequate technology.

Subdivision of Ownership and Land Fragmentation

Subdivision of landownership can take place through two methods: (1) transactions, i.e. sale and purchase; (2) transmission to heirs after the demise of the legal owner. In practice, it is observed that the latter often leads to a significant net increase in the total number of owners of the lot. This is because the Islamic law of inheritance requires distribution of the deceased's land between the surviving spouse and the children in various proportions. Though legally the original lot is subdivided into two or more separate lots with individual owners and new lot numbers, the usual result is that the lot remains physically intact although it may be owned by a number of co-owners with legally registered shares in the title.

A "fragmented farm" is defined as a farm composed of more than one parcel[4] where at least one parcel is not contiguous with the rest. More often than not, it is assumed that a "fragmented" farm indicates a stage in the process of breaking up the original holding and is a sign of the influence of the Islamic law of inheritance. There is evidence which suggests that the above assumption is wrong for the following reasons: (1) it confuses what happens to the ownership of a piece of land upon inheritance (which is subdivided into shares) and what happens to the operation of that land; and (2) subdivision of ownership upon inheritance does not cause the degree of fragmentation to increase, and it may even reduce it (Lim 1976).

Usually fragmentation takes place not through subdivision but through growth in the farm size. If a man already has a parcel of land, he may acquire another parcel through inheritance and marriage (if he chooses to operate both parcels, his farm is now bigger and fragmented) or through squatting, purchase, lease, etc. As a consequence, and contrary to the common view, fragmented farms are often larger than average.

The findings of the study on farm fragmentation in the Muda district, Kedah, (Lim et al. 1976) show that the degree of fragmentation is not as severe as in some countries where action has been taken to consolidate the scattered parcels into compact farms (Table 9.5).

Many studies pertaining to farm fragmentation assume that there is a great loss of time in a highly fragmented farm when moving labour and machinery from parcel to parcel during the working day. However, it is of importance to note that what matters is the size of the individual parcels in a fragmented farm rather than their number.

For example, given a job which requires a total of eight days' work, it makes little difference whether the eight days are spent on a single large parcel or on eight separate small parcels. Provided that the size of each parcel is sufficiently large, there may be relatively little disadvantage in a fragmented farm except for longer journeys required for inspection trips to each parcel. The research conducted by Lim et al. found that the sizes of the parcels are reasonably big (Table 9.6). Therefore, farm operations should first be studied to determine at what degree of fragmentation diseconomies become sufficiently severe to justify reorganization before one decides on the consolidation of fragmented farm lands for increased efficiency. On the basis of all this, we may refute the argument that the Islamic law of inheritance has fragmented the rural farm land into uneconomically-sized pieces.

TABLE 9.5
Farm Fragmentation in the Muda Irrigation Scheme Area, 1976

No. of Parcels	No. of Farms	Percentage of Farms
1	24,652	54.0
2	10,862	23.8
3	4,941	10.8
4	2,478	5.4
5	1,247	2.7
6	667	1.5
7	368	0.8
8–10	358	0.8
11–15	78	0.2
16 and over	16	0.0
Total	45,667	100.0

SOURCE: Lim Teck Ghee et al., "Land Tenure in the Muda Irrigation Area: Final Report, Part 2: Findings" (1976).

TABLE 9.6
Farm Size Category by Number of Parcels, Number of Farms and Mean Number of Parcels Per Farm, Muda Irrigation Scheme Area, 1976

Size of Farms (*relong*)[1]	Total No. of Parcels	Total No. of Farms	Mean No. of Parcels Per Farm
Below 1.0	3,415	3,053	1.12
1.0 – 2.9	16,874	13,138	1.28
3.0 – 5.9	23,134	14,046	1.65
6.0 – 8.9	16,168	7,077	2.28
9.0 –11.9	10,716	3,983	2.69
12.0 –14.9	6,329	1,857	3.41
15.0 and over	11,759	2,513	4.68
Missing Data	16		
Total	88,411	45,667	1.94

[1] There is no fixed equivalent of a *relong*. *Relong* in various states have different standards. In addition, one *relong* of very good paddy land is less than a *relong* of poorer quality land.

SOURCE: Lim Teck Ghee et al., ibid.

The widespread subdivision of ownership of paddy land in the Muda area in itself is not necessarily undesirable. Since ownership of the paddy land is an important determinant of income for the farmers, a subdivision of the ownership of paddy land among farmers would result in a wider and more equitable distribution of income than would otherwise be the case. However, if the original holding was already small the new owners will not be able to derive much benefit from their tiny shares. The actual result of such extreme subdivision of ownership, therefore, may well be shared poverty (Lim et al. 1976).

Landownership and Use in the District of Bachok, Kelantan

A survey was conducted on 250 households involved in the cultivation of tobacco and paddy in the district of Bachok, Kelantan. The purpose of the survey was to collect information pertaining to landownership and use, and the income status of the Malay farmers.

The state of Kelantan is located at the northeastern part of Peninsular Malaysia. It covers an area of 5,713 square miles. The population of the state was enumerated at 893,800 with a total number of 172,000 households (Census of Population and Housing, Malaysia 1980). The state of Kelantan consists of nine administrative districts. The district of Bachok is located in the northeastern part of Kelantan. It is situated to the southeast of Kota Bahru, the capital of Kelantan, and its eastern shore faces the South China Sea.

Bachok is one of the poorest districts in Peninsular Malaysia. The major economic activities of the households in the district are farming and fishing. The main crops planted in the district are paddy and tobacco. The landholdings of these farmers are small with more than 80 per cent of the farm lands falling below five acres. Coconut palms are found around the farmers' houses, but of late this crop is of little economic value to the farmers.

Most of the fishing activities are carried out in the coastal areas. Like most fishermen in the state, many of them operate with rented fishing vessels and gear. The remuneration for the labour they put in are small relative to the returns that accrue to the owners of fishing vessels and gear.

Most of the farmers and fishermen in this district are poor. Their living conditions have not shown any significant improvement over the last ten years or so. In fact, there are indications which suggest that the conditions have worsened. This, to a certain extent, could well explain the severe problem of out-migration experienced by the district, which has resulted in insufficient labour and the numerous patches of paddy land left idle.

The district of Bachok in the state of Kelantan was chosen for the study because more than 90 per cent of the population are Malays and all of them are Muslims. The majority of them are farmers and fishermen and most of them are poor. For these farmers, the land that they own is the most important factor in their traditional farming activities. The district of Bachok was chosen also because it is one of the few districts involved in the cultivation of tobacco, and tobacco is one of the rare crops that yield high returns.

In the district of Bachok, similar to other districts in Kelantan or other districts in the rural areas of Peninsular Malaysia, the size of land owned by the farmers is small. Based on the information that was obtained from the farmers and the officers of the district office, it appears that the land owned by the farmers have undergone a series of subdivision through the process of inheritance. However, there are also many instances where the subdivided, inherited lands added more land to the farmers' existing farms, thus increasing their farm size.

Findings

As mentioned earlier, land is an essential factor in traditional agricultural production. It is an integral asset of the rural Malays. The incomes and well-being of the rural Malays, very often, are measured by the acreage and quality of land they own. The Agricultural Census 1988 provides valuable information on the status of landownership and land use of the farmers in the state of Kelantan.

Table 9.7 briefly describes the types of landownership in Bachok, Pasir Puteh, Pasir Mas, and Kota Bahru districts in Kelantan. Generally, there are three types of landownership, namely Grant, TOL, and "Others". "Others" refers to illegally occupied land, sharecropping land, rented land, etc. On the average, lands belonging to farmers in these districts are small, ranging between 2.22 to 3.46 acres for Grant land; 2.55 to 4.80 acres for TOL land; and 1.39 to 4.22 acres for "Others". It is important to note that these sizes are too small to generate income above the subsistence level, assuming that they are used for traditional agricultural purposes.

Kelantan is very much rural in character compared to most other states in Peninsular Malaysia. The economy of the state is essentially agricultural and the major crops cultivated in the state are paddy, rubber, oil palm and tobacco. Tobacco is planted in the district of Pasir Mas and the coastal districts of Kota Bahru, Tumpat, Pasir Puteh, and Bachok.

Except for the estate sector where the Federal Land Development Authority (FELDA), and the Kelantan State Economic Authority (KESEDAR) are involved in planting oil palm and rubber on a commercial scale, the agricultural practices in the state are still traditional. Agricultural production is carried out on a small-scale basis, characterized by small land area and redundant family labour. In fact, the actual average land owned by the farmers is much smaller than that reported in Table 9.7. This is because a piece of land may well belong to a number of owners through subdivision. As can be seen in Table 9.8, the average land size in the four districts is small, ranging between 1.0 to 1.6 acres. The rented land and the land left idle are significant in acreage, ranging from 33–41 per cent, 9–20 per cent and 15–28 per cent, respectively.

TABLE 9.7
Landownership in Selected Districts of Kelantan
(Acres)

District	Ownership		
	Grant	TOL	Others
Bachok	7,412 (2.48)	139 (4.80)	315 (1.39)
Pasir Putih	8,198 (3.27)	449 (2.72)	637 (1.87)
Pasir Mas	10,726 (3.46)	243 (2.55)	275 (4.22)
Kota Bahru	13,881 (2.22)	194 (3.20)	173 (2.71)
Total	40,217	1,025	1,400

Note: Figures in parentheses refer to average land size.
Some states in Malaysia still use Imperial measures, i.e. acres instead of hectares, and official statistics reflect this difference.

SOURCE: Agriculture Census of Peninsular Malaysia, 1985.

TABLE 9.8
Landownership and Land Use in Selected Districts of Kelantan
(Acres)

District	Own Land	Average	Rented Land	Idle
Bachok	14,980	1.2	6,570	2,654
Pasir Mas	27,447	1.6	13,684	6,350
Pasir Putih	22,557	1.6	13,684	6,350
Kota Bahru	23,433	1.0	12,472	3,533
Total	88,417		46,410	18,887

SOURCE: Agriculture Census of Peninsular Malaysia, 1985.

TABLE 9.9
Family Land Size

Acres	Frequency	Percentage
0	35	14
0.0 < 1.0	66	25
1.0 – 2.5	104	42
2.6 – 3.5	18	7
3.6 – 4.5	19	8
4.6 – 6.0	4	2
Above 6.0	4	2
Total	250	100

Table 9.9 provides a profile of the landholdings of the 250 tobacco growers interviewed. Of the total respondents, 35 (14 per cent) do not own land. The land that they use for the cultivation of tobacco and other crops was either rented, illegally owned or operated on a revenue sharing basis (better known as the *pawah* system). The data also reveals that the majority (82 per cent) of the tobacco growers own land within the category of 4.5 acres and below, with 25 per cent in the category of one acre and below, while 42 per cent fall in the category of one to 2.5 acres. Most of the tobacco growers in the district of Bachok operated on small pieces of landholdings, an important characteristic that could well explain their low income status.

Table 9.10 describes the nature of landownership of the 250 tobacco growers. Of the 250 respondents, 55 (22 per cent) indicated that the land they own were inherited, 43 (17 per cent) of them had purchased the land they own, while 19 (8 per cent) work on rented land.

The 250 respondents interviewed are all farmers. Their main source of income is from the sale of tobacco leaves. Besides tobacco, the farmers are also involved in the production of other cash crops such as paddy, coconut, vegetables and fruits. Crops other than tobacco are planted on a small-scale basis and are mainly consumed within the households.

The agricultural produce consumed within the households is substantial, and, if sold, will form a significant component of the household income. In a study conducted by Salleh (1987) on the *Determinants of the Level of Living of the Residents of Tumpat, Kelantan*, it was found that the non-cash income, if converted to cash, will form up to 20 to 30 per cent of the total family income.

Table 9.11 presents the income distribution of the 250 Bachok households

TABLE 9.10
Type of Landownership

	Type of Ownership	Frequency	Percentage
I	Temporary Occupation Licence (TOL)	3	1.2
II	Rent	19	7.6
III	Inherited	55	22.0
IV	Purchased	43	17.2
V	Illegal	1	0.4
VI	TOL & Purchased	1	0.4
VII	Rent & Inherited	38	15.2
VIII	Rent & Purchased	23	9.2
IX	Inherited & Purchased	25	10.0
X	Inherited & Illegal	1	0.4
XI	Purchased & Illegal	1	0.4
XII	Rent, Inherited & Purchased	17	6.8
XIII	Inherited, Purchased & Illegal	1	0.4
XIV	Missing Value	22	8.8
	Total	250	100.0

that were interviewed. The family monthly incomes of the tobacco farmers in the district are low. Of the 250 households interviewed, 59 (24 per cent) of the households obtained monthly incomes of M$100 and below, while 133 (53 per cent) of the households received incomes between M$113 and M$292. Taking a monthly income of M$300 as the poverty line for the rural household in Peninsular Malaysia, 192 (77 per cent) of the total respondents are living in poverty. Of the total 57 households not living in poverty, only 16 (6.4 per cent) are in the M$500 and above monthly income group.

To reflect the true or more accurate income status of the respondents, their reported family incomes were adjusted by 30 per cent. On the basis of the adjusted monthly family income, it appears that 154 (62 per cent) of the respondents are living in poverty, while 40 (16 per cent) respondents had monthly incomes of M$500 and above.

Revenue derived from the sale of tobacco is the main source of income for all the 250 respondents, who are mainly tobacco growers. As all the tobacco leaves are for commercial purposes, the income reported from the sale of tobacco is, therefore, not adjusted for household consumption. The income and its distribution generated from this crop are illustrated in Table 9.12. Annual family incomes (column 1 of the table) are derived mainly from the sale of tobacco.

TABLE 9.11
Current Family Income
(In Malaysian dollars)

Family Annual Income	Adjusted Family Monthly Income	Adjusted Family Annual Income	Family Monthly Income	Frequency	Percentage
41	3	53	5	1	0.4
99	8	129	11	1	0.4
20	17	260	22	3	1.2
300	25	390	33	3	1.2
400	33	520	43	2	0.8
450	38	585	48	1	0.8
500	42	650	54	4	1.6
700	58	910	76	2	0.8
800	67	1,040	87	6	2.4
1,000	83	1,300	108	35	14.0
1,200	100	1,560	130	1	0.4
1,350	113	1,755	146	1	0.4
1,500	125	1,950	163	21	8.4
2,000	167	2,600	217	62	24.8
2,500	208	3,250	271	11	4.4
3,000	250	3,900	325	34	13.6
3,009	251	3,912	326	1	0.4
3,500	292	4,550	380	3	1.2
4,000	333	5,200	433	14	5.6
4,500	375	5,850	488	3	1.2
5,000	417	6,500	542	20	8.0
6,000	500	7,800	650	9	3.6
7,000	583	9,100	759	3	1.2
7,500	625	9,750	813	1	0.4
8,000	667	10,400	867	3	1.2
N.A.	–	–	–	4	1.6
Total				250	100.0

As reported in Table 9.12, only 60 respondents (24.8 per cent) are in the monthly income category of M$100 and below derived from the sales of tobacco, while many of the respondents (54 per cent) are able to generate a monthly income of M$100 to M$300 from the same source. Only a small number of the respondents (54) are able to generate a monthly income of over M$300 (47 within

TABLE 9.12
Family Income from the Sale of Tobacco
(In Malaysian dollars)

Annual Family Income from Tobacco	Family Monthly Income	Frequency	Percentage
0	0	1	0.4
3	–	1	0.4
150	13	2	0.8
200	17	2	0.8
250	21	1	0.4
300	25	1	0.4
400	33	2	0.8
500	42	5	2.0
600	50	2	0.8
700	58	2	0.8
800	67	6	2.4
1,000	83	35	14.0
1,200	100	2	0.8
1,350	113	1	0.4
1,500	125	2	8.0
2,000	167	6	24.8
2,500	208	1	4.0
3,000	250	3	14.4
3,500	292	3	1.2
4,000	333	1	5.6
4,500	375	3	1.2
5,000	417	21	8.4
6,000	500	9	3.6
7,000	583	3	1.2
7,500	625	1	0.4
8,000	667	3	1.2
9,999	–	2	0.8
		250	100.0

the range of M$301 to M$500, and seven in the range of M$501 and above).

Some interesting observations may be made by comparing the percentage contribution of tobacco sales to the family income. As shown in Table 9.13, 24 per cent of the income derived from tobacco are in the category of less than M$100 a month, while only nine per cent of the respondents actually belong to this income category. This suggests that in the lower income group, much of the income

TABLE 9.13
Comparison Between Family Income and Income Derived from Tobacco

Income Group	Monthly Family Income (%)	Monthly Income From Tobacco (%)
<$100	9	24
$100–$300	52	24
$301–$500	22	20
>$500	14	1

is derived from sources other than the sale of tobacco. Within the M$100–M$300 and the M$301 to M$500 income groups, the percentage differential between that contributed by tobacco sales to family incomes is marginal, implying that the contribution of tobacco sales to the aggregate family income is significant for the "middle" income groups.

The high income group (M$500 and above) illustrates a different picture. Of the total 14 per cent of the respondents whose household incomes are in this category, only 1 per cent depended on the cultivation and sale of tobacco. This means that other sources of income are of greater importance to the high income group.

The land used for cultivation of tobacco in the district of Bachok is relatively small in size (Table 9.14). It was found that 228 or 94 per cent of the

TABLE 9.14
Land Use for Tobacco

Size	Frequency	Percentage
<1.0	109	45
1.0–2.5	119	49
2.6–3.5	3	1
3.6–4.5	9	5
4.6–6.0	1	–
Above 6.0	1	–
Total	242	100

TABLE 9.15
Family Income by Land Size

Income ($)	Land Size (in acres) <1.0	1.0–2.0	2.1–3.0	3.1–4.0	>4.0	Total
< 100	9	8	2	0	0	19
	(47.4)	(42.1)	(10.5)	(0.0)	(0.0)	(9.2)
	13.4	8.8	10.5	0.0	0.0	
	4.3	3.9	1.0	0.0	0.0	
100 – 300	40	52	7	4	5	108
	(37.0)	(48.1)	(6.5)	(3.7)	(4.6)	(52.2)
	59.7	57.1	36.8	33.3	27.8	
	19.3	25.1	3.4	1.9	2.4	
301 – 500	16	17	7	4	3	47
	(34.0)	(36.2)	(14.9)	(8.5)	(6.4)	(22.7)
	23.9	18.7	36.8	33.3	16.7	
	7.7	8.2	8.4	1.9	1.4	
> 500	2	14	3	4	10	33
	(6.1)	(42.4)	(9.1)	(12.1)	(33.3)	(15.9)
	3.0	15.4	15.8	33.3	55.6	
	1.0	6.8	1.4	1.9	4.8	
Total	67	91	19	12	18	207
	(32.4)	(44.0)	(9.2)	(5.8)	(8.7)	(100.0)

Notes: There are 43 missing cases. Values in parentheses are percentages.

respondents cultivated their crops on land areas of 2.5 acres and below; of these, 109 (or 45 per cent) had less than an acre each. Although tobacco cultivation yields much higher returns than most other crops, the land size is too small to generate an income above the subsistence level.

The size and quality of land are two important factors in determining the level of income of the farmers. As variables pertaining to the quality of land are not available, the size of land is used as the more important determinant of income. Table 9.15 shows how the size of land is correlated to the household income of tobacco growers in the district of Bachok. Low-income households tend to own two acres of land or less. Most households in the income category of M$100 to M$300, (85 per cent or 92 households) also own two acres or less. Only 16 (15 per cent) of them own land exceeding two acres. In the high income group, 17 respondents

TABLE 9.16
Landownership and Idle Land for Selected Districts in Kelantan

District	Land Owned (acres)	Idle land	Percentage
Bachok	14,980	2,654	18
Pasir Mas	27,447	6,350	23
Pasir Puteh	22,557	6,350	28
Kota Bahru	23,433	3,533	15
Total	88,417	18,887	21

SOURCE: Agriculture Census 1986, Ministry of Agriculture, Malaysia.

(54 per cent) own more than two acres of land each. There are, however, 14 households in this income category who own land between one to two acres, and the high income is presumably derived from sources other than the cultivated land.

Idle Land

While land represents an important factor input in agriculture, idle agricultural land is not an unusual sight in the rural areas of Peninsular Malaysia, especially in the state of Kelantan. A sample of the magnitude of agricultural land left idle in the state of Kelantan can be seen in Table 9.16. Of the total 88,417 acres of farm land owned by the farmers, 18,887 acres (21 per cent) were left idle. Most of these idle lands were once used for the cultivation of paddy.

The incidence of idle agricultural lands in the rural areas is thus alarmingly high. If these idle lands were to be cultivated, they could generate increased output and employment in the rural sector.

The Economics of Land and Agricultural Production

Land is the most important factor input in traditional farming activities. Its size, quality and location are the three important criteria determining the productivity and value of land.

In Malaysia, it has been established that returns from land used in agriculture has always been low. This is generally true both in the Less Developed Countries (LDCs) and in the developed countries. This is one of the reasons why the agricultural sector is sometimes heavily subsidized, even in a highly developed country like Japan. In Malaysia, the subsidies and infrastructural support provided to traditional farmers are huge, yet returns from their farm production are low.

There are many explanations for the low returns derived from land used in the traditional agricultural sector. Small farm size is one of the explanations. There are several equally valid reasons, which include (1) rising costs of factor and intermediate inputs, (2) deteriorating terms of trade of the agricultural sector *vis-à-vis* the non-agricultural sector (3) inelastic supply conditions, and (4) price instability.

Much would, however, depend on the types of crops grown and the types of agricultural husbandry practised. Crops like tobacco, for example, can generate high income even when it is planted on one acre of land. The report by the Malaysian Tobacco Authority indicates that an acre of tobacco cultivation can generate a revenue of about M$6,200 to M$8,000 a year, compared to an acre of paddy cultivation which can only generate revenue equal to one third that of tobacco (*Berita Tembakau* 1988).

The non-farm occupations in the rural areas have become increasingly important as a source of income for the rural households. In fact, a number of studies have been carried out to determine the effect of non-farm jobs on rural households' income. The studies found that farmers or farm families with higher income tend to work longer hours in the non-farm sector than on their farm land (Jonathan Haughton 1987).

The traditional agricultural sector of Peninsular Malaysia has always been associated with surplus labour and underemployment. Like many other LDCs, Malaysia experiences high population growth rates (Table 9.17). At the same time,

TABLE 9.17
Population Size and Rates of Change, Malaysia, 1947–80

	Population Size ('000)	
Year	Malaysia	Peninsular Malaysia
1947	5,775	4,908
1957	7,383	6,279
1960	8,036	6,837
1970	10,439	8,810
1980	13,136	10,945
1980 (Revised)	13,745	11,427
Average Annual Growth Rate (per cent)		
1947–57	2.5	2.5
1957–60	2.8	2.8
1960–70	2.6	2.5
1970–80	2.3	2.2

SOURCE: Population and Housing Census of Malaysia, 1980.

the modern industrial sector is unable to absorb the surplus labour emanating from the rural areas (Fong 1987). Consequently, those who choose to remain in the rural areas usually work on family farms. Hence, there is still a considerable amount of underemployment which has led to low productivity and poor returns.

Income and wages are much higher in the non-agricultural sectors. As a result, the rural population, especially the economically active segment, tends to move out of agriculture and venture into the industrial sector in the urban areas. Only the aged, the under-aged and females remain in the rural areas; hence the idle land phenomenon and economic stagnation there.

Conclusion

For the Malay farmers in the rural areas of Malaysia, land is the most important factor input in traditional agriculture. Most of the Malay-owned land in the rural areas are used for agricultural purposes.

Agricultural land belonging to Malay farmers are generally small. The rubber smallholders constitute the largest group of Malay farmers. It is estimated that 52 per cent of their rubber holdings are less than two hectares. The second largest group of Malay farmers are the paddy planters, with an average farm size of 1.25 hectares. Their farm sizes are clearly much below the optimum.

The size and quality of land used in traditional agriculture is an important factor determining the income of the rural Malay households. Rural household income is assumed to be inversely related to land size. Based on this assumption, many are of the opinion that low income and persistent prevalence of poverty among Malays in the rural areas are caused by, among other factors, low agricultural productivity associated with small farm land. Some have extended this argument further by asserting that the existence of small Malay farms was due to the Islamic inheritance laws. However, several studies conducted by a number of researchers have suggested that land fragmentation has helped bring about equitable income distribution among the farm families. The implication is that land fragmentation is not the real cause of low productivity and income among the rural Malay farmers. The issue at hand is how efficiently can these small pieces of scattered land be utilized to extract the maximum returns out of them.

In response to the issue of land fragmentation, the Government of Malaysia, through its agencies, has adopted the "mini-estates" approach in rural agricultural production. Under this scheme, the small farm lands are integrated into a bigger entity to grow commercial crops, managed by a team of skilled managers. This approach helps overcome the problems of redundant labour, and absence of scale economies in traditional agriculture. The landowners whose lands are used in the mini estate become shareholders of the estate. The equity of the shareholders are determined by the sizes of their land.

It is also important to note that through this concept, the producers, or more appropriately, the farm managers, will have a better bargaining position in the pricing and marketing of farm products. It is hoped that this will result in better and more stable prices of farm products.

From the discussion thus far, it is therefore inaccurate to suggest that the Islamic law of inheritance necessarily contributes to low productivity in agriculture. The real issue of land fragmentation and subdivision of ownership is the inefficient management of small farm lands.

Nevertheless, it is important to recognize that the supply of agricultural land is finite, while the population of the country, especially in the rural areas, is growing rapidly. As a result, we can expect the man: land ratio to increase over time, resulting in increased scarcity of land for agricultural production in future. It is, therefore, imperative that continuous efforts are directed at limiting the fragmentation of agricultural land and ensuring that these lands are strategically conglomerated in the production process.

APPENDIX A

Dzu Fardlin

There are six types of heirs in the Dzu Fardlin. Each type is entitled to receive different portions of the inherited property. According to the Qur'an, the types of heirs and their apportion are as follows:

a. The heirs who are entitled to receive half ($\frac{1}{2}$) of the inheritance include:
   1. The daughter, when she is the only child.
   2. The daughter of the son (granddaughter), when she is the only child of the son.
   3. The only sister from the same father, and without any brother and in the absence of No. 1 and 2.
   4. The husband in the absence of children or grandson from the son.

b. Those who are entitled to receive a quarter ($\frac{1}{4}$) of the inheritance. There are two categories of heirs in this group:
   1. The husband, when there is a son or grandson from the son.
   2. Wife or wives in the absence of any child or grandchild from the son.

c. The heirs who are entitled to one eighth ($\frac{1}{8}$) of the inheritance: The wife or wives when there are sons or sons of the sons (grandsons).

d. The heirs who are entitled to two-thirds ($\frac{2}{3}$) of the inheritance. There are four categories of heirs in this group:
   1. Two or more daughters in the absence of sons.
   2. Two or more daughters from the son (granddaughters) when the granddaughters do not have brothers or daughters of their son.
   3. Two or more sisters from the same mother in the absence of daughters or grandchildren from the sons.
   4. Two or more sisters from the same father in the absence of brother and those in No. 1, 2 and 3.

e. The heirs who are entitled to one-third ($\frac{1}{3}$) of the inheritance:
   1. The mother, in the absence of children or grandson from the sons, or in the absence of two sibling brothers or sisters from the same father and mother or from the same father or mother.
   2. Two or more brothers and sister from the same mother.

f. The heirs who are entitled to one sixth ($\frac{1}{6}$) of the inheritance. There are six categories of heirs who belong in this group:
   1. The mother, when there are children, or grandsons from the sons, or when there are two or more brothers or sisters.
   2. The father, when there are children or grandchildren from the son.
   3. The grandmother in the absence of mother.
   4. The grand daughters from the son if the son has a sister from the same mother.
   5. Sisters from the same father if there is a sister from the same mother.
   6. Grandfather in the absence of father.

'Ashabah

The heirs that belong to the 'Ashabah are those that do not belong to the six groups of heirs mentioned in the Dzu Fardlin. The heirs that belong to this group are divided into two categories: those who will inherit all of the inheritance in the absence of the Dzu Fardlin; and those who will receive the balance of the inheritance after the Dzu Fardlin have taken their portions of the shares.

The heirs who belong to the 'Ashabah are:

1. The sons.
2. The sons of the son (grandsons) of the sons (great-grandsons) and so forth.

3. The father.
4. Grandfather, great-grandfather and so forth.
5. Brothers from the same father and mother.
6. Brothers of same father.
7. The sons of brothers of same father and mother.
8. The sons of brothers of same father.
9. Uncle of same father and mother.
10. Uncle of same father.
11. Sons of uncles of same mother and father.
12. Sons of uncles of same father.
13. Men who free slaves.
14. Women who free slaves.

The above listing of heirs are in the sequence of priority, with No. 1 as the highest order of priority. Once a particular heir who belongs to a group, for example group No. 1, inherits a property, the subsequent groups will automatically not be eligible. However, there is an exception to this rule which involves grandfather and brothers from the same mother and father or from the same father. It is also a rule that the father and grandfather as heirs belonging to the Dzu Fardlin can also belong to the 'Ashabah in the absence of sons or grandsons.

The portions of shares and the conditions of eligibility to 'Ashabah are as follows:

1. An 'Ashabah will receive the whole of the inheritance when the deceased has no other heirs.
2. Properties are divided equally among the heirs when the heirs belong to the same or similar status, for example among the two sons, among brothers, etc.
3. An 'Ashabah will receive all the balance of inheritance already received by heirs of Dzu Fardlin.
4. If there are females of the same status as the 'Ashabah, the males will get two shares and the female will get one share.
5. An 'Ashabah will not receive anything, if nothing is left after the heirs of Dzu Fardlin have received their shares.

NOTES

1 Land in this chapter refers to agricultural land, unless otherwise stated.

2 In this chapter, Malaysia refers to Peninsular Malaysia.

3 Include other agricultural farmers such as oil palm smallholders, pepper smallholders, pineapple and tobacco farmers, and livestock and poultry farmers.

4 Parcel refers to a piece of land operated by a single operator under a single tenurial arrangement, whether as owner or as tenant. A parcel can be a part of a lot or can comprise the whole lot; it is also possible for an operator to work two continuous parcels on the same lot if they represent the shares of different owners and so are subject to different tenurial arrangements. It has been used as the unit of enquiry into the operation of paddy land.

REFERENCES

Ahmad Ibrahim. *Islamic Law in Malaysia*, edited by Shirley Gordan. Kuala Lumpur: Malaysia Sociological Research Institute Ltd., 1975.

Bondestam, J. and T.S. Bergstrom. *Poverty and Population Control*. London: Academic Press Inc. Ltd., 1980.

Chamhuri Siwar. *Kehendak dan Bentuk Reformasi Tanah di Malaysia*. Kuala Lumpur: Dewan Bahasa dan Pustaka, Kementerian Pelajaran Malaysia, 1978.

Department of Statistics. *Census of Population and Housing, 1980*. Kuala Lumpur: 1982.

Fong, Chan Onn et. al. "Changes in the Industrial Structure and the Role of Small and Medium Industries in Asean Countries: The Case of Malaysia". Tokyo: Institute of Developing Economies, 1987.

Gibbons, D.S., Lim Teck Ghee and Shukor Kassim. "Land Tenure in the Muda Irrigation Area: Final Report, Part 2: Findings". Centre for Policy Research, University Sains Malaysia, 1981.

Government of Malaysia. *Fifth Malaysia Plan: 1985–1990*. Kuala Lumpur: Government Printers, 1985.

——. *Economic Report 1988/89*. Kuala Lumpur: Ministry of Finance, 1988.

H. Mohammad Rifai. *Ilmu Fiquih Islam Lengkap*. Singapore: Pustaka National Pte. Ltd., 1981.

Husna Sulaiman, Laily P., Zailina H., Poh S.C. "Rural Development and Technology: An Analysis of Farm Family's Levels of Living in Muda Agriculture". Paper presented at the AAACU 7th Biennial Conference at Universiti Pertanian Malaysia, Kuala Lumpur, 1988.

Haughton, Jonathan. "Are the Incomes of the Rural Poor Rising? Evidence for Single-Crop Padi Cultivators in West Malaysia". *Journal of the Malaysian Economic Association*, XXIV, no. 1 (June 1987).

Lim Teck Ghee et. al. "Land Tenure in the Muda Irrigation Area: Final Report, Part 2: Findings". 1976.

Malaysia. Lembaga Tembakau Negara, Taklimat Lembaga Tembakau Negara kepada mesyuarat Jawatankuasa Pembangunan dan Tindakan Jajahan Bachok pada 5hb April 1985.

——. *Agriculture Census of Peninsular Malaysia*. Kuala Lumpur: Ministry of Agriculture, 1985.

——. *National Land Code of Malaysia*, Kuala Lumpur: Government Printers, 1987.

——. Lembaga Tembakau Negara, *Berita Tembakau*, Bil 27, 1988.

Nik A. Rashid. "Land Law and Land Administration". Faculty of Economics & Administration, University of Malaya, 1971.

Salleh Ismail. "Population Growth and Poverty Eradication in Malaysia", *Current Population Policy and Research in Malaysia*, Population Studies Unit, Faculty of Economics & Economics, University of Malaya, Kuala Lumpur, 1985.

——. "Programme and Policies on Poverty Eradication in Peninsular Malaysia: An Assessment". *Proceedings from ISIS First National Conference*, Kuala Lumpur, 1986.

——. *Determinants of the Level of Living of Tumpat, Kelantan*. Papers of the Asean and Japan Project, No. 17. Tokyo: Nihon University, 1987.

Shukor Kassim. "Persistence of Poverty under the New Economic Policy". Paper presented at the Eighth Malaysia Economic Convention on The Malaysia Economy: Challenge and Response, Penang, 1985.

——. "Poverty Monitoring System". *Proceedings from ISIS First National Conference*, Kuala Lumpur, 1986.

Tunku Shamsul Bahrin. "Poverty and Land Issues". Paper presented at the Seminar on Rural Poverty, 21–23 April 1983, organized by Agriculture Institute of Malaysia and KEDA, 1983.

Ungku A. Aziz. "Poverty and Rural Development in Malaysia". *Kajian Ekonomi Malaysia* 1, no. 1 (June 1964).

World Bank. *Malaysia: Selected Issues in Rural Poverty*, World Bank Report No: 2685–MA, 1980.

David S.W. Yong, *Tenure and And Dealings in the Malay States*. Singapore: Singapore University Press, 1975.

10 ISLAM AND THE PRIVATE SECTOR: SOUTHEAST ASIAN PERSPECTIVES

Mohamed Ariff

Introduction

The presence of Islam is readily visible in Southeast Asia not only in terms of the large number of religious institutions such as places of worship with distinguishing features but also in terms of the distinctiveness of the Muslims themselves. Presumably, all Muslims of the region are conscious of the fact that they belong to the *ummah*. It is perhaps not incorrect to state that most Southeast Asian Muslims have always been proud of their faith. Recent Islamic resurgence and spiritual revivification have made all this all the more manifest.

Notwithstanding all this, Islam has ceased to be a way of life in Southeast Asia, having been relegated to a religion of rituals under the impact of alien influences. To be sure, there are conflicts between Islamic ethics to which Southeast Asian Muslims obstensibly subscribe in theory, and the socio-economic norms that they actually adopt in practice. Some "resolved" this conflict by becoming totally oblivious to it while others resort to rationalization. In the midst of them, there is a hard core of people who choose to fight it out from within and stay close to the path of Islam.

The behavioural pattern of those Muslims who do not conform to Islamic injunctions may be attributed to such factors as ignorance (*jahl*), weakness of their belief (*iman*) and expediency or pragmatism on the part of the actors. Some freely take the escape route of *dharurat* which allows things (under emergency situations) that are normally disallowed. It cannot be denied that it is sometimes extremely difficult for Muslims to strictly observe the Islamic jurisprudence (Shariah) simply because they are not operating in an Islamic economy. But for the exogenous factors over which individuals have little or no control, Islamic ethics are really not difficult to practise, as demonstrated by those who derive pleasure and joy from such practices.

It is important to make three pertinent observations at the outset. First, a common denominator of the countries covered in this study is the market orientation of their economies where the private sector plays a dominant role. Second, Islam recognizes the prowess of the private sector and is not opposed to anonymous market forces. Third, it was through trade that Islam was brought to Southeast Asia, an observation that underscores the close affinity between commerce and the Islamic mission. Seen in this light, it is not surprising that Southeast Asian Muslims play an active role in the private sector.

An attempt is made in this chapter to identify the strengths and weaknesses of Muslim enterprises and to assess the involvement of Muslims in the private sector activities, with Islam acting both as a catalyst and as a constraint. Although this chapter draws heavily on the preceding chapters, no effort is made here to summarize the preceding discussions. For, the scope of this chapter is by no means limited by the depth and width of the various country studies presented in this volume. The primary purpose of the present chapter is to plough through the case studies presented in this volume so as to shed additional light on key issues.

Profile of the Muslim Private Sector

In Brunei, Indonesia and Malaysia, Muslims constitute a majority. Elsewhere in Southeast Asia they represent a small minority. The sultanate of Brunei is small with a population of 250,000. Much of Brunei's income and wealth is generated by the petroleum sector, owned by the royalty, while the people are engaged in traditional activities such as farming and fishing, and more recently in commerce and trade. Manufacturing is a new phenomenon in Brunei Darussalam. The private sector in the non-oil sector is relatively free from government intervention. In Indonesia, where Muslims form over 90 per cent of the population of some 180 million, the Pancasila ideology permits the private sector to play a dominant role in the economy. The private sector is active in almost all sectors, including agriculture, manufacturing, and services. In the plural society of Malaysia, Muslims account for roughly 55 per cent of the total population of 17 million. The private sector's role in the open economy of Malaysia has grown increasingly important over the years, but the share of Muslims in the lucrative modern sector still remains disproportionately small.

In countries where Islam is a minority religion, Muslims understandably tend to keep a low profile but their stake in the private sector is by no means insignificant. In the Philippines, there are over 4.5 million Muslims, forming about 9 per cent of the total population. The Filipino Muslims, referred to as the Moros,[1] are concentrated in the South especially in the provinces of Mindanao, Sulu and

Palawan. The majority of them are farmers and fishermen, although a sizeable section of the Muslim community is active in trade as well. In Singapore, Muslims account for about l6 per cent of the island's total population of 2.5 million. The Muslims of Singapore are ethnically a heterogenous lot with the Malays forming the majority, while the rest are mainly of Indian and Middle-Eastern origins. However, it is the latter groups which actively participate in Singapore's thriving private sector. In Thailand, according to official statistics, Muslims constitute 4 per cent (which probably is a gross underestimate) of the country's 52 million population. The Muslims of Thailand are also of diverse ethnicity, but the Malays make up the single largest group. In fact, the Malays constitute the majority in the southern provinces of Pattani, Yala, Narathiwat and Santul. The Muslims of Thailand seem to keep a somewhat low profile in the buoyant Thai private sector, through playing an active role in other traditional sectors such as fishing and farming.

A striking characteristic of the Muslim private sector in Southeast Asia is the small size of the Muslim enterprises. This, however, does not reflect the preference of Muslims for small-sized units, as firm size is constrained largely by the amount of capital available and management styles. This pattern, in fact, is typical of the private sector in the countries of Southeast Asia and has little correlation to religion or ethnicity. Thus, for instance, about 90 per cent of the manufacturing establishments in the region are small-scale operations.

The most common type of organization in the Muslim business communities of Southeast Asia is the sole proprietorship, followed by partnership arrangements. The corporate structures constitute the exceptions. Many well-known Muslim businesses in the region are "family enterprises" steered by influential personalities. Outstanding examples include the Sakaluran, Usman, Camlian and Nunio families of Zambaonga in the Southern Philippines. The Moro business "tycoons" are big names in the plantation and barter trade sectors, although some have diversified into real estate, agri-business, aqua-culture and shipping.

The Moros are active participants in the barter trade of the region and have organized their barter trade by forming co-operatives. There are nine such barter trade associations with about 8,000 members, of which 70 per cent are Muslims. Many Moro traders have also resorted, rather informally, to equity participating (*musharaka*) and profit-sharing (*mudaraba*) arrangements, which represent the two well-known Islamic modes. Nonetheless, sole proprietorship seems to be the norm for the Moro businessmen.

In Singapore, the Malay Muslims are inconspicuous in the commercial sector. Indian Muslims are involved in a wide range of business activities as hawkers, moneychangers, booksellers, stationers, jewellers, etc. Many trade in manufactured goods such as garments, chemicals, and computer software. They also play an active role in the entrepôt trade as exporters and importers of tropical products (e.g. timber, spices and foodstuffs). The Muslims of Arab descent in Singapore are essentially traders dealings in goods such as textiles, batik and perfumes. Some of the minority Muslims in Singapore run firms which act as agents for manufacturers, but some of them have gone into manufacturing in a big way. Manpower shortage seems to be a constraint on the expansion of their activities, as they have traditionally relied on their own kith and kin who are now in short supply as there is a tendency for the younger ones to go for tertiary education.

In Thailand, the Muslims of South Asian extraction are more active in their commercial pursuits than other Muslims, especially in the major urban centres such as Bangkok, Pattaya and Chiengmai. The nature of trade, scale of operation and management styles of the Thai Muslims are somewhat similar to those practised by their compatriots in Singapore. However, Muslims play only a marginal role in the booming tourist trade of Thailand. For instance, none of the 97 hotels in Bangkok is Muslim-owned. There are many Muslim restaurants in Bangkok,[2] but only a few of them cater to the tourists and not all of them are run strictly along Islamic lines. Again, sole proprietorship seems to be the most common form of business organization within the Muslim business community of Thailand, although partnerships have also emerged as an important variant.

In Malaysia, the involvement of non-Malay Muslims in commerce and trade is quite similar to the role played by their brethren in Singapore and Thailand. In the seventies and eighties, the Malays have emerged as an important component of the Muslim business community in Malaysia, thanks chiefly to the New Economic Policy which was designed among other things to increase the equity stakes of the Malays and other indigenous people in the economy. As a result, many Malay business units have come into existence together with some large Malay concerns.

The latter notwithstanding, the average Malay firm is rather small, and usually is a sole proprietorship. There are cases of partnerships involving two or more Malay entrepreneurs. In addition, there are cases of partnerships not only between Malays and other Muslims, but also between Malays and non-Muslims. Malays are fairly well represented in wood processing, rice milling, printing, batik manufacturing and the retail business, especially in the state of Kelantan.[3] Despite the New Economic Policy, the Malays still play only a minor role in the manufacturing sector and their involvement in this sector is limited mainly to batik production, songket weaving, and the making of gold and silverware. In Kelantan, a striking feature of the Muslim private sector is the high incidence of women's participation. In fact, the major market centres in Kelantan are overwhelmingly dominated by Malay women traders who account for about 90 per cent of all traders in the market places.

In the agricultural sector of Southeast Asia, Muslims have traditionally played an important role. In the Philippines, the Moros have practised a customary land tenure system based on communal landownership referred to as *harta pusaka*, with ancestral domains being treated as tribal preserves or trust lands. Some private trust lands handed down from ancestors still remain undivided among the members of the clans or families. As a rule, the communal land is "partitioned" into portions which are cultivated by individual members of the clan. It is not uncommon to find some of these "portions" being leased out to others.

In Malaysia, Muslim-owned agricultural land is subjected to the Islamic law of inheritance which clearly spells out the shares of daughters, sons, wives and others under different conditions. This apparently has resulted in land being subdivided into smaller lots. More than one-half of the paddy lands are below two hectares each, and more than one-half of the rubber smallholdings are below five hectares each. In some districts, the average land holding of the Malay farmers is as small as 0.6 hectares per family. Even in secular societies, including Indonesia and Thailand, Muslims have long practised the Islamic law of inheritance with the endorsement of the judiciary.

Finance and Insurance

The Islamic modes of finance and insurance are very different from the conventional modes operated by modern institutions. Islam has serious objections to modern financial instruments as they contain elements which Islam has forbidden in no uncertain terms. Since interest (*riba*) is prohibited in Islam, most financial transactions operated through modern banks and other financial institutions, which are interest-based, are deemed unislamic. Likewise, modern insurance is found unislamic as it incorporates such elements as gambling (*maisir*), indeterminancy or ambiguity (*gharar*) and *riba*, all of which are disallowed in Islam.

It appears that the Southeast Asian Muslims have, by and large, ignored the Islamic injunctions on matters relating to finance and insurance. Some of them do not even realize that their financial dealings are in violation of the Shari'ah, while others condone such infringements for lack of better alternatives. Conversely, there are Muslims who attempt to circumvent the problem through informal arrangements, while others would actively seek out Islamic means.

Needless to say, the number of Muslims who heed the Islamic injunctions in this regard seems pretty small compared with those who do not. Even in Malaysia, where organized Islamic banking and insurance exist, only a small proportion of Muslims have availed themselves of such facilities. As of the end of 1988, the number of depositors of Bank Islam Malaysia stood at 220,400 which presumably represent only a small share of the Muslim clientele in the country. The total deposits of Bank Islam Malaysia, as of the end of 1988, amounted to M$1.285 billion or 2.11 per cent of the total commercial bank deposits in the country.[4] Even if one assumes that only one-fifth of the total deposits in the country belong to Muslims, this would mean that only 10.55 per cent of the deposits of the Muslims in Malaysia is accounted for by Bank Islam Malaysia. This probably overestimates the Muslim patronage of Islamic banking in the country, since about one-tenth of the Bank Islam Malaysia's financial transactions is accounted for by non-Muslims. In other words, over 90 per cent of the financial transactions of the Muslims in Malaysia are still conducted through conventional banks.

Philippine Amanah Bank (PAB), which was established in 1973 to serve the Muslim Filipinos, operates an Islamic "window" in addition to the interest-based conventional counter. Thus, strictly speaking, PAB is not an Islamic banking institution. In fact, it appears that the Islamic banking component of PAB is limited to the Pilgrims Special Savings Deposits which was launched in 1983. The loan transactions of PAB are still interest-based. It is of interest to note that non-Muslims account for 75 per cent of the total loans and 91 per cent of the total deposits of PAB.[5]

The Moro traders in need of capital have traditionally resorted to partnership (*musharaka*) or profit-sharing (*mudaraba*) arrangements rather than to borrowings based on interest. An interesting case in point is the barter trade arrangement whereby the Moro traders, in groups of ten per team, pool their resources and entrust their capital to the team leader to undertake trips to East Malaysia and Singapore, sharing the expenses of the trip and distributing the merchandise in accordance with individual orders and capital contributions. It is significant to note that this transaction, which resembles *wakala* (agency) with partnership features, is *riba*-free. The Moros usually invest their surplus in gold so as to avoid interest earnings. All this, however, does not mean that they are completely averse to *riba*. It is not uncommon for the Moros to pawn their gold and borrow money on interest payments.

In Indonesia, Singapore and Thailand where Islamic banking does not exist, Muslims have either rationalized the institution of interest as a necessary evil or resorted to *riba*-free informal arrangements to meet their financial needs. One form of traditional *riba*-free borrowing in Indonesia is the rural credit known as *ijon* which allows loans to be secured on the standing crop.[6] Another is the *arisan* system practised among the Indonesian consumers, traders and craftsmen whereby each member contributes regularly a certain sum and obtains interest-free loans from the pool by drawing lots.[7] In Thailand, Muslims have organized cooperatives and savings clubs that provide assistance to the members without interest. An example of these is the Baitul Maal set up by the Jamaat Nasratul Muslimin in the province of Nakorn Sri Thammarat.[8]

Venture capital financing can provide a viable alternative to interest-based loan financing. The Indonesian experiment in venture capital financing is particularly instructive. The Islamic modes of *musharaka* and *mudaraba* can be useful implements in venture capital financing. Venture capital financing represents equity investment in new ventures which are subsequently "sold" after they have developed. The returns are derived from capital appreciation upon divestment which may take the form of an initial public offering, a sale to another company, a buy-back arrangement with the entrepreneur or the major shareholders, etc. In Indonesia, where the label of "Islam" in economic transactions can cause considerable uneasiness to the ruling regime which is openly committed to the Pancasila ideology, *riba*-free venture capital financing can provide a way out.

However, in this regard, the experience of Bahana in Indonesia is disheartening. Bahana has relied heavily on loans from Bank Indonesia involving *riba* (at the interest rate of 3–12 per cent per annum). It is particularly disturbing to note that Bahana's outstanding loan as of December 1987 (Rp8.5 billion) exceeded its total paid-up capital (Rp6 billion). Bahana has also been charging interest rates of 12 to 18 per cent per annum on its credit facilities, in addition to a front-end fee of 1 per cent and a commitment fee of 0.25 per cent on the undrawn sum of the total loan. In short, Bahana's modus operandi is unislamic, although venture capital financing can be operated along Islamic lines.

The insurance needs of the Muslims in Southeast Asia have long been "served" by conventional insurance companies. Islamic insurance does not exist in the region except in Malaysia where it was introduced in 1984. Islamic insurance is referred to as "*takaful* insurance", an Arabic term that embodies the principles of co-operation, mutual help, and shared responsibility. It is called "Islamic" because it is cleansed of unislamic elements such as *maisir*, *gharar* and *riba* and is based on the concept of justice (*adl*) which ensures that everyone benefits from the scheme and that risks are distributed fairly. Thus, a portion of the insurance contribution goes into an investment account which earns profits that is shared between the clients and the insurance company, in addition to providing protection against risks covered by the insurance scheme.

Islamic insurance in Malaysia, however, appears to be still at the experimental stage. One reason why *takaful* insurance has not made much impact on the local insurance scene is because Muslims are apparently more comfortable with conventional insurance than the Islamic one simply because they are more familiar with the former than the latter.

Ethical Dilemma

As was alluded to earlier, Islam apparently has ceased to be a way of life for most Muslims in Southeast Asia where Islamic rituals are observed without much attention being paid to Islamic values. Thus, it is not unusual to find Muslims who would pray and fast on a regular basis but would behave like non-Muslims in almost all other respects. This dualism is largely the result of years of deislamization of the region under the influence of Western capitalism and secularism.

All this, however, does not mean that Islam has lost its attraction in Southeast Asia or that the Southeast Asian Muslims have no qualms about compromising their Islamic values. The recent Islamic resurgence has led many conscientious

Muslims to take a hard look at themselves. It cannot be denied that such self-appraisals have heightened the tension between the rigour of the Islamic faith one subscribes to and the demands of the secular society one lives in.

It is sometimes argued that Islamic values impose additional constraints which blunt the competitive edge of the Muslims against others who could not care less. But the objective of the latter is to maximize their worldly returns while the former's concern is *falah* (prosperity in this world *and* in the Hereafter). The tension would then amount to a trade-off between worldly pursuits and the Hereafter. This tension would not arise if everyone conforms to the letter and spirit of the Islamic precepts. Even in an Islamic state this would not be the case, human beings being what they are. The tension assumes critical proportions in societies where the rules of the game are less stringent than those prescribed by Islam.

To what extent are the Muslims of today willing or prepared to compromise their faith? Admittedly, questions of this kind are hard to answer. Case studies such as those contained in this volume can shed some light but cannot produce unmistakable evidence. It will be extremely costly to conduct studies that cover every Muslim in a country, and practically impossible to derive foolproof methodologies that can fathom the minds and souls of individuals. In other words, case studies, especially those based on random samples, can lead to incomplete and incorrect inferences. It would be dangerous to make generalizations based on particular observations. The ethical dilemma faced by Muslims is brought out forcefully in the case of Thailand's tourist trade which is associated with sins of all sorts.

The observation that Muslims keep a very low profile in Thailand's tourism industry suggests that the mainstream Muslims in Thailand prefer to distance themselves from economic activities that blatantly violate Islamic injunctions. This does not mean that tourism *per se* is frowned upon in Islam. In fact, Muslims are encouraged to travel far and wide so that they can see the wondrous manifestations of God and feel the universality of the Islamic message and the unity or the oneness of the source of all creations (the concept of *tauhid*). And, Islam confers special privileges on travellers, and it is an Islamic virtue to be hospitable to wayfarers (*ibnus-sabil*). Needless to say, all this has nothing to do with tourism of modern times which is seen as "commercialized hospitality" where the sky is the limit, at a price.

The extent to which one is willing to "compromise" would depend crucially on the strength of one's belief (*iman*). All Muslims refrain from saying or doing things that would go against *tauhid*, but the behavioural pattern of Muslims is far from uniform with respect to the lesser sins. Nonetheless, the Muslim private sector by and large avoids activities that are visibly unislamic. Thus, it is rare to find Muslim enterprises that specialize in the moneylending business. In the same vein, Muslim restaurants and shops selling liquor or pork are no more than aberrations.

It is probably not incorrect to conjecture that the "average" Muslim entrepreneur would refrain from practices that are unambiguously unislamic, if he can help it, that is if it is well within his control. Thus, for instance, he will not accept interest on the money that he lends, but will not mind paying interest on the loan he secures, although both are forbidden in Islam. Paradoxically, some Muslims seem to think that receiving interest is a greater sin than paying interest, since the latter, unlike the former, is beyond one's own control. This explains why the Kelantanese women in Malaysia and the Moros in the Philippines convert their savings into gold (to avoid bank interest on deposits) which they pawn to get loans on which they pay interest. It also appears that many Muslim small-scale operators do not resort to bank loans not because of Islamic injunctions against interest but because of lack of collateral.

Rationalization provides a way out of the dilemma for some. For instance, some Muslims have no qualms about accepting interest rates offered by banks, thinking that the return from institutions is not usurious, unlike interest received from individuals. There are also those who would argue that there is no harm in receiving interest from non-Muslims. Some others think that *riba* prohibited in Islam refers to exorbitantly high rates charged by unscrupulous individual money lenders and not to the low rates charged by institutions under state supervision. Yet another variant of this line of reasoning is that *riba* condemned by Islam refers to returns on consumptive loans and not on productive loans.

All this sounds confusing, but the confusion is the product of the rationalization exercise referred to above. There is consensus (*ijma*) among the jurists (*ulama*) that Islam prohibits Muslims from taking or giving interest, regardless of the purpose for which loans are made and regardless of the rates at which interest is charged. Those who accept this as a dictum, however, find it difficult to live with in situations where there are no lawful (*halal*) substitutes offered by Islamic financial institutions. In societies where Islamic banks do not exist, Muslims have tended to invoke the "emergency" clause, namely *dharurat* which permits things that are otherwise prohibited, tolerating interest payments as a "necessary evil".

There is, however, the danger of the *dharurat* principle being misused or abused. In Islam, *dharurat* can be invoked only in the event of extreme compulsion (i.e. as a last resort after everything else has been tried), which however provides no excuse to partake of the unlawful more than absolutely necessary.[9]

It would then follow that the doors of *dharurat*, insofar as interest is concerned, are closed for Muslims in Malaysian towns where Islamic banking is available. However, as observed earlier, many continue to use conventional banking facilities despite the availability of Islamic substitutes. One may advance three possible explanations for this: (1) they do not take the Islamic injunction against interest seriously (2) they question the Islamicity of the facilities offered by Bank Islam Malaysia, and (3) they do not really understand the Islamic modes of finance. It is hard to ascertain which of these explanations really counts.

Islamic Values and Economic Progress

As is well known, Westerners have attempted to attribute the economic backwardness of Muslim societies to the Islamic values which they claim are inimical to economic progress. The truth of the matter, however, is that Islam contains all the necessary ingredients for economic progress and development. For, Islam protects individual freedom, encourages private enterprise, sanctions private ownership and upholds social justice. Indeed, Islamic values are conducive to economic development. Thus, for example, the Islamic virtues such as hard work, acquisition of knowledge and skills, saving and investment, and moderation in consumption are all congenial to economic development. Among the explanations frequently advanced by Western analysts for the economic backwardness of Muslim societies are: (1) the fatalist attitude (*takdir*) has caused Muslims not to be achievement-oriented, (2) the Islamic injunction against *riba* has forced Muslims to be constrained by internal finance, and (3) the Islamic law of inheritance has led to fragmentation of farms into uneconomic units. The concept of *takdir* is misunderstood by many. Islam clearly states that God will not change the status of a community that does not attempt to have it changed in the first place. Seen in the light of the Qur'anic Revelation, the notion of predestiny (*takdir*) has a *positive* influence on human efforts, as it enables a Muslim to cope with disappointments and failures so that they do not act as obstacles to further efforts.

The causal relationship between economic underdevelopment and the Islamic stance on *riba* is rather dubious. Indeed, one may argue that the institution of interest is a bane rather than a boon to economic development. High interest rates in modern times have tended to retard investment activities and frustrate development efforts. It also contributes to economic instability by forcing many firms in financial difficulties to close down and by slowing down economic recovery. In contrast, profit-sharing arrangements can protect the economy from such economic ailments. Be that as it may, it appears from our casual empiricism that most Muslims are not wary of dealing with interest-based financial institutions. By implication, one cannot attribute the economic backwardness of Muslims to the Islamic injunction on *riba*.

In the Southeast Asian context, the contribution of Muslims to the economic development of the countries in which they live appears to be significant. However, the fact that there are many poor Muslims in this region need not be blamed on the Islamic virtues which they subscribe to. The causes of poverty may lie elsewhere, as there is poverty among non-Muslims as well. A detailed analysis of the causes of poverty in the Southeast Asian countries is outside the scope of this chapter. Suffice to note in this context that religion is sometimes used as a red herring to divert attention.

It would be instructive to take a close look at Kelantan which is the least developed state in Malaysia. It would be wrong to attribute the economic backwardness of Kelantan to the strong Islamic orientation of the Kelantanese. It is an open secret that, under the federal structure of Malaysia, the allocation of federal funds to the various component states is often determined by political considerations. It is, therefore, not surprising that Kelantan's share of federal funds was affected by the fact that the state was ruled for many years by an Islamic party (Party Islam Se-Malaysia or PAS) which was in the opposition at the federal level.

As regards the Islamic law of inheritance, which is based on the concept of justice (*adl*), one needs to only underscore the fact that the Islamic law does not insist on *physical* fragmentation of farms. There is no reason why a farm cannot remain as one unit even after inheritance has been executed. There is provision in Islam for joint ownership (*musharaka*) and lease (*ijara*) which pave the way for small farms to be integrated into bigger lots to take advantage of scale economies.

A major cause of rural poverty appears to be the small size of the farm lands. The farms cultivated by rural Muslims are too small to generate income above the subsistence level, as shown by the study of the Bachok district of Kelantan. It would, however, be wrong to blame it all on the Islamic law of inheritance. For, as the study shows, only 22 per cent of the land owned by the operators were inherited and that the rest were purchased. By the same token, it would be wrong to construe that the Islamic law of inheritance, by fragmenting the land into smaller pieces, has caused land to be left idle. As the Bachok study reveals, many large pieces of land are also lying idle.

Upon close scrutiny, in the final analysis, it appears that rural poverty in Malaysia is attributable to the inappropriate division of labour, i.e. specialization in production where there is no comparative advantage, such as the cultivation of paddy. Government assistance has only served to persuade the farmers to stay in their traditional occupations and to inadvertently obstruct structural adjustments and transformations that would have otherwise occurred.

Nevertheless, it appears that Southeast Asian Muslims are rather conservative. They seem to be somewhat slow in adapting themselves to changing circumstances. Thus, they hang on to their traditional occupations and activities and fail to take advantage of structural changes taking place in the economy, as shown by the experience in Singapore, for example. This conservatism, however, is a manifestation of the withdrawal syndrome that Muslim communities all over the world have exhibited after the collapse of the Islamic empires under the onslaught of Western colonization. It probably will take a few more generations for Muslim societies to completely rid themselves of this hang-up.

That important changes are taking place in Muslim societies is evident in the transformation seen in Kelantan, the least developed state in Malaysia. The entrepreneurial role played by the Kelantanese women clearly demonstrates that Islam has not confined women to their kitchens, as is often alleged. Small farms have been converted from paddy cultivation into tobacco growing as the latter lends itself more economically to small-scale operation unlike the former. Nor is it unusual for small farmers to lease adjacent pieces of land so that scale economies can be better exploited.

Concluding Remarks

All available evidence seems to suggest that the Muslim private sector in Southeast Asia is doing reasonably well, although it faces many problems, not all of which are peculiar or specific to itself. Muslims are experiencing tensions of sorts in Southeast Asia where the blend of pluralism, secularism and capitalism pose problems especially for those who accept Islam as a way of life.

It would have been easier for Muslims to practise Islam *in toto* in an Islamic state. It is mainly in this sense, that the environment in Southeast Asia is "hostile" to Muslims. However, the situation is not as "hostile" as it may appear at first sight. Even in countries where Muslims constitute a minority, Muslims enjoy freedom of worship and religious practices. There is a display of considerable tolerance and understanding between Muslims and non-Muslims. It would be very wrong to assume that the latter's ethical norms diverge from those of the Muslims in all respects. In fact, the ethical values of Islam and those of other faiths often do converge, although there are fundamental differences.

History tells us that Muslims had often migrated to places where they could practise their faith freely, whenever the situation at home became unbearable. However, this notion of *hijrah* has become increasingly inapplicable, as the world has been firmly divided into nation-states, making emigration and immigration almost impossible. At the same time, *hijrah* has also become increasingly irrelevant in the sense that there are not many places in today's world that can be described as Islamically superior to others. Seen in this perspective, it appears that Southeast Asia is no more "hostile" than other places in the world insofar as Islam is concerned.

The Muslims of Southeast Asia have learned to live with the environment in which they operate, without losing their identity and distinctiveness as Muslims. Although some "compromises" have been made here and there in the process, mainly through "rationalization" and "exemptions" under the *dharurat* provision, the fundamentals of Islam remain intact and untarnished in Southeast Asia.

NOTES

1 The Spaniards who conquered the Philippines named the Filipino Muslims "Moros" after the Moroccans, South of Spain.

2 According to the Muslim Telephone Directory of 1987, there were 32 Muslim restaurants in Bangkok. The list, in all probability, is incomplete.

3 Mohd. Fauzi Hj. Yaacob, *Peniaga dan Perniagaan Melayu* (Kuala Lumpur: Dewan Bahasa dan Pustaka, 1981).

4 See M. Ariff, "Islamic Banking in Malaysia: Framework, Performance and Lessons", *Journal of Islamic Economics* (forthcoming).

5 The Philippine Amanah Bank, *Annual Report*, 1987.

6 A. Partadireja, "Rural Credit: the Ijon System", *Bulletin of Indonesian Economic Studies* 10, no. 3 (1974): 54–71.

7 See Rahardjo, "The Question of Islamic Banking in Indonesia". In *Islamic Banking in Southeast Asia*, edited by M. Ariff (Singapore: Institute of Southeast Asian Studies, 1988).

8 S. Pitsuwan, "The Islamic Banking Option in Thailand", in ibid.

9 Abdur Rahman Doi, "Duties and Responsibilities of Muslims in Non-Muslim States: A Point of View", *Journal of the Institute of Muslim Minority Affairs* 8, no. 1, (January 1987).